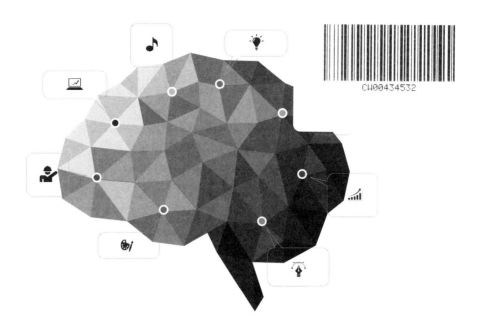

COUNTING
WHAT COUNTS

REFRAMING EDUCATION OUTCOMES

YONG
ZHAO

Ross C. Anderson
Kendra Coates
Brian Gearin
Yue Shen
Sarah Soltz
Michael Thier
Daisy Zhang-Negrerie

Solution Tree | Press

555 North Morton Street
Bloomington, IN 47404
800.733.6786 (toll free) / 812.336.7700
FAX: 812.336.7790
email: info@solution-tree.com
solution-tree.com

Visit **go.solution-tree.com/leadership** to access materials related to this book.

Printed in the United States of America

19   18   17   16   15   1   2   3   4   5

Library of Congress Cataloging-in-Publication Data

Names: Zhao, Yong, 1965-

Title: Counting what counts : reframing education outcomes / editor, Yong

   Zhao ; Contributors, Ross C. Anderson, Kendra Coates, Brian Gearin, Yue

   Shen, Sarah Soltz, Michael Thier, Daisy Zhang-Negrerie, and Yong Zhao.

Description: Bloomington, IN : Solution Tree Press, [2016] | Includes

   bibliographical references and index.

Identifiers: LCCN 2015032129 | ISBN 9781936763580 (perfect bound)

Subjects: LCSH: Educational evaluation. | Educational tests and measurements.

   | Educational change.

Classification: LCC LB2822.75 .C68 2015 | DDC 379.1/58--dc23 LC record available at http://
lccn.loc.gov/2015032129

Solution Tree
Jeffrey C. Jones, CEO
Edmund M. Ackerman, President

Solution Tree Press
President: Douglas M. Rife
Senior Acquisitions Editor: Amy Rubenstein
Editorial Director: Lesley Bolton
Managing Production Editor: Caroline Weiss
Senior Editor: Kari Gillesse
Proofreader: Elisabeth Abrams
Text Designer: Laura Kagemann
Cover Designer: Rian Anderson

Table of Contents

About the Editor

 **Yong Zhao, PhD,** is presidential chair and director of the Office of Global and Online Education in the College of Education at the University of Oregon and a professor in the Department of Educational Measurement, Policy, and Leadership. He is also a Professorial Fellow with the Mitchell Institute for Health and Education Policy, Victoria University in Australia. He was previously University Distinguished Professor in the College of Education at Michigan State University, where he was founding director of the Office of Teaching and Technology and the US-China Center for Research on Educational Excellence, and executive director of the Confucius Institute. He is an elected fellow of the International Academy of Education.

Dr. Zhao is an internationally known scholar, author, and speaker whose works focus on the implications of globalization and technology on education. He has designed schools that cultivate global competence, developed computer games for language learning, and founded research and development institutions to explore innovative education models. The author of more than one hundred articles and twenty books, he was named one of the ten most influential people in educational technology in 2012 by the journal *Tech & Learning*.

Dr. Zhao received a BA in English language education from Sichuan Institute of Foreign Languages in Chongqing, China, and an MA and PhD in education from the University of Illinois at Urbana-Champaign.

To book Yong Zhao for professional development, contact pd@solution-tree.com.

The Danger of Misguiding Outcomes: Lessons From Easter Island

YONG ZHAO

The stone statues on Easter Island have a lot to teach us about education. The hundreds of stone statues on Easter Island have been one of the greatest mysteries on earth (Diamond, 2005). Located in the southern Pacific Ocean, Easter Island is over 2,000 miles away from the closest land, Chile, and 1,400 miles away from the nearest island, which is uninhabited. It is also a very small island, only fifteen miles long and ten miles wide. Yet, on this remote and small island are over eight hundred giant statues carved out of stone. They are large and heavy—ranging from fifteen feet to seventy feet and from ten to two hundred-seventy tons. The largest ever erected weighed over eighty tons. Some of them have a separate headpiece, a cylinder of red scoria that weighs up to twelve tons. When the first European explorers discovered it in 1722, the island was almost uninhabited, with just a few thousand people living in poor conditions without any advanced technology. The explorers did not find any large animals or trees that could be used to help move and lift the statues.

How could the islanders have carved, transported, and erected the statues because "organizing the carving, transport, and erection of the statues required a complex populous society living in an environment rich enough to support it" (Diamond, 2005, p. 81), and such a society was apparently nonexistent when Easter Island was discovered?

Early Europeans did not believe that the "Polynesians, 'mere savages,' could have created the statues or the beautifully constructed stone platforms" (Diamond, 2005, p. 82). They attributed these grand works to other civilizations and even intelligent space aliens. Unless you believe in aliens, Pulitzer Prize–winning scientist Jared Diamond (2005), a professor of geography and physiology at the University of California–Los Angeles (UCLA), provides a compelling and sobering account of how a civilization destroyed itself by diligently pursuing the wrong outcome in his book, *Collapse: How Societies Choose to Fail or Succeed*. The giant statues were created by the Polynesians who began to occupy Easter Island between 1100 and 1680, when it was covered with forests of big and tall trees, some of which reached to about one hundred feet in height and seven feet in diameter. These trees were used to make seafaring canoes that enabled more productive fishing. Coupled with a rather sophisticated agriculture, Easter Islanders developed a civilization that once had an estimated population of fifteen thousand. Such a population provided a sufficient labor force to carve, transport, and raise the statues. The tall trees provided the necessary tools and materials to transport and raise the statues.

There are competing theories pointing out that human activities may not be the only cause of deforestation and ecosystem collapse on Easter Island (for example, some scientists suggest rats as another contributing factor), but Diamond (2005) provides a convincing "example of a society that destroyed itself by overexploiting its own resources" (p. 118). A significant driving force behind the overexploitation was the race to erect bigger statues, and in fact, this ambition was one of the primary causes of the collapse of the Easter Island civilization. The island was divided into about a dozen territories, and each belonged to one clan. Diamond suggests the statues were raised to represent their ancestors, and there was a competition going on between rival clans. Each chief was trying to outdo his rivals by erecting larger and taller statues, and later adding the heavy headpiece on the statues. The statues became a symbol of status, power, and prestige to impress and intimidate rivals. Building bigger statues became a race among the clans. As a result, the statues got bigger, taller, and fancier.

The race was costly. It took tremendous resources to carve, transport, and erect these statues. It demanded surplus food to feed the people working on the statues and thus required more farming land. Trees were cut down to build vehicles for transporting and supporting the erection. Ropes used to pull the statues were made from barks of the tall trees. As more, bigger, and taller statues were built, more trees were cut down. Slowly, all tree species on Easter Island disappeared, resulting in dire consequences for the people living there: "Immediate consequences for the islanders were losses of raw materials, losses of wild-caught foods, and decreased crop yields . . . The further consequences start with starvation, a population crash, and a descent into cannibalism" (Diamond, 2005, pp. 107, 109). Eventually, the Easter Island civilization collapsed, leaving hundreds of broken, fallen, and unfinished stone statues littered on a barren island.

Test Scores as Education's Stone Statue

Today's education reform movement in many parts of the world resembles the Easter Islanders' race to erect stone statues in many ways. The Finnish education scholar and author of *Finnish Lessons: What Can the World Learn From Educational Change in Finland?*

Pasi Sahlberg (2011) has termed the movement the GERM, or Global Educational Reform Movement. Those infected with the GERM or countries engaged in this reform movement have embarked on a race to produce students with excellent test scores—in the belief that scores in a limited number of subjects on standardized tests accurately represent the quality of education a school provides, the performance of a teacher, and students' ability to succeed in the future—not unlike the chiefs and priests on Easter Island who believed that the statues represented the health and power of their clans, the performance of their members, and promise for a more prosperous future.

Test scores have no doubt become the stone statue in education for many countries today. Countries examine their rankings on international tests such as the Programme for International Student Assessment (PISA) and the Trends in International Mathematics and Science Study (TIMSS) with great joy or sorrow, admiration and agony, and a determination to outscore others in the next round, just like Easter Island's rival clans wanted to outbuild each other. National accountability policies are made to force states, schools, and teachers to outscore each other. National education systems are judged according to their test scores; so are schools. Teachers are evaluated based on test scores their students produce. Students' learning and progress are assessed with standardized tests as well. Achievement is equated with test scores, and the achievement gap becomes the test-score gap.

In their race to build bigger statues, Easter Islanders put increasingly more resources into carving, transporting, and erecting statues. Likewise, in the race to obtain higher test scores, schools have invested more resources in raising those scores. A large proportion of schools has spent significantly more time on the tested subjects (math and reading) and reduced time for other subjects and activities. Teachers have spent more time preparing students for standardized tests and focused more time on tested content. Millions of hours are spent each year for students to take the standardized tests. Billions of dollars are spent each year on testing (Chingos, 2012)—or simply measuring whose statue is larger.

Just like the Easter Islanders' obsession with building statues damaged their ecosystem, the obsession with test scores has already begun and will continue to damage the education ecosystem. The high stakes attached to test scores have already forced states, schools, and teachers to improve test scores at any cost—manipulating standards, cheating, teaching to the tests, and only focusing on those students who can bring the most gains in scores. Students who are talented and interested in things that do not contribute to improving scores are considered at risk and put in special sessions to improve their scores. Teachers' professional autonomy is taken away so they can more easily be forced to raise test scores. Local education leaders are rendered assistants of the central government to raise scores.

Perhaps even more dangerous is the failure to see the consequences such a single-minded focus may have. Easter Islanders perhaps did not realize their imminent collapse before it was too late. Blinded by the short-term glory of their magnificent statues, they were preoccupied with creating even more magnificent ones while the last palm tree was cut down. Equally blinded by the potential of common standards and testing programs to improve test scores, reform leaders are ignoring the real challenges facing our children: poverty, unsafe neighborhoods, and unequal access to educational resources.

Ultimately, just like Easter Island ended up a barren island filled with big statues, countries may succeed in raising test scores, but they will likely end up as nations of great test takers in an intellectually barren land; test scores do not count nearly as much as reformers believe for the success of individuals or nations. Moreover, great test scores can come at a huge cost.

Problems With Current Measures

What is measured by today's tests is "almost exclusively cognitive skills" (Brunello & Schlotter, 2010, p. 31). As practiced today,

> World-class education is largely measured by the high test scores of students in one country relative to those in other countries. That is, in evaluating world-class performance, those countries and schools whose students earn the highest scores on common achievement tests set the benchmarks for other countries. In this respect, a world-class educational system is judged strictly by measures of cognitive achievement, rather than on any of the other types of human development that schools produce. (Levin, 2012, p. 270)

Judgments based solely upon measurement of cognitive achievement surely have their limitations. In five critical ways, the focus on assessing cognitive achievement fails to address the skills and competencies a world-class education must deliver.

More Than Just Test Scores: The Importance of Noncognitive Skills

One primary purpose of education is to prepare students to become productive citizens. What makes one productive, however, is much more than the cognitive proficiencies measured in test scores. There is growing evidence from international longitudinal studies (Brunello & Schlotter, 2010; Heckman, 2008; Levin, 2012) that clearly suggests noncognitive factors play a critical role in one's success as a citizen. Noncognitive factors such as personality traits, motivation, interpersonal skills, and intrapersonal skills have been found to correlate significantly with educational attainment, workplace productivity, and life earnings. As a result, among the most highly valued personal qualities, academic achievement ranked lower than communication skills, motivation/initiative, teamwork skills, and leadership skills (Kuhn & Weinberger, 2005).

The importance of noncognitive qualities is also partially evidenced by the relatively inadequate explanatory power of international test scores and economic development. For example, despite the long history of poor performance on international assessments of the United States and some other Western nations in comparison to Eastern Asian countries, their economic performance remains strong and competitive (Baker, 2007; Tienken, 2008; Zhao, 2009, 2012, 2014). The lack of a direct link between nations' long-term economic performance and international test scores suggests that what is measured by these assessments—mainly cognitive proficiencies in math, science, and reading—may not be as critical as the noncognitive skills that have been ignored.

The Rise of the Undervalued: The Importance of Diversity

The second limitation of the current definition and measure of quality lies with its tendency to exclude competencies in domains outside the primary academic subjects—math, science, and literacy. As practiced now, test scores reflect the effectiveness of a teacher, a school, or an educational system in producing a homogenous population of students in the tested subjects. They say little about a teacher, school, or system's capacity in fostering a diversity of talents. But research has shown that diverse talents, skills, knowledge, and perspectives are powerful assets to create better societies, groups, and businesses (Page, 2007). Moreover, as technology and globalization drastically transformed our world from a mass-production industrial society into a society that is more personal, customizable, and hyperspecialized, traditional undervalued talents become highly valuable (Pink, 2005). Thus, a world-class education may be one that enhances diversity rather than reduces it.

Job Creators, Not Job Seekers: The Importance of Creativity and Entrepreneurship

The third limitation is that the current definition and measure of quality has little to do with creativity and other entrepreneurial qualities required of every citizen in the 21st century. Due to globalization and technological advancement, jobs that require routine knowledge and skills can be easily outsourced to other countries or replaced by technology (Friedman, 2005; Goldin & Katz, 2008). Consequently, the future world needs creative and entrepreneurial talents (Auerswald, 2012; Barber, Donnelly, & Rizvi, 2012; Florida, 2012; Wagner, 2012; Zhao, 2012). However, the current assessments measure students' abilities to solve existing problems and give answers to predefined questions. Such assessments are antithetical to challenging, encouraging, and measuring students' abilities to create new solutions, identify new problems, and ask new questions.

Globalized World, Globalized Economy: The Need for Global Competency

The fourth limitation with the current definition and measure of quality of education is its failure to consider the fact that in the globalized world, the ability to interact across cultural, linguistic, and political boundaries has become essential (Ang & Dyne, 2008; Hunter, White, & Godbey, 2006; Reimers, 2010; Suarez-Orozco & Qin-Hilliard, 2004). One's perspective of, attitude toward, and ability to work with people from different cultures and nations have direct impacts on one's own success as well as the well-being of the world as a whole. Australia's emphasis on Asia literacy is but one compelling example of the importance of global competency. Recognizing the vital importance of Asia to Australia's economic, social, and cultural development, Australia has been working on developing Asia literacy. For example, the Australian Curriculum includes Asia literacy as a priority. Asia literacy includes knowledge and understanding of Asian cultures and diversity, as well as the ability to communicate and interact with the diverse populations in Asia (Australian Curriculum, 2015).

When the Floor Becomes the Ceiling: Mediocrity vs. Greatness

The fifth problem with the practice of using scores as the measure of educational quality is that it encourages mediocrity in students and schools. Standardized tests do not measure how great exceptional students can be in their own way. Rather, they measure the extent to which students meet the expectations of the test maker. The best a student can do on a test is to get 100 percent of the questions correct. Since there is nothing beyond that, it discourages students to exert more effort than getting the required or desired scores.

The Costs of High Scores: Side Effects of Improving Test Performances

There is abundant evidence to show that actions to improve scores on standardized tests can damage the development of other important skills such as noncognitive skills, creativity, and entrepreneurship. This is akin to the side effects of medicine. All medicines have side effects. When it cures, it can harm the body as well. To put it another way, there is no free lunch. Everything comes at a cost.

Education cannot escape this simple and obvious law of nature for a number of reasons. First, time is a constant. When one spends it on one thing, it cannot be spent on others. Thus, when all time is spent on studying and preparing for exams, it cannot be spent on visiting museums. By the same token, when time is spent on activities not necessarily related to academic subjects, less time is available for studying the school subjects and preparing for exams. Second, certain human qualities may be antithetical to each other. When one is taught to conform, it will be difficult for him to be creative. When one is punished for making mistakes, it will be hard for her to take risks. When one is told she is wrong or inadequate all the time, it will be difficult for her to maintain confidence. In contrast, when students are allowed freedom to explore, they may question what they are asked to learn and may decide not to comply. Finally, resources are finite as well. When a school or society devotes all resources to certain things, it doesn't have them for others. For example, when all resources are devoted to teaching math and language, schools will have to cut out other programs. When more money is spent on testing students, less will be available for actually helping them grow.

Evidence suggests that students in countries with high scores on the TIMSS and PISA show lower confidence, enjoyment, and interest in the subjects than those with lower test scores (Loveless, 2006; Zhao, 2014). The damage is best evidenced by China, a country that has often been praised for its students' outstanding performance on tests. China's imperial testing system, *keju*, enticed generations of Chinese to study for the test so as to earn a position in government and bring glory to the family. But it has been blamed as a cause of China's failure to develop modern science, technology, and enterprises as well as for China's repeated failures in wars with foreign powers because good test takers are just that: good at taking tests and nothing else. Even today, China is still working hard to move away from a test-oriented education in order to have the talents to build a knowledge-based economy (Zhao, 2014).

Seeking the Alternative

As destructive as using scores to judge the quality of teaching and learning is, we cannot just get rid of it. Governments and the public need measures to hold schools and teachers accountable and know how their schools are doing. Parents need to know if their children are making progress and are on target. Schools and teachers need a way to know if their students are learning and progressing. Finally, universities and employers need to determine how well students are qualified. Thus, we have to seek alternative tools to supplant the presently dominating standardized tests as measures of educational quality.

There is a large and growing body of literature in a variety of fields that can serve as the foundation for building the alternative measures. This body of literature includes both theoretical postulations and empirical evidence about the various noncognitive factors that matter to individual productivity as well as various measurement tools. It also includes new constructs that have been proposed in the 21st century skills movement. Additionally, there is a long history of research and measurement of creativity and multiple intelligences. Research on entrepreneurship has been growing as well.

But the research and development work has typically been conducted and published in different fields independent of each other, with each focusing on its own set of factors. Rarely have these factors been placed in a unifying framework to be examined together. Moreover, although some of these factors have been considered in education, often separately in different contexts, most of them have not been examined carefully in the context of student and teacher evaluation or treated as important educational outcomes.

This book attempts to bring the literature together under a unifying framework for the purpose of expanding the definition of educational quality. It will first present a synthesis of qualities and constructs that have been hypothesized or identified as important contributors to the success of individuals and organizations with analysis of their supporting empirical evidence. Following the synthesis, the book will discuss its implications for education evaluation and raise questions related to developing high-quality education. Chapter one presents further evidence of the limitations of test scores as indicators of quality of education. Chapter two considers how rising productivity has changed the economy and society and created opportunities for the whole spectrum of human talents, and proposes that education should no longer aim to homogenize individuals. Chapter three examines the value of personality traits for success. Chapter four focuses on motivational factors. Chapter five investigates the importance of creativity and the entrepreneurial spirit. Chapter six reviews the literature on developing and measuring global competencies. Chapter seven discusses qualities related to social intelligence and social capital, as well as their impact on life's success. Chapter eight reviews research concerning the development of noncognitive qualities. Lastly, chapter nine summarizes the state of educational evaluation and outcomes and presents a new framework for thinking about high-quality education.

References and Resources

Ang, S., & Dyne, L. V. (Eds.). (2008). *Handbook of cultural intelligence: Theory, measurement, and applications*. Armonk, NY: Sharpe.

Auerswald, P. E. (2012). *The coming prosperity: How entrepreneurs are transforming the global economy*. New York: Oxford University Press.

Australian Curriculum, Assessment and Reporting Authority. (2015). Asia and Australia's engagement with Asia. *Australian Curriculum*. Accessed at www.australiancurriculum .edu.au/crosscurriculumpriorities/asia-and-australias-engagement-with-asia on July 30, 2015.

Baker, K. (2007). Are international tests worth anything? *Phi Delta Kappan, 89*(2), 101–104.

Barber, M., Donnelly, K., & Rizvi, S. (2012). *Oceans of innovation: The Atlantic, the Pacific, global leadership and the future of education*. London: Institute for Public Policy Research.

Brunello, G., & Schlotter, M. (2010). *The effect of non cognitive skills and personality traits on labour market outcomes*. Munich, Germany: European Expert Network on Economics of Education.

Chingos, M. M. (2012). *Strength in numbers: State spending on K–12 assessment systems.* Washington, DC: Brown Center on Education Policy at Brookings. Accessed at www .brookings.edu/~/media/research/files/reports/2012/11/29-cost-of-assessment-chingos/11 _assessment_chingos_final_new.pdf on August 3, 2015.

Cohen, J. E., & Malin, M. B. (Eds.). (2010). *International perspective on the goals of universal basic and secondary education.* New York: Routledge.

Diamond, J. (2005). *Collapse: How societies choose to fail or succeed.* New York: Viking.

European Commission. (2007). *Key competences for lifelong learning: European reference framework.* Luxembourg: Office for Official Publications of the European Communities.

Florida, R. (2012). *The rise of the creative class: Revisited.* New York: Basic Books.

Friedman, T. L. (2005). *The world is flat: A brief history of the twenty-first century.* New York: Farrar, Straus & Giroux.

Goldin, C., & Katz, L. F. (2008). *The race between education and technology.* Cambridge, MA: Harvard University Press.

Heckman, J. J. (2008). Schools, skills and synapses. *Economic Inquiry, 46*(3), 289–324.

Hunter, B., White, G. P., & Godbey, G. C. (2006). What does it mean to be globally competent? *Journal of Studies in International Education, 10*(3), 267–285.

Kuhn, P., & Weinberger, C. (2005). Leadership skills and wages. *Journal of Labor Economics, 23*(3), 395–436.

Levin, H. M. (2012). More than just test scores. *Prospects: Quarterly Review of Comparative Education, 42*(3), 269–284.

Loveless, T. (2006). *The 2006 Brown Center Report on American Education: How well are American students learning?* Washington, DC: Brookings Institution.

Means, B., Toyama, Y., Murphy, R., Bakia, M., & Jones, K. (2009). *Evaluation of evidence-based practices in online learning: A meta-analysis and review of online learning studies.* Washington, DC: U.S. Department of Education.

National Governors Association Center for Best Practices & Council of Chief State School Officers. (n.d.). *Common Core State Standards Initiative.* Accessed at www.corestandards.org on November 24, 2011.

Page, S. E. (2007). *The difference: How the power of diversity creates better groups, firms, schools, and societies.* Princeton, NJ: Princeton University Press.

Partnership for 21st Century Skills. (n.d.). *Framework for 21st century learning.* Accessed at www.p21.org/our-work/p21-framework on March 23, 2015.

Pink, D. H. (2005). *A whole new mind: Why right-brainers will rule the future.* New York: Riverhead Books.

Reimers, F. (2010). Educating for global competency. In J. E. Cohen & M. B. Malin (Eds.), *International perspective on the goals of universal basic and secondary education* (pp. 183–202). New York: Routledge.

Sahlberg, P. (2011). *Finnish lessons: What can the world learn from educational change in Finland?* New York: Teachers College Press.

Sahlberg, P. (2012, June 29). How GERM is infecting schools around the world. *The Washington Post.* Accessed at www.washingtonpost.com/blogs/answer-sheet/post/how-germ -is-infecting-schools-around-the-world/2012/06/29/gJQAVELZAW_blog.html#comments on March 23, 2015.

Suarez-Orozco, M. M., & Qin-Hilliard, D. B. (Eds.). (2004). *Globalization: Culture and education in the new millennium.* Berkeley: University of California Press.

Tienken, C. H. (2008). Rankings of international achievement test performance and economic strength: Correlation or conjecture? *International Journal of Education Policy and Leadership, 3*(4), 1–15.

Wagner, T. (2012). *Creating innovators: The making of young people who will change the world.* New York: Scribner.

Zhao, Y. (2009). *Catching up or leading the way: American education in the age of globalization.* Alexandria, VA: Association for Supervision and Curriculum Development.

Zhao, Y. (2012). *World class learners: Educating creative and entrepreneurial students.* Thousand Oaks, CA: Corwin Press.

Zhao, Y. (2014). *Who's afraid of the big bad dragon? Why China has the best (and worst) education system in the world.* San Francisco: Jossey-Bass.

Yong Zhao, PhD, is presidential chair and director of the Office of Global and Online Education in the College of Education at the University of Oregon and a professor in the Department of Educational Measurement, Policy, and Leadership. He is also a Professorial Fellow with the Mitchell Institute for Health and Education Policy, Victoria University in Australia. He was previously University Distinguished Professor in the College of Education at Michigan State University, where he was founding director of the Office of Teaching and Technology and the US-China Center for Research on Educational Excellence, and executive director of the Confucius Institute. He is an elected fellow of the International Academy of Education.

Dr. Zhao is an internationally known scholar, author, and speaker whose works focus on the implications of globalization and technology on education. He has designed schools that cultivate global competence, developed computer games for language learning, and founded research and development institutions to explore innovative education models. The author of more than one hundred articles and twenty books, he was named one of the ten most influential people in educational technology in 2012 by the journal *Tech & Learning*.

Dr. Zhao received a BA in English language education from Sichuan Institute of Foreign Languages in Chongqing, China, and an MA and PhD in education from the University of Illinois at Urbana-Champaign.

To book Yong Zhao for professional development, contact pd@solution-tree.com.

CHAPTER 1

Numbers Can Lie: The Meaning and Limitations of Test Scores

YONG ZHAO

Test scores carry high—and sometimes extremely high—stakes. IQ scores have been used to justify racism and support eugenics, resulting in depriving certain groups of immigration, education, and even reproduction rights in the United States (Gould, 1996). College admissions tests such as the SAT and ACT in the United States have been playing a significant role in determining who gets what kind of education, and the *gaokao* in China, or the country's rigorous college entrance exam, has been almost exclusively used to decide a person's fate (Zhao, 2014). International test scores such as the Programme for International Student Assessment (PISA) and Trends in International Mathematics and Science Study (TIMSS) have been used to drive massive reform efforts and education investment that affect millions of children around the world (Meyer & Benavot, 2013). Recent years have seen a rising trend in using standardized test scores to determine the performance and income of teachers and school leaders (Pathe & Choe, 2013).

One of the reasons that test scores are given such power is that they are believed to reliably measure some human intellectual quality. Such quality is believed to contribute significantly to, if not determine, the "success" of an individual, group, or nation. Therefore, test scores are believed to be able to predicate whether or to what extent an individual, a group, or a nation can be successful. In other words, test scores indicate whether or how much individuals and groups have the potential to succeed. Thus, decisions regarding allocation of limited resources, such as opportunities for advanced education, are made according to test scores. Similarly, nations must possess or develop individuals with such potential for their future prosperity and thus must find ways to raise test scores, ranging from limiting immigration of certain groups to holding schools and teachers accountable for improving test scores.

All these sound rational and logical. The only problem is that human beings are simply too complex to be reduced to a single number, let alone to allow a number to make life-changing decisions about them. So far, there is no test that has been proven to capture all the qualities that lead to the success and prosperity of a person, group, or nation, despite some of the outlandish claims of proponents of certain tests at the time. History has disproved most of the claims made about certain tests, even though some of them were once believed to be valid or extremely reliable.

Tests and Individual Success

Various standardized test scores have been used to predict life success of individuals. IQ tests, the SAT, the GRE, and the ACT are some of the well-known ones in the United States. Many other countries have some form of high-stakes entrance exams for college admissions. These tests have been used to determine who is "ready for" or "worthy of" more education because they supposedly measure one's capacity for handling complex cognitive tasks and achieving success in life. But how good are they?

IQ Tests and Life Success

IQ tests have perhaps been one of the most widespread attempts to predicate individuals' future success in the United States. Over the past century, numerous studies have reported the connections between IQ scores and achievement in life (for example, see Firkowska-Mankiewicz, 2002; Lynn & Vanhanen, 2002; Rindermann, 2007). While there are plenty of studies that show IQ scores at a young age to have a significant impact on job performance, income, and other indicators of success in later life, there is also a large number of studies showing the limitations of IQ tests (for example, see Gardner, 1999; Goleman, 1995a; Sternberg, 1987). Regardless of the controversies, the general consensus today is that IQ indeed matters, but it alone cannot explain why some people are more successful than others.

One of the most well-known and earliest attempts to study IQ and life success is the Genetic Studies of Genius launched by Stanford psychologist Lewis Terman, the man who introduced IQ tests to the United States in 1916. Later renamed the Terman Study of the Gifted, the study is still ongoing, making it the longest-running psychology study in the world. The study follows the life of 1,528 children identified as having extremely high IQ scores and thus deemed most intelligent in the 1920s. The study will continue until the last participant dies or withdraws.

The children included in the study, nicknamed Termites, must have scored above 135 (Leslie, 2000). They were the top 1 percent geniuses. So if IQ scores mattered as much as

Terman believed, the Termites should have a much more successful life than 99 percent of the population.

The Termites did pretty well. In the follow-up study thirty-five years after Terman's study began, Terman's geniuses "were taller, healthier, physically better developed, and socially adept" (Kaufman, 2009). They had excellent education: two-thirds of them earned a bachelor's degree, which was ten times the national average at the time of the follow-up study. They also earned a substantially higher income than the national average: the Termites earned a median salary of $10,556, twice the national median salary for white-collar jobs in 1954. The group also had excellent careers, and many of them became prominent professionals: ninety-seven PhDs, fifty-seven MDs, and ninety-two lawyers (Leslie, 2000). They were also creative and productive: two thousand scientific and technical papers; sixty books and monographs in sciences, literature, arts, and the humanities; at least 230 granted patents; thirty-three novels; 375 short stories, novelettes, and plays; and hundreds of radio, TV, and movie scripts were reported by Terman in the thirty-five-year follow-up study (Kaufman, 2009).

No doubt these were impressive accomplishments. But do they match the rarity of their IQ scores? The answer is no, according to Dean Simonton's (1994) book, *Greatness: Who Makes History and Why*. Simonton compared the per capita output of Terman's group with that of other top scientists and found the Termites were not nearly as impressive. The Termites produced about half of what the Nobel scientists did around the same age. "Hence, Terman's intellectual elite was not of the same caliber as the true scientific elite of the same nation and era," concludes Simonton (1994, p. 222). Moreover, while there are a number of Termites who gained professional prominence, none have been awarded a Nobel. Ironically, two Nobel laureates, William Shockley and Luis Alvarez, were excluded from the Terman study because their IQ scores were not high enough.

In fact, the late Harvard sociologist Pitirim Sorokin (1956) argued that the achievement of the Termites could have been achieved by a randomly selected group of individuals from similar backgrounds. The Termites were overwhelmingly white coming from urban and middle-class families in California. The group had only two African Americans, six Japanese Americans, and one American Indian. The group had more males than females (856 versus 672) as well. Their advantaged background, other than IQ, may have been the contributing factor to their success. According to Sorokin, the Termites' accomplishments are within the expectations of superiority regardless of their IQs. "The IQ scores of these 'geniuses' appear to have added little to the prediction of their life outcomes over that gained simply from a consideration of their parental income, education, and occupational status," writes Cornell University professor Stephen Ceci (1996, p. 89).

Additionally, doubts have been raised whether Lewis Terman's personal involvement with the Termites and occasional intervention with their life had helped with the Termites' success. While we do not know the full extent of his personal involvement, "it's clear that Terman helped several get into Stanford and other universities. He dispatched numerous letters of recommendation mentioning that individuals took part in his project" (Leslie, 2000). He also pulled strings to help a Japanese American participant's family stay freed from internment during World War II.

Yet not all the Termites are equally accomplished. Terman's research associate Melita Oden compared the life accomplishments of the most successful hundred and the least successful hundred Termites in 1968. She found that the top hundred were in professions that matched their expectations—law, medicine, university professors, or business executives—while the bottom hundred were in occupations such as sales clerks, earning a slightly higher-than-average income, and had a higher rate of alcoholism and divorce than the top hundred (Oden, 1968). The two groups' IQ scores had a slight difference, with the top hundred scoring an average of 7 points higher (157 versus 150). When the scores are so high, such a difference barely matters; in fact, "Such a difference is 'meaningless'" (Goleman, 1995b). But why the stark difference in accomplishment?

The difference lies in other areas, according to Daniel Goleman (1995a), author of *Emotional Intelligence*. The top achievers "were more motivated from the start; they skipped more grades in grammar school, and went further in their education" than the bottom hundred (Goleman, 1995b). The top hundred participated in more extracurricular activities and were rated as more lively and engaged (Goleman, 1995a). "Perhaps most significant in explaining the difference in career success […] were character traits," writes Goleman (1995b) in a *New York Times* article; the top achievers "already showed greater 'will power, perseverance and desire to excel'" at a very young age.

More longitudinal studies of IQ and life success have been conducted around the world. In 1992, Boston University psychologists David McClelland and Carol Franz (1992) looked at the achievement and income of a group of individuals in the Boston area as a follow-up to a study conducted in 1951, when these adults were five-year-olds. They found that childhood IQ scores were not as powerful a predicator as parenting styles.

Another longitudinal study came up with similar findings. Anna Firkowska-Mankiewicz (2002), a Polish sociologist, conducted a study in Warsaw, Poland, from 1974 to 1999. She writes that "we do not know how to disentangle IQ scores from many environmental factors that are colinear with them" because "in the limited cases of persons with identical IQ scores but different social backgrounds, we discovered that the predictive power of intelligence was limited" (Firkowska-Mankiewicz, 2002, p. 41). Firkowska-Mankiewicz (2002) suggests the same as Goleman: "Personality variables, particularly high and stable self-esteem, are decisive for a sense of achieving life success." She concludes: "The value of the IQ scores should not be overestimated" (p. 41).

The SAT, the ACT, and Success in College and Life

The SAT and ACT are the two most widely used standardized tests for college admissions in the United States. In 2014, over 1.6 million people took the SAT, and more than 1.8 million took the ACT (National Center for Fair and Open Testing, 2015). Students and parents take them seriously. In 2011, for example, it was estimated that 1.5 million students spent about $530 million annually on test preparation and tutoring for the SAT (Marte, 2011). While an increasing number of colleges and universities have decided not to require the SAT or ACT or are flexible with them, the majority of U.S. universities and colleges continue to consider the scores an important factor in admission decisions because they supposedly measure the degree to which individuals have the ability to succeed in college. In other words, a good SAT or ACT score should correlate with good performance in college, or put in academic jargon, the scores have good predictive validity.

Many studies have been carried out to detect the predictive validity of the SAT and ACT. The general conclusion is that they matter, but not as much as commonly believed. A study conducted by the University of California (UC) system looked at the relationship between SAT and academic records of nearly seventy-eight thousand first-time freshmen who entered UC between 1996 and 1999. The study (Geiser, 2002) found that, averaged across the four cohorts, SAT I scores explained about 13.3 percent of variations in freshman grade point average (GPA). This finding is consistent with other studies. For example, a meta-analysis study by the College Board, the owner of the SAT, found the average correlation between SAT I scores and undergraduate GPA to be .36 based on results from predictive studies between 1980 and 2000 (Burton & Ramist, 2001). That is, about 13 percent of the variation in undergraduate GPA can be explained by SAT I scores. High school GPA had a higher correlation coefficient of .42, which explains about 18 percent of the variation in GPA. The study also found that the best combination of SAT scores explains about 10 percent of the variation in college graduation. A more recent College Board study of 151,316 students from 110 colleges and universities produced similar findings; for example, the changes in the SAT did not affect its predictive power (Kobrin, Patterson, Shaw, Mattern, & Barbuti, 2008).

There are fewer studies on the predictive power of the ACT, but available studies paint a similar picture. In a study commissioned by ACT Inc., researchers found that the median correlation across 129 colleges between the current four ACT subject scores (English, mathematics, reading, and science) and college freshman GPA is .43, which is lower than the correlation between high school grades and freshman GPA (.48) (Noble & Sawyer, 2002). A more recent study conducted by researchers at the National Bureau of Economic Research studied over twenty-five thousand college students who matriculated to universities and colleges in Ohio in 1999. They found the ACT composite scores explain about 13 percent of the variation in freshman GPA. In terms of subscores, they found mathematics and English scores to have more significant predictive power than reading and science scores. In fact, reading and science scores have almost no predictive power on freshman GPA, with science scores negatively correlated with freshman GPA (Bettinger, Evans, & Pope, 2011).

Looking across the many studies of the SAT and ACT, the percentage of variations in college success is as high as about 18 percent, with an estimated range between 7 percent and 25 percent, according to Stanford professor Claude Steele. He best summarized the power of the SAT in a 1999 interview:

> SAT is not going to get you very far with predicting who's going to do well in college. And certainly not far with regards to who is going to do well in society or contribute to society. It's just not that good a tool and that's the first thing to realize about it. ("Interview: Claude Steele," 1999)

This is why a study of nearly 123,000 students in over thirty different types of colleges and universities that have made standardized tests optional found no significant difference between those who submitted SAT or ACT scores and those who did not. Released in 2014, the report of a study led by a former dean of admissions at Bates College said that "the differences between submitters and non-submitters are five one-hundredths of a GPA point, and six-tenths of one percent in graduation rates. By any standard, these are trivial differences" (Hiss & Franks, 2014, p. 3).

So what do we make of standardized tests? No doubt they measure *something* and that something apparently plays a contributing role in success for college and life, and the contribution is even statistically significant. However, it is unclear whether the *something* measured by standardized tests is innate ability or qualities acquired later, or the socioeconomic conditions one is born into. A more important fact is that after reaching a certain level of the *something* measured by standardized tests, other factors come into play. This is recognized by the ambitious Common Core State Standards Initiative, which claims to help American students prepare for college and career. Despite the Common Core's general claim, one of its two assessment consortia, the Partnership for Assessment of Readiness for College and Careers (PARCC, 2012), acknowledges that academics do not encompass the full range of knowledge and skills students need to be ready for college and careers, such as those described by Conley (2012), which include persistence, motivation, time management, and "awareness of postsecondary norms and culture" (PARCC, 2012, p. 2).

Tests and National Success

"We cannot conceive of any worse form of chaos than a democracy in a population of average intelligence of a little over thirteen years," proclaimed Colgate University president G. G. Cutten in 1922 (as quoted in Gould, 1996, p. 254). The president was referring to the average IQ scores of white draftees in the U.S. Army found by psychologists Robert Yerkes and Carl C. Brigham. Brigham later led the development of the SAT. Both Yerkes and Brigham were strong supporters of eugenics, as was Lewis Terman. Yerkes found the average mental age of drafted whites to be 13.08. Yerkes was apparently deeply troubled because he wrote:

> A moron has been defined as anyone with a mental age from 7 to 12 years. If this definition is interpreted as meaning anyone with a mental age less than 13 years, as has recently been done, then almost half of the white draft (47.3 percent) would have been morons. Thus it appears that feeble-mindedness, as at present defined, is of much greater frequency of occurrence than had been originally supposed. (as quoted in Gould, 1996, p. 253)

The "fact" was used to advocate immigration quotas. To ensure the United States' future success, the country could not take more feeble-minded people from other countries. Brigham's 1923 book *A Study of American Intelligence* "became a primary vehicle for translating the army [IQ tests'] results on group differences into social action" (Gould, 1996, p. 254). It was believed that IQ scores measure one's innate mental ability and different racial groups have different innate abilities. For example, Brigham worked out the IQ scores of three different groups of Europeans: Nordic, 13.28; Alpine, 11.67; and Mediterranean, 11.43 (Gould, 1996). Brigham and like-minded psychologists' data were factored in heavily in the congressional immigration debates leading to the passage of the Immigration Act of 1924, which greatly restricted immigration from southern and eastern Europe.

Of course, as history shows, Brigham was wrong, and he recanted six years after his test scores had profoundly affected the establishment of the national immigration quota, as did many of his contemporaries sharing the same view. He realized that the data "were worthless as measures of innate intelligence" and "recognized that a test score could not be reified as an entity inside a person's head" (Gould, 1996, p. 262).

The ugly episode of using IQ test scores as a racist tool in hopes of building a more prosperous nation ended in the United States, but its spirit has not. Test scores have actually gained more power in people's thinking about national success. The theory of "intelligent wealth" proposes that cognitive ability is a major causal component of national wealth (Rindermann, 2012). Northern Ireland psychologist Richard Lynn and Finnish political scientist Tatu Vanhanen made the proposition in their book *IQ and the Wealth of Nations* (Lynn & Vanhanen, 2002). Using average IQ scores they calculated for eighty-one countries based on published reports and some statistical manipulation, they concluded that national productivity measured with gross domestic product (GDP) is significantly correlated with IQ scores (.82). So is economic growth rate, according to the authors. Their data and conclusion have been challenged by economists and psychologists alike (for example, see Barnett & Williams, 2004; Berhanu, 2007).

But when the word *IQ* is removed, test scores seem to have broader acceptance as an indicator of national wealth. For example, international assessments such as the PISA and the TIMSS have been assigned the power to predict nations' future economic prosperity in the world (Hanushek & Woessmann, 2008). Hoover Institution economist Eric Hanushek and University of Munich professor Ludger Woessmann wrote a report sponsored by the Organisation for Economic Co-operation and Development (OECD) in 2010:

> This report uses recent economic modelling to relate cognitive skills—as measured by PISA and other international instruments—to economic growth. The relationship indicates that relatively small improvements in the skills of a nation's labour force can have very large impacts on future well-being. (p. 3)

They assert:

> A modest goal of having all OECD countries boost their average PISA scores by 25 points over the next 20 years . . . implies an aggregate gain of OECD GDP of USD 115 trillion over the lifetime of the generation born in 2010. . . . Bringing all countries up to the average performance of Finland, OECD's best performing education system in PISA, would result in gains in the order of USD 260 trillion . . . Other aggressive goals, such as bringing all students to a level of minimal proficiency for the OECD (*i.e.* reaching a PISA score of 400), would imply aggregate GDP increases of close to USD 200 trillion according to historical growth relationships . . . (Hanushek & Woessmann, 2010, p. 6)

The assertion has gained wide reception by national governments around the world and of course further reinforced the value of the PISA test. The basis of Hanushek and Woessmann's prediction is the results of statistical modeling based on outcomes of international assessments and economic growth. Since PISA did not exist in most of the time period they examined, they used other international tests such as the First International Mathematics Study (FIMS), First International Science Study (FISS), Second International Mathematics Study (SIMS), Second International Science Study (SISS), and Third International Mathematics and Science Study (TIMSS), which became the Trends in International Mathematics and Science Study. The first problem is that not all countries participated in all the studies. Moreover, Hanushek and Woessmann (2010) write:

> The fact that the scales of their test-score results are not directly equated across tests is a major drawback in comparative uses of the various ISATs [International Student Achievement Tests]. They do not use the same test questions; nor do they even use the same technique

and scale of mapping answers into test scores. The early tests mainly used aggregate scores in "percent correct" format, but with questions of varying difficulty in the different tests, these scores will not be comparable across tests. The later tests use a more sophisticated scale, constructed using Item Response Theory (IRT). Among other things, IRT weighs different questions by their revealed difficulty and then maps answers onto a pre-set scale set to yield a given international mean and standard deviation among the participating countries. However, the questions on which the mapping is based are not the same in the different tests. Even more, the set of participating countries varies considerably across tests, making the separately developed scales incomparable across ISATs. (p. 38)

They developed a way to project "the performance of different countries on different tests . . . onto a common metric" (Hanushek & Woessmann, 2010, p. 39), meaning they created scores for countries through statistical manipulations. Regardless of the quality of the data and the appropriateness of the statistical approach, they came up with quite unequivocal and shocking conclusions that test scores matter, and a lot, to nations' economic success. This is contrary to the findings of other researchers. For example, former U.S. Department of Education researcher Keith Baker (2007) found no or a negative relationship between the FIMS test scores and national wealth, economic growth rate, democracy, productivity, or creativity. Christopher Tienken (2008), education professor at Seton Hall University, found that test scores better predict economic growth in low-performing countries than in developed countries.

The United States is a prime example. According to historical data, the United States never achieved greatness in test scores. In the 1960s, when the FIMS and the FISS were conducted, U.S. students ranked at the bottom in virtually all categories (Medrich & Griffith, 1992):

- Eleventh out of twelve (eighth grade—thirteen-year-old mathematics)
- Twelfth out of twelve (twelfth-grade mathematics for mathematics students)
- Tenth out of twelve (twelfth-grade mathematics for nonmathematics students)
- Seventh out of nineteen (fourteen-year-old science)
- Fourteenth out of nineteen (twelfth-grade science)

In the 1980s, when the SIMS and SISS were conducted, U.S. students inched up a little bit, but not much (Medrich & Griffith, 1992):

- Tenth out of twenty (eighth-grade arithmetic)
- Twelfth out of twenty (eighth-grade algebra)
- Sixteenth out of twenty (eighth-grade geometry)

- ◆ Eighteenth out of twenty (eighth-grade measurement)

- ◆ Eighth out of twenty (eighth-grade statistics)

- ◆ Twelfth out of fifteen (twelfth-grade number systems)

- ◆ Fourteenth out of fifteen (twelfth-grade algebra)

- ◆ Twelfth out of fifteen (twelfth-grade geometry)

- ◆ Twelfth out of fifteen (twelfth-grade calculus)

- ◆ Fourteenth out of seventeen (fourteen-year-old science)

- ◆ Fourteenth out of fourteen (twelfth-grade biology)

- ◆ Twelfth out of fourteen (twelfth-grade chemistry)

- ◆ Tenth out of fourteen (twelfth-grade physics)

In the 1990s, in the TIMSS, American test performance was not the best either, albeit with some improvement (National Center for Education Statistics, 1999):

- ◆ Twenty-eighth out of forty-one (but only twenty countries performed significantly better) (eighth-grade mathematics)

- ◆ Seventeenth out of forty-one (but only nine countries performed significantly better) (eighth-grade science)

In 2003, in the TIMSS (now called the Trends in International Mathematics and Science Study), U.S. students were not great, but again improved (National Center for Education Statistics, 2003):

- ◆ Fifteenth out of forty-five (only nine countries performed significantly better) (eighth-grade mathematics)

- ◆ Ninth out of forty-five (only seven countries performed significantly better) (eighth-grade science)

In 2007, the United States improved again in the TIMSS, though it was still not the top-ranking country (National Center for Education Statistics, 2007):

- ◆ Ninth out of forty-seven (only five countries performed significantly better) (eighth-grade mathematics)

- ◆ Tenth out of forty-seven (only eight countries performed significantly better) (eighth-grade science)

American students have not done well on the PISA, either. The PISA was first introduced in 2000 to test fifteen-year-olds in math, literacy, and science. It is conducted every three years. Because the PISA is fairly new, there is not a clear trend to show whether the

United States is doing better or worse, but it is clear that U.S. students are not among the strongest (www.oecd.org/pisa/keyfindings):

PISA Reading Literacy

+ Fifteenth out of thirty countries in 2000

+ Seventeenth out of seventy-seven countries in 2009

+ Twenty-fifth out of sixty-five countries in 2012

PISA Math

+ Twenty-fourth out of twenty-nine countries in 2003

+ Thirty-first out of seventy-four countries in 2009

+ Thirty-sixth out of sixty-five countries in 2012

PISA Sciences

+ Twenty-first out of thirty countries in 2003

+ Twenty-third out of seventy-four countries in 2009

+ Twenty-eighth out of sixty-five countries in 2012

There are still other studies and statistics, but this long list of ranks should be sufficient to prove that U.S. students have been awful test takers for over half a century. Some have taken this to mean U.S. education has been awful in comparison to that of other countries. This interpretation has been common and backed up by media reports, scholarly books, and documentary films, for example:

+ 1950s–1960s: Worse than the Soviet Union (1958 *Life* magazine cover story "Crisis in Education")

+ 1980s–1990s: Worse than Japan and others (*A Nation at Risk* [National Commission on Excellence in Education, 1983]; *The Learning Gap: Why Our Schools Are Failing and What We Can Learn From Japanese and Chinese Education* [Stevenson & Stigler, 1992])

+ 2000s: Worse than China and India *(Two Million Minutes: A Global Examination* documentary film [Compton & Heeter, 2008]; *Surpassing Shanghai: An Agenda for American Education Built on the World's Leading Systems* [Tucker, 2011])

According to the statistical models of Hanushek and Woessmann (2008), the awful test scores American students have received over the past half century should have rendered the United States an economic backwater. The country should have hit rock bottom in national security, jobs, and economy by now. But facts suggest otherwise:

The Soviet Union, the United States' archrival during the Cold War, which supposedly had better education than the United States, disappeared. The United States remains the dominant military power in the world. Japan, which was expected to take over the United States because of its superior education in the 1980s, has lost its number-two status in terms of size of economy. The United States is still the largest economy in the world. There are more indicators of the United States' leading standing today:

- Third out of 142 countries in global competitiveness in 2014–2015 (World Economic Forum, 2015)

- Sixth out of 143 in Bloomberg Innovation Index in 2015 (Bloomberg, 2015)

- Second out of 82 countries in global creativity, behind only Sweden in 2011 (Florida, 2011)

- First in the number of patents filed or granted by major international patent offices in 2013 (World Intellectual Property Organization [WIPO], 2014).

Hanushek and Woessmann (2008) acknowledge that the United States is an anomaly to their model: "The United States has never done well on these international assessments, yet its growth rate has been very high for a long period of time" (p. 637). Asserting that "the reconciliation is that quality of the labor force is just one aspect of the economy that enters into the determination of growth," they believe other factors such as "appropriate market, legal, and governmental institutions" worked to "overcome any deficits in quality" of education indicated by test scores (p. 637).

But there are other anomalies. For example, the United Kingdom did not have a stellar history of high scores on international tests, but remains a strong democracy. Perhaps the explanation lies with the measure of quality itself. Heiner Rindermann (2007), a German psychologist at Otto-von-Guericke University Magdeburg, found that international assessment scores are strongly correlated with IQ scores. In other words, scores of the TIMSS or PISA, for example, may be measuring the same thing as IQ tests. This finding led him to conclude that "different scales of student assessment studies and different cognitive test approaches appear to have measured essentially the same construct, namely general national cognitive ability" (Rindermann, 2007, p. 687). That is, the quality measured by international tests that claim to measure educational quality may actually be measuring no more than the good old IQ.

Thus, the limitation of IQ test scores in predicting individual success should equally apply to predicting national success. In other words, as these numbers shouldn't be taken to measure education quality, they shouldn't be used to measure the entire spectrum of human qualities needed to build strong and prosperous economies of a nation, even if the qualities required for different economies can probably be different, as Tienken (2008) has found. As Keith Baker (2007) concludes after studying the relationship between international test scores and national prosperity,

> Among high-scoring nations, a certain level of educational attainment, as reflected in test scores, provides a platform for launching national success, but once that platform is reached, other factors become more important than further gains in test scores. Indeed, once the platform is reached, it may be bad policy to pursue further gains in test scores because focusing on the scores diverts attention, effort, and resources away from other factors that are more important determinants of national success. (p. 104)

A plausible alternative explanation of the U.S. situation can be developed from what I argue in my book *World Class Learners: Educating Creative and Entrepreneurial Students* (Zhao, 2012), in which I propose two paradigms of education: *employee-oriented* and *entrepreneur-oriented*. The employee-oriented paradigm aims to transmit a prescribed set of content (the curriculum and standards) deemed to be useful for future life by external authorities, while the entrepreneur-oriented paradigm aims to cultivate individual talents and enhance individual strengths. The employee-oriented paradigm produces homogenous, compliant, and standardized workers for mass employment, while the entrepreneur-oriented paradigm encourages individuality, diversity, and creativity.

Although in general all mainstream education systems in the world currently follow the employee-oriented paradigm, some may not be doing so as effectively and successfully as others. The international test scores may be an indicator of how successful and effective the employee-oriented paradigm has been executed. In other words, these numbers are measures of how successful the prescribed content has been transmitted to all students. But the prescribed content does not have much to do with an already industrialized country such as the United States, whose economy relies on innovation, creativity, and entrepreneurship. As a result, although American schools have not been as effective or successful in transmitting knowledge as the test scores indicate, they have somehow produced more creative entrepreneurs, who have kept the country's economy going. Moreover, it is possible that on the way to produce those high test scores, other education systems may have discouraged the cultivation of the creative and entrepreneurial spirit and capacity.

Where Do We Go From Here?

Numbers don't lie, but they can be used to endorse lies. A single number rarely tells the whole truth. As we have seen, test scores, particularly test scores that purport to measure cognitive skills, tell a partial truth about important human qualities. As measures of educational outcomes, their power should be questioned and limited. In education, we should attempt to escape from what David Boyle (2000) calls the tyranny of numbers.

His "Counting Paradox 8" is good caution; as he notes, "the more sophisticated you are, the less you can measure" (p. 58). He observes,

> We have reached a point where measuring things doesn't work anymore. When you're in politics or business and you need to measure the unmeasurable in order to make things happen—and your career and our lives may depend on you being able to do so—then you have crisis. It is a counting crisis, born out of using numbers to distil the sheer complexity of life into something manageable. The closer you get to measuring what's really important, the more it escapes you. Because number crunching brings a kind of blindness with it. When we measure life, we reduce it. (p. 60)

But it looks like in education we cannot fully escape the tyranny of numbers. There is a strong desire and sometimes the necessity for measuring our students, teachers, and schools; let's at least expand what we measure. Moreover, let's treat any number, any test score, with suspicion because it can never fully capture the entirety of a human being.

References and Resources

Baker, K. (2007). Are international tests worth anything? *Phi Delta Kappan, 89*(2), 101–104.

Barnett, S. M., & Williams, W. (2004). National intelligence and the emperor's new clothes. *Contemporary Psychology: APA Review of Books, 49*(4), 389–396.

Berhanu, G. (2007). Black intellectual genocide: An essay review of *IQ and the Wealth of Nations. Education Review, 10*(6), 1–28.

Bettinger, E. P., Evans, B. J., & Pope, D. G. (2011, June). *Improving college performance and retention the easy way: Unpacking the ACT exam* (Working Paper No. 17119). Cambridge, MA: National Bureau of Economic Research.

Bloomberg. (2015). *The Bloomberg Innovation Index.* Accessed at www.bloomberg.com/graphics /2015-innovative-countries/ on July 30, 2015.

Boyle, D. (2000). *The tyranny of numbers: Why counting can't make us happy.* New York: HarperCollins.

Brigham, C. C. (1923). *A study of American intelligence.* Princeton, NJ: Princeton University Press.

Burton, N. W., & Ramist, L. (2001). *Predicting success in college: SAT studies of classes graduating since 1980* (College Board Research Report No. 2001-2). New York: College Board.

Ceci, S. J. (1996). *On intelligence: A bioecological treatise on intellectual development* (Expanded ed.). Cambridge, MA: Harvard University Press.

Chandler, M. (Director & Writer). (1999). Secrets of the SAT [Television series episode]. In D. Fanning & M. Sullivan (Executive Producers), *Frontline.* Arlington, VA: Public Broadcasting Service.

Compton, R. A. (Executive Producer), & Heeter, C. (Director). (2008). *Two million minutes: A global examination* [Motion picture]. Arlington, VA: Broken Pencil.

Conley, D. T. (2012). *A complete definition of college and career readiness*. Eugene, OR: Educational Policy Improvement Center. Accessed at www.epiconline.org/publications /documents/College%20and%20Career%20Readiness%20Definition.pdf on March 23, 2015.

Crisis in education. (1958, March 24). *Life, 44*(12), 27. Accessed at http://books.google.com /books?id=PlYEAAAAMBAJ&printsec=frontcover&source=gbs_ge_summary_r&cad=0#v =onepage&q&f=false on March 23, 2015.

Firkowska-Mankiewicz, A. (2002). Intelligence (IQ) as a predictor of life success. *International Journal of Sociology, 32*(3), 25–43.

Florida, R. (2011, October 5). *The Global Creativity Index*. Accessed at www.citylab.com/work /2011/10/global-creativity-index/229 on March 23, 2015.

Gardner, H. (1999). *Intelligence reframed: multiple intelligences for the 21st century*. New York: Basic Books.

Geiser, S. (2002). UC and the SAT: Predictive validity and differential impact of the SAT I and SAT II at the University of California. *Educational Assessment, 8*(1), 1–26.

Goleman, D. (1995a). *Emotional intelligence*. New York: Bantam Books.

Goleman, D. (1995b, March 7). 75 years later, study still tracking geniuses. *The New York Times*. Accessed at www.nytimes.com/1995/03/07/science/75-years-later-study-still-tracking -geniuses.html on March 23, 2015.

Gould, S. J. (1996). *The mismeasure of man* (Revised and expanded ed.). New York: Norton.

Hanushek, E. A., & Woessmann, L. (2008). The role of cognitive skills in economic development. *Journal of Economic Literature, 46*(3), 607–668.

Hanushek, E. A., & Woessmann, L. (2010). *The high cost of low educational performance: The long-run economic impact of improving PISA outcomes*. Paris: Organisation for Economic Co-operation and Development.

Hiss, W. C., & Franks, V. W. (2014). *Defining promise: Optional standardized testing policies in American college and university admissions*. Arlington, VA: National Association for College Admission Counseling. Accessed at www.nacacnet.org/research/research -data/nacac-research/Documents/DefiningPromise.pdf on March 23, 2015.

Interview: Claude Steele. (1999). *Frontline: Secrets of the SAT*. Accessed at www.pbs.org/wgbh /pages/frontline/shows/sats/interviews/steele.html on August 3, 2015.

Kaufman, S. B. (2009, September 9). The truth about the "termites." *Psychology Today*. Accessed at www.psychologytoday.com/blog/beautiful-minds/200909/the-truth-about-the-termites on March 23, 2015.

Kobrin, J. L., Patterson, B. F., Shaw, E. J., Mattern, K. D., & Barbuti, S. M. (2008). *Validity of the SAT for predicting first-year college grade point average* (College Board Research Report No. 2008-5). New York: College Board.

Leslie, M. (2000, July/August). The vexing legacy of Lewis Terman. *Stanford Magazine*. Accessed at https://alumni.stanford.edu/get/page/magazine/article/?article_id=40678 on March 23, 2015.

Lynn, R., & Vanhanen, T. (2002). *IQ and the wealth of nations.* Westport, CT: Praeger.

Marte, J. (2011, April 5). *10 things test-prep services won't tell you.* Accessed at www.marketwatch
.com/story/10-things-testprep-services-wont-tell-you-1301943701454 on January 15, 2015.

McClelland, D. C., & Franz, C. E. (1992). Motivational and other sources of work
accomplishments in mid-life: A longitudinal study. *Journal of Personality, 60*(4), 679–707.

Medrich, E. A., & Griffith, J. E. (1992). *International mathematics and science assessment:
What have we learned?* (NCES 92-011). Washington, DC: National Center for Education
Statistics, U.S. Department of Education. Accessed at http://nces.ed.gov/pubs92/92011.pdf
on March 23, 2015.

Meyer, H.-D., & Benavot, A. (Eds.). (2013). *PISA, power, and policy: The emergence of global
educational governance.* Providence, RI: Symposium Books.

National Center for Education Statistics. (1999). *Highlights from TIMSS: The Third
International Mathematics and Science Study* (NCES 1999-081). Washington, DC: Office of
Educational Research and Improvement, U.S. Department of Education. Accessed at http://
nces.ed.gov
/pubs99/1999081.pdf on March 23, 2015.

National Center for Education Statistics. (2003). *Trends in International Mathematics and
Science Study (TIMSS) 2003 results.* Accessed at http://nces.ed.gov/timss/results03.asp on
March 23, 2015.

National Center for Education Statistics. (2007). *Trends in International Mathematics and
Science Study (TIMSS) 2007 results.* Accessed at http://nces.ed.gov/timss/results07.asp on
March 23, 2015.

National Center for Fair and Open Testing. (2015). *University admissions test takers 1986–2014.*
Accessed at www.fairtest.org/sites/default/files/ACT-SAT-Annual-Test-Takers-Chart.pdf on
January 15, 2015.

National Commission on Excellence in Education. (1983). *A nation at risk: The imperative for
educational reform.* Washington, DC: U.S. Government Printing Office. Accessed at http://
datacenter.spps.org/uploads/SOTW_A_Nation_at_Risk_1983.pdf on March 23, 2015.

Noble, J., & Sawyer, R. (2002). *Predicting different levels of academic success in college using high
school GPA and ACT composite score.* Iowa City, IA: ACT.

Oden, M. H. (1968). The fulfillment of promise: 40-year follow-up of the Terman gifted
group. *Genetic Psychology Monographs, 77,* 3–93.

Partnership for Assessment of Readiness for College and Careers. (2012). *PARCC college-
and-career-ready (CCR) determination policy in and policy-level performance descriptors.*
Washington, DC: Author.

Pathe, S., & Choe, J. (2013, February 4). *A brief overview of teacher evaluation controversies.*
Accessed at www.pbs.org/newshour/rundown/teacher-evaluation-controversies on July 30,
2015.

Rindermann, H. (2007). The g-factor of international cognitive ability comparisons: The
homogeneity of results in PISA, TIMSS, PIRLS and IQ-tests across nations. *European
Journal of Personality, 21*(5), 667–706.

Rindermann, H. (2012). Intellectual classes, technological progress and economic development: The rise of cognitive capitalism. *Personality and Individual Differences*, *53*(2), 108–113.

Simonton, D. K. (1994). *Greatness: Who makes history and why.* New York: Guilford Press.

Sorokin, P. A. (1956). *Fads and foibles in modern sociology and related sciences.* Chicago: Regnery.

Sternberg, R. J. (1987). *Beyond IQ: A triarchic theory of human intelligence.* Cambridge [Cambridgeshire]; New York: Cambridge University Press.

Stevenson, H. W., & Stigler, J. W. (1992). *The learning gap: Why our schools are failing and what we can learn from Japanese and Chinese education.* New York: Simon & Schuster.

Tienken, C. H. (2008). Rankings of international achievement test performance and economic strength: Correlation or conjecture? *International Journal of Education Policy and Leadership*, *3*(4), 1–15.

Tucker, M. S. (Ed.). (2011). *Surpassing Shanghai: An agenda for American education built on the world's leading systems.* Cambridge, MA: Harvard Education Press.

World Economic Forum. (2015). *Competitiveness rankings.* Accessed at http://reports.weforum .org/global-competitiveness-report-2014-2015/rankings/ on July 30, 2015.

World Intellectual Property Organization. (2014, March 13). *US and China drive international patent filing growth in record-setting year.* Accessed at www.wipo.int/pressroom /en/articles/2014/article_0002.html on July 30, 2015.

Zhao, Y. (2012). *World class learners: Educating creative and entrepreneurial students.* Thousand Oaks, CA: Corwin Press.

Zhao, Y. (2014). *Who's afraid of the big bad dragon? Why China has the best (and worst) education system in the world.* San Francisco: Jossey-Bass.

Sarah Soltz is a doctoral candidate in the Department of Educational Methodology, Policy, and Leadership at the University of Oregon, and a Title I reading specialist in the Scappoose School District in Oregon. She is a former early childhood educator at a large corporate child development program near Portland, Oregon, where she worked as a head classroom teacher with children ages newborn to three years. She has been an educator for over ten years and worked with learners aged three months through adulthood.

Soltz's core beliefs in equity and social justice inform her work with children and adults. She is a member of the National Association for the Education of Young Children (NAEYC). She is a Master Trainer on the Oregon Registry, and has presented professional development workshops for early childhood educators throughout Oregon. She presents on a variety of topics including equity and inclusion, Positive Behavior Intervention and Support (PBIS), and early literacy. Soltz's areas of research include literacy, adult learning, and leadership.

Soltz received a bachelor's degree in philosophy and politics from New York University and a master's degree in elementary education from Teachers College at Columbia University. She will defend her dissertation in 2016.

To book Sarah Soltz for professional development, contact pd@solution-tree.com.

CHAPTER 2

Celebrity for Nothing: The Rise of the Undervalued

SARAH SOLTZ

In purely economic terms, Alana Thompson, better known as Honey Boo Boo, was more successful at age eight than most college graduates or PhDs. The star of the reality TV series *Here Comes Honey Boo Boo* was worth $800,000 in 2014, according to Celebrity Net Worth (n.d.), a website that tracks the assets of celebrities. She, together with her family members who also appear on the show, was paid between $5,000 and $15,000 per episode (TMZ, 2012). The series aired on TLC for four seasons from 2012 to 2014 ("Here Comes Honey Boo Boo," n.d.). Alana's mother, Mama June Shannon, was said to have a net worth of $1 million before the show was cancelled later in 2014.

Honey Boo Boo is one of the "celebrities for nothing," people who are famous for the banality of their existence. She lives in the town of McIntyre, Georgia, with a population of just under seven hundred. Alana is a juvenile beauty pageant contestant made famous by the television series *Toddlers and Tiaras*, which first aired on TLC in 2009. In its third season (2014), *Here Comes Honey Boo Boo* attracted slightly under two million viewers per episode, and in its first season, it was among the highest-rated shows on TLC ("Here Comes Honey Boo Boo," n.d.).

The show's reviews include more criticism than praise, and it has not been necessarily a smash hit. Not many people believe Alana and her family members have great talent or expertise. In other words, they are rewarded financially simply for being famous. They are celebrities for nothing. The Shannons spend their days like many Americans, concerned with work and taking care of the family. They are not rewarded for their skills, certainly not skills that traditional education would consider valuable.

The Shannon family offers a sample of contemporary American culture and insight to the changing nature of celebrity and success. There are numerous celebrities for nothing in the modern world. If Honey Boo Boo does not fit your definition of success, and indeed criticism abounds about the show, here is Dancing Matt. Matt Harding is an ordinary American and average dancer. Matt is a celebrity, an icon of pop culture. He travels to different countries and makes appearances dancing with different folks. Matt has been dancing publicly since 2008 and maintains a website, wherethehellismatt.com. Matt's dancing videos on YouTube have more hits than videos of choreographer and *Nutcracker* dancer Mikhail Baryshnikov.

Or consider the success of the Shaytards. The Shaytards are an American family with a lucrative YouTube channel, featuring a daily vlog upload of banal family affairs. The family's Christmas videos have received over three million hits on their channel, SHAYTARDS. Father Shay, mother Colette, and three children, affectionately dubbed "babytards" by Mom and Dad, can be found engaging in typical antics of American middle-class family life. Footage of shopping for groceries, playing practical jokes, or cooking dinner is commonplace on the Shaytard's channel. The Shaytards represent a slice of American life, having done everything ordinary and nothing extraordinary.

The list of celebrities for nothing continues. The Kardashians, Paris Hilton, and Kevin Federline all experience this cyclical fame and fortune. They are famous for being well known. The Shannons, Dancing Matt, and the Shaytards, among other celebrities, illustrate what Neal Gabler (2001) calls the "Zsa Zsa Factor." Gabler presents the Zsa Zsa Factor as a way to reconcile cognitive dissonance people experience when reflecting on the nature of the success of the aforementioned celebrities. He explains, "There are obviously people who have gained recognition for having done virtually nothing of significance" (Gabler, 2001, p. 2). Gabler emerges from Daniel Boorstin's (1961) roots as a postmodern social critic popularizing the phrase "famous for being famous." Any public appearance capturing the banality of existence can now be a sufficient cause of fame.

How the Useless Becomes Useful

Honey Boo Boo, the Kardashians, Matt Harding, and other celebrities for nothing may be disagreeable to many people, certainly educators. But examined from a broader perspective, they simply exemplify an emerging social phenomenon: the increasing consumption of nothingness. The human society, particularly in developed countries, has begun to consume unnecessary things. We are all guilty of consuming choices, for example. We are no longer satisfied with just one type, one brand, or one flavor of potato chips. Thus, supermarkets offer hundreds of different types of chips. Unlike centuries ago when we were happy if we had a bar of soap, today we want to be able to choose the right one for our unique, individualized hair quality from hundreds of varieties. The choices are absolutely unnecessary. Human survival does not depend on the number of varieties of chips, shampoo, or TV channels, nor does it rely on buying a new cell phone every two years.

But we want them. And our wants become the reason the traditionally useless talents, skills, and knowledge become useful, and the traditionally undervalued become valuable. There are two major reasons for the rise of the traditionally undervalued talents: (1) the age of abundance, and (2) a global customer base.

The Age of Abundance

Human beings differ from other animals in many different aspects. One of them is psychological and spiritual activity beyond physiological need. Humans have a long history of creating and enjoying art, music, dance, literature, drama, sports, and other forms of entertainment, as well as seeking beauty, spiritual life, and psychological counseling. As a result, human societies have often put a value on talents and skills that help meet these needs. But until recently, human consumption of spiritual and psychological products and services has remained a luxury, typically reserved for the wealthy and powerful. The majority of the ordinary worked to meet their physiological needs and could only consume psychological and spiritual products and services on rare occasions. Thus, talents and skills in producing spiritual and psychological products have been historically undervalued. Except for a few lucky ones, those who possessed these talents and skills have been considered useless.

The arrival of the era of abundance, marked by the growth in consumer opportunities available since the 1970s (Pink, 2005), has dramatically increased the value of the historically undervalued talents. Technology has increased human productivity, and increased productivity has enabled human beings to devote less time and energy to securing necessities, resulting in a growth of wealth, more disposable income, and more free time. Many humans thus have the means, time, and desire to pursue unmet and even unrecognized needs in the age of necessity. Economist Gregory Clark (2007) writes in his book *A Farewell to Alms: A Brief Economic History of the World,*

> The average person in the world of 1800 was no better off than the average person of 100,000 BC. Indeed in 1800 the bulk of the world's population was poorer than their remote ancestors. The lucky denizens of wealthy societies such as eighteenth-century England or the Netherlands managed a material lifestyle equivalent to that of the Stone Age. But the vast swath of humanity in East and South Asia, particularly in China and Japan, eked out a living under conditions probably significantly poorer than those of cavemen. (p. 1)

It is not hard to imagine that, when humans were worried about their next meal, they were not deeply concerned about what brand of shampoo they should use. But today, despite the uneven distribution of wealth, the majority of the seven billion people are not worried about their next meal. In fact, some are worried about which gym to go to or what equipment to use in order to get rid of their last meal. In 2013, average global wealth reached $51,600 per adult (Clark, 2013). In the United States, the average yearly household income increased by sixty-seven-fold from $750 in 1901 to $50,302 in 2002 (U.S. Bureau of Labor Statistics, 2006). Even after adjustment for inflation, the average income in the United States would have increased three- to fourfold.

Increased income means increased spending. The average U.S. household expenditures increased from $769 in 1901 to $40,748 in 2002. More important, the percentage of expenditures on necessities (food, clothing, and housing) has fallen dramatically from nearly 80 percent in 1901 to just about 50 percent in 2002. Americans allocate a much higher proportion of their income (49.9 percent versus 20 percent) on psychological and spiritual products and services, the non-necessities—such as entertainment, charity, education, personal care, vacationing, and health—than they did in the early 1900s (U.S. Bureau of Labor Statistics, 2006).

Increased spending on non-necessities has created opportunities for traditionally undervalued talents and skills. For example, while entertainment has always accompanied the human society, it did not become a lucrative business until the modern world. Industries such as film, video and TV, video games, music, and online entertainment did not even exist in the early 1900s, but today they employ millions of people and make a significant contribution to the economy. In the United States, for example, the number of jobs in the arts, entertainment, and recreation sector doubled from a little over one million in 1990 to over two million in 2014, while jobs in automobile manufacturing decreased from over one million in 1990 to fewer than nine hundred thousand in 2014 (U.S. Bureau of Labor Statistics, 2015). The entertainment and media industry is projected to reach $555 billion in the United States and $1.9 trillion worldwide by 2015 (PricewaterhouseCoopers, 2011).

Spiritual and psychological needs are more diverse than physiological needs. In the age of necessity when food was scarce, the primary task was to secure enough nutrition. It would have been difficult for most people to be picky about what form the nutrition came in or what shape of plate the food was served on. But today, even food has become a psychological product and service. The mushrooming of TV cooking shows, boutique and artisan restaurants, and inventive cuisine and restaurant settings exemplifies human needs for diversity, as do the hundreds of TV channels, the over twenty-six million songs available for download on iTunes (Apple, Inc., 2012), and perhaps thousands of different cases for smartphones. Personalized consumption is a hallmark of the age of abundance, when people want choices and the ability to customize consumption to fit their individual needs. Personalization helps create demands for more unique products and services. This is why, among the many available entertainment programs, even not-so-great shows like *Here Comes Honey Boo Boo* have viewers.

The arrival of the age of abundance has increased the demand for nonmaterial non-necessity products and services, which has led to the emergence of new industries. The emergence and expansion of new industries such as entertainment, fashion design, video gaming, social media, and many others provide opportunities for the traditionally undervalued talents and skills to gain economic and social value.

A Global Customer Base

Like Honey Boo Boo, if Madonna lived in the 1800s, her talent would perhaps at best be rewarded with some applause and perhaps a few free beers in the village bar instead of the millions of dollars she makes today. The same goes for sports talents like Michael Jordan, David Beckham, and Derek Jeter. Take the Chinese basketball player Yao Ming as an example. He earned a salary totaling $93 million during the ten years he played for the National Basketball Association (NBA) ("Yao Ming," n.d.). He is tall and skilled in playing basketball, of course. But his height and skills would not have earned him much long ago.

What brings Honey Boo Boo, Madonna, Michael Jordan, and Yao Ming their fortune is the access to a global consumer pool of seven billion people made possible by technology, coupled with the diverse needs in the age of abundance. It is estimated that about 40 percent of this seven billion have Internet access, with access growing daily ("Internet Users," n.d.). With such a vast potential base of consumers, even if only a small fraction of the potential consumers choose to have something, the eventual total number can be staggering. This is the *long tail* phenomenon.

Best-selling author Chris Anderson (2006) writes about this phenomenon in his book *The Long Tail: Why the Future of Business Is Selling Less of More*. Traditional physical stores such as Costco, Best Buy, or Barnes & Noble must consider carefully what items they can put on the shelf based on their potential appeal to the local customers. So do local music stores, restaurants, and furniture stores because these businesses count on "hits"—items that appeal to a large percentage of customers who can visit them physically. As a result, only a very limited number of products make it to the market. But online stores like Amazon, eBay, and iTunes are different. They benefit from selling "misses"—items that may appeal to only a small fraction of people. Given the large number of people they can reach globally, they can always find somebody who is interested in something, however odd it may be.

The same thing can happen and has happened for human talents and skills. There are certain talents or skills that may just be needed by a very small percentage of people. Thus, if the total number of people who can gain access to these talents and skills is small, there would not be enough people in one location to turn the talent or skill into viable businesses. Worse, there might be no one in a local community who needs the available talent or skill. Thus, these rare talents are in essence useless.

However, when made available on a global scale, the number of those who may need or appreciate this unique talent or skill can become large enough to make it economically viable. Soccer is a telling example. Long ago, it was hard to believe that the ability to kick a ball would become the multibillion-dollar business that it is today. Not counting all the revenues of national and local soccer activities and related businesses, Fédération Internationale de Football Association, better known as FIFA (n.d.), had over $4 billion in revenue during the period of 2007 to 2010. Its 2010 World Cup games in South Africa received $2.4 billion in television rights and $1 billion in marketing rights. The most recent World Cup held in Brazil in 2014 was estimated to generate over $4 billion for FIFA (Ozanian, 2014). This is possible because the games are broadcast globally. Even if a small percentage of the total seven billion people watch the games, the viewership can be extraordinary. For example, an average of 188.4 million people watched one game of the 2010 tournament, while the total number of viewers reached nearly three billion (Voigt, 2014). This means that many people had access to and consumed the ball-kicking talents of the players. By comparison, only ninety-three thousand people watched the final game of the first FIFA World Cup tournament when it was held in Montevideo, Uruguay, in 1930 ("1930 FIFA World Cup Final," n.d.).

Technology has transformed how humans interact with one another in such a way that many talents and skills that had little economic and social value have become more valuable. With increased productivity and wealth, humans can now better attend to their spiritual and psychological needs. With a globally interconnected economy, individual talents have gained the potential to reach a large consumer base. Taken together, the human society now offers opportunities for anyone to become valuable, to enjoy the broad spectrum of human capacities, and to reward the broad range of human diversity and variability.

Human Diversity: Strengths and Weaknesses

Human differences themselves make such a multiplicity of talents possible and valued. Over the past three decades since the first publication of Howard Gardner's seminal book *Frames of Mind: The Theory of Multiple Intelligences* in 1983, the idea that there is more than one "intelligence" and each of us possesses a unique set of intelligences has been generally accepted. Gardner initially suggested that the "multiple intelligences" included seven different types: (1) linguistic, (2) logical-mathematical, (3) musical, (4) bodily-kinesthetic, (5) spatial, (6) interpersonal, and (7) intrapersonal. Later, more types were added.

Gardner suggests that each individual manifests varying levels of these different intelligences. That is, we are intelligent in different domains, more or less intelligent in some areas than others. In other words, we are born to be good at some things but poor at others. As a result, each of us has a unique talent profile.

Of course, most of us are not extremely polarized in that we can do something extremely well but cannot do other things at all. This is why the majority of the population, regardless of race or sex, can learn to read and write, sing, dance, speak different languages, do basic math, play soccer, paint, and swim. But not everyone can paint as well as Pablo Picasso or play basketball as well as Michael Jordan because aptitude matters.

The difference in aptitude, or our predisposition to learn, may not be huge in the majority of the human race. However, it does result in differences in how fast one learns something and the ultimate level one can reach. Anthropologist Jane Goodall (1971) writes in her book *In the Shadow of Man*, "Some humans are mathematicians; others aren't" (p. 245). This partially explains why some people can learn foreign languages faster than others, why some children learn to read earlier than others, and why some excel in math while others paint better.

Nature, or what we are born with, gives the potential. But nurture, our experiences after birth, can either suppress or enhance that potential, as the British popular science writer Matt Ridley (2003) explains the dynamics between nature and nurture in his book *Nature via Nurture: Genes, Experience, and What Makes Us Human*. Someone may be born with great potential in art, but that potential needs training in arts to be realized. Someone may not be a genius in writing, but excellent writing lessons can certainly help improve his writing skills. Thus, human talents become further diversified due to culture and educational experiences.

Human beings cannot be equally talented in everything. They may be mediocre at lots of things, but they cannot be great at many because to become great requires lots of time. Popular writer Malcolm Gladwell (2008) suggests if one wants to succeed in something, ten thousand hours are needed. Author Daniel Coyle (2009) has similar observations and added the need for good feedback and aptitude. The ten-thousand-hour rule may not be precise; it could be nine thousand or eleven thousand hours, for instance. But it is a fact that if one wishes to be great at something, lots of time is needed, for sure. Time is a constant. If one spends ten thousand hours on learning one thing, he cannot spend the same ten thousand hours on something else. As a result, a person can only choose to be great in a few domains.

Whether it is nature or nurture, or nature via nurture, human beings can become great in some areas and at the same time not great, even very weak, in other domains. The other side of the coin is then when one is weak at something, she can be great at other things. Even the same trait can be both an advantage and a disadvantage at the same time. For example, there is increasing evidence to support the hypothesis that dyslexia may be a blessing in disguise (West, 2005). While people with dyslexia may have difficulty reading, they are likely blessed with more talent in creativity and working with images. But for a long time, visual talents have not been as valued as the ability to read. Dyslexia has been considered a deficit.

Fixing Deficits: Bias Against Diversity

Human beings have made much progress toward accepting diversity. It is not just nice to be tolerant of people who are different; it is actually beneficial. University of Michigan sociology professor Scott Page (2007) brings much evidence to show the value of diversity in his book, *The Difference: How the Power of Diversity Creates Better Groups, Firms, Schools, and Societies*. In the United States, for example, it is illegal to discriminate against people based on race, gender, religion, or national origin. Americans are encouraged to celebrate the diversity of cultures, languages, and family styles reflected in our communities. However, American schools, and schools all over the world, are some of the most intolerant institutions with regard to talents. They explicitly favor certain types of talents and skills and discriminate against others. Children who are talented or equipped with better skills in math, language arts, and sciences are viewed as talented and gifted. For example, in order to be identified as Talented and Gifted (TAG) in Oregon, students must score in the 97th percentile on a standardized test of either reading, math, or mental ability (Oregon Department of Education, 2015). These students are celebrated and given more resources to further develop their talents and skills. Children who are talented or interested in some areas such as arts, music, interpersonal skills, or intrapersonal skills are given fewer opportunities and resources, if they can keep up with reading and math. If not, they are considered "at risk" and sent to remedial lessons to help fix their deficits. The euphemism for these students is *special education*. But it is possible that the students who are good at math and reading may be horrible at arts, music, or swimming. Why should their deficits not be fixed?

Schools also allocate many more resources to cultivate their favored talents and skills. Math and language arts are given much more attention than any other subjects, as evidenced by the subject areas addressed in the Common Core State Standards. Federal Title I funds can be used to implement activities within a school to increase student achievement in reading or math, but not in the creative arts. No Child Left Behind and the Common Core State Standards movement have shifted the focus to mathematics and English language arts in U.S. schools. Arts, music, sports, and other subjects are only available in wealthier schools, to students who have done well in mathematics and reading, and when the school is not pressed to show adequate performance on standardized tests in mathematics and reading. At tax-supported public educational institutions, why do some taxpayers' children deserve to have their talents and interests better supported than others?

The usual justification goes something like this: it's for their own good because mathematics and reading skills are more important than others. Everyone needs the fundamentals in reading and math. People are suggesting that if a child does not learn to read by third grade, he is doomed for life. This may have been true in the past because most jobs required similar left-brain-directed thinking skills in a narrow spectrum—verbal, quantitative, and logical. Most jobs also required these skills at a mediocre level in order to follow instructions and perform routine jobs. However, society has changed. We have entered a society in which all talents, when fully developed, can be valuable. We now live in a world where all talents, even the ones "once disdained or thought frivolous," have become very valuable (Pink, 2005, p. 3).

More importantly, routine jobs are rapidly disappearing due to automation and off-shoring. Today, we need great talents to create new jobs and opportunities. Thus, not only must we cease discrimination against other talents, we need to actively change the education paradigm into one that cultivates all talents and supports the development of greatness and creativity in all children (Zhao, 2012).

The Science and Education of the Individual

The new paradigm of education should be about the individual. It is a radical departure from the traditional paradigm that is about the group and the average. The Center for Individual Opportunity (www.individualopportunity.org) is a pioneer in advocating for understanding and creating opportunities for the individual because it recognizes the mistakes we have committed in the past.

Since the mid-19th century, we have used averages to understand individuals. The assumption has been that either the average itself represents everyone, or else it is your deviation from average that defines you. Today, the average determines how we study individuals, the way that we design institutions, and how we measure potential and performance. There is just one problem with this approach: it is fundamentally wrong.

The center calls the past paradigm "science of nobody" because "averages rarely tell you about individuals" (Center for Individual Opportunity, n.d.). To understand individuals, we need a new science of the individual (Rose, Rouhani, & Fischer, 2013) that ignores the averages but focuses on understanding individual variability. While celebrating the progress of the new science of the individual, the Center for Individual Opportunity (n.d.) laments on the lack of progress "in our institutions of opportunity," such as education.

Despite the diversity of our society and the economic necessity of developing more talent, our institutions remain firmly committed to average. The way we design educational materials, assess learning, measure intelligence, hire employees, and evaluate performance—all of it is based on the myth of average, and none of it is based on insights about real-life individuals. No wonder we have a problem.

Built on the new science of the individual, we can imagine a shift in education as a major social institution of opportunities, from the education of the average to the education of the individual. Such a shift starts with the definition of what matters, or what skills are worth learning, or what talents are worth developing.

Counting Valuable Talents: A Brief History of the Expansion of Definitions

Our understanding of the nature of human talents has evolved over time, and fortunately, it has become increasingly broadened. The late scientist Stephen Jay Gould (1996) provides a very critical account of early development in understanding and measuring human abilities in his book, *The Mismeasure of Man*. Charles Spearman (1904) was one of the first to popularize the concept of intelligence as a single variable, *g*, that can be objectively measured through testing. There are significant flaws to Spearman's theory. Spearman makes the circular assumption that intelligence is singular and fixed in order to arrive at the conclusion that there exists a general mental ability. Admitting a singular mental ability opens up the possibility for creating rankings and hierarchies, a prized outcome for experimental sciences. The historic conception of intelligence as a singular quantity as suggested by Spearman lingers in the policies and practices of current structures of education.

The work of Alfred Binet, Théodore Simon, and Lewis Terman at the turn of the 20th century influenced the development of the intelligence quotient, or IQ, which has become a popular way to indicate the "smartness" of people with a single number (Binet, Simon, & Terman, 1916). One result of using a composite score to indicate intelligence is that scores can be ranked and individuals compared to one another based on a quantitative summary. The Binet-Simon Scale supported the development of the contemporary concept of IQ and other measures of intelligence. The Wechsler Adult Intelligence Scale, WAIS-IV, was developed during World War II and is the leading adult intelligence test.

In the years since the introduction of Spearman's *g*, IQ, and the WAIS-IV, many psychologists and educators have embraced a multifaceted understanding of intelligence as advanced by Howard Gardner (1993, 2011). Contemporary versions of Gardner's theory of multiple intelligences include eight intelligences, shown in table 2.1. All individuals construct an understanding of the world using multiple intelligences rather than a singular, general mental ability or function. Individuals often use combinations of intelligences to solve problems and make sense of the world.

Around the mid-1990s, emotional intelligence (EI) began to be added as a valuable human quality. Science writer Daniel Goleman's (1995) book *Emotional Intelligence* made the term *EQ*, or *emotional quotient*, a household concept. There are different theories about emotional intelligence and abundant controversy about the various EI measures. But it has been generally accepted that human ability to regulate one's emotions and process emotional information is a critical quality, perhaps even more important than IQ in determining one's success.

Table 2.1: Multiple Intelligences

Intelligence	Attributes
Language and Communication	Uses words to communicate ideas
Mathematical and Logical	Uses reasoning chains and abstraction
Construction and Spatial Design	Uses mental visualization of shapes and relationships
Physical and Sport Activity	Uses muscular movement to learn
Musical and Rhythmic	Uses songs or rhythms to learn
Social and Leadership	Uses interpersonal relationships to develop empathy
Self-awareness	Uses introspection and self-reflection to arrive at understanding
Nature and Environmental	Uses natural classification and nurturing

Source: Adapted from Gardner, H. (1983, 2011). Frames of mind: The theory of multiple intelligences. *New York: Basic Books.*

Toward the end of the 20th century, the concept of 21st century skills began to spread. The argument is the 21st century needs a different set of skills than the 20th century (Trilling & Fadel, 2009). While *21st century skills* is a catchall phrase to describe a wide range of skills traditional education does not typically address, it has many different interpretations (European Commission, 2007; Partnership for 21st Century Skills, n.d.). The commonly mentioned interpretation of 21st century skills includes the four Cs: creativity, critical thinking, communication, and collaboration (Kay & Greenhill, 2013). Harvard researcher Tony Wagner (2008) proposes seven "survival skills" for the new world: (1) critical thinking and problem solving, (2) collaboration across networks and leading by influence, (3) agility and adaptability, (4) initiative and entrepreneurialism, (5) effective oral and written communication, (6) accessing and analyzing information, and (7) curiosity and imagination.

Besides the expansion in defining valuable talents beyond a single cognitive measure to include many more factors, Daniel Pink (2005) brings evidence to support the rising value of six "high concept and high touch" skills, namely the *R*-directed skills, or the creative and human-centered skills. These *R*-directed skills include (1) design, (2) story, (3) symphony, (4) empathy, (5) play, and (6) meaning. These skills create artists, inventors, designers, storytellers, caregivers, consolers, and big-picture thinkers, all of whom are in high demand in the new age, according to Pink (2005).

Counting Individual Strengths: Personalized Assessment

Unfortunately while the definition of valuable skills has dramatically expanded, the practice of counting what's valuable has not changed. In fact, the practice in schools has gotten worse with the introduction of high-stakes standardized testing in only a few subjects. Worse yet, the mindset of *average* still persists.

With these newly developed and expanded definitions of valuable talents, skills, and qualities, the dominant view is still that all children should develop all these talents, skills, and qualities, which is utterly impossible. Instead of expecting every child to be equally good or average in all the domains, we need to look at the strength of each individual child. Further, we also need to count and value talents, skills, and qualities that may not be included in any of the proposed valuable skills.

Countering the traditional deficit model of assessment, there is an emerging trend in assessing strengths thanks to new research and perspectives. The increasing acceptance of the view that wellness is more than the absence of deficits has gradually shifted from focusing on repairing the worst thing in life to building the best, positive qualities in life (Jimerson, Sharkey, Nyborg, & Furlong, 2004). A number of strength-based assessments have been developed. University of California–Santa Barbara scholar Shane Jimerson and colleagues reviewed a sample of strength-based assessments school psychologists can use. The assessments include the Behavior Assessment System for Children (BASC), Behavioral and Emotional Rating Scale (BERS), California Healthy Kids Survey Resilience and Youth Development Module (RYDM), Developmental Assets Profile (DAP), Multidimensional Students Life Satisfaction Scale (MSLSS), School Social Behavior Scales-2 (SSBS-2), and Social Skills Rating System (SSRS) (Jimerson et al., 2004).

These assessments, however, do not include all possible strengths, particularly strengths beyond psychological traits. Because each individual is a unique combination of a variety of aptitudes, experiences, contexts, interests, and passions, what we need is personalized assessment of valuable talents. A strength profile for each student is necessary, as suggested by Jenifer Fox (2008) in her book, *Your Child's Strengths: Discover Them, Develop Them, Use Them.*

A strength profile is an evolving record that can be compiled by students, teachers, parents, and the school. The profile can include the student's interests, passions, hobbies, academic and nonacademic activities and achievements, and what he or she is good at or wants to be good at. The profile also can include artifacts the student has produced.

Where Do We Go From Here?

We must reconsider the role and significance of talents and skills that have been traditionally undervalued. Students with these skills and talents have traditionally not been supported. But as this chapter has well documented, we have entered a new society where all talents have become valuable. We can no longer hold all students to the same standard or expectations and consider those unable or unwilling to meet the standards as liabilities. Instead we need to adopt a new paradigm that does not look at what the student cannot do but attempts to discover what he or she can do and help enhance that. After all, if Honey Boo Boo's talent is valuable to someone, any talent can be valuable!

References and Resources

Anderson, C. (2006). *The long tail: Why the future of business is selling less of more*. New York: Hyperion Books.

Apple, Inc. (2012). *Apple unveils new iTunes* [Press release]. Accessed at www.apple.com/pr /library/2012/09/12Apple-Unveils-New-iTunes.html on July 12, 2015.

Binet, A., Simon, T., & Terman, L. M. (1916). *The development of intelligence in children*. (Limited ed., Publications of the Training School at Vineland, New Jersey, Department of Research; no. 11). Nashville, TN: Williams Print.

Boorstin, D. J. (1961). *The image: A guide to pseudo-events in America*. New York: Vintage Books.

Celebrity Net Worth. (n.d.). *Honey Boo Boo child net worth*. Accessed at www.celebritynetworth .com/richest-celebrities/actors/honey-boo-boo-child-net-worth on March 23, 2015.

Center for Individual Opportunity. (n.d.). *The science*. Accessed at www.individualopportunity .org/overview on January 2, 2015.

Clark, G. (2007). *A farewell to alms: A brief economic history of the world*. Princeton, NJ: Princeton University Press.

Clark, M. (2013, October 11). Global wealth hits all-time high, largely from US growth: Credit Suisse (CS) global wealth report. *International Business Times*. Accessed at www .ibtimes.com/global-wealth-hits-all-time-high-largely-us-growth-credit-suisse-cs-global -wealth-report-1421278 on March 23, 2015.

Coyle, D. (2009). *The talent code: Greatness isn't born. It's grown. Here's how*. New York: Bantam Books.

European Commission. (2007). *Key competences for lifelong learning: European reference framework*. Luxembourg: Office for Official Publications of the European Communities.

Fédération Internationale de Football Association. (n.d.). *Income*. Accessed at www.fifa.com /aboutfifa/finances/income.html on January 1, 2015.

Fox, J. (2008). *Your child's strengths: Discover them, develop them, use them*. New York: Viking.

Gabler, N. (2001). *Toward a new definition of celebrity*. Los Angeles: Norman Lear Center. Accessed at www.learcenter.org/images/event_uploads/Gabler.pdf on September 21, 2014.

Gardner, H. (1983, 2011). *Frames of mind: The theory of multiple intelligences*. New York: Basic Books.

Gardner, H. (1993). *Multiple intelligences: The theory in practice*. New York: Basic Books.

Gladwell, M. (2008). *Outliers: The story of success*. New York: Little, Brown.

Goleman, D. (1995). *Emotional intelligence*. New York: Bantam Books.

Goodall, J. (1971). *In the shadow of man*. Boston: Houghton Mifflin Harcourt.

Gould, S. J. (1996). *The mismeasure of man* (Revised and expanded ed.). New York: Norton.

Here Comes Honey Boo Boo. (n.d.) In *Wikipedia*. Accessed at http://en.wikipedia.org/wiki /Here_Comes_Honey_Boo_Boo on May 25, 2015.

"Internet Users." (n.d.). *Internet Live Stats*. Accessed at www.internetlivestats.com/internet-users / on July 12, 2015.

Jimerson, S. R., Sharkey, J. D., Nyborg, V., & Furlong, M. J. (2004). Strength-based assessment and school psychology: A summary and synthesis. *California School Psychologist, 9*(1), 9–19.

Kay, K., & Greenhill, V. (2013). *The leader's guide to 21st century education: 7 steps for schools and districts.* Boston: Pearson.

1930 FIFA World Cup Final. (n.d.). In *Wikipedia.* Accessed at https://en.wikipedia.org/wiki /1930_FIFA_World_Cup_Final on July 12, 2015.

Oregon Department of Education. (2015). *TAG: Frequently asked questions.* Accessed at www .ode.state.or.us/search/page/?id=2321 on July 12, 2015.

Ozanian, M. (2014, June 5). World Cup Brazil will generate $4 billion for FIFA, 66% more than 2010 tournament. *Forbes.* Accessed at www.forbes.com/sites/mikeozanian/2014/06/05 /the-billion-dollar-business-of-the-world-cup on January 1, 2015.

Page, S. E. (2007). *The difference: How the power of diversity creates better groups, firms, schools, and societies.* Princeton, NJ: Princeton University Press.

Partnership for 21st Century Skills. (n.d.). *Framework for 21st century learning.* Accessed at www.p21.org/our-work/p21-framework on March 23, 2015.

Pink, D. H. (2005). *A whole new mind: Why right-brainers will rule the future.* New York: Riverhead Books.

PricewaterhouseCoopers. (2011, November 22). *Global entertainment and media outlook 2011–2015.* Accessed at http://pwc.blogs.com/north/2011/11/global-entertainment-and -media-outlook-2011-2015.html on March 23, 2015.

Ridley, M. (2003). *Nature via nurture: Genes, experience, and what makes us human.* New York: HarperCollins.

Rose, L. T., Rouhani, P., & Fischer, K. W. (2013). The science of the individual. *Mind, Brain, and Education, 7*(3), 152–158.

Spearman, C. (1904). "General intelligence," objectively determined and measured. *American Journal of Psychology, 15*(2), 201–292. Accessed at www.jstor.org/stable/1412107 on March 23, 2015.

TMZ. (2012, October 1). *Honey Boo Boo family: TLC gave them huge raise.* Accessed at www .tmz.com/2012/10/01/here-comes-honey-boo-boo-family-tlc-raise on March 23, 2015.

Trilling, B., & Fadel, C. (2009). *21st century skills: Learning for life in our times.* San Francisco: Jossey-Bass.

U.S. Bureau of Labor Statistics. (2006). *100 years of U.S. consumer spending: Data for the nation, New York City, and Boston* (Report No. 991). Washington, DC: U.S. Department of Labor. Accessed at www.bls.gov/opub/uscs/report991.pdf on March 23, 2015.

U.S. Bureau of Labor Statistics. (2015). *Databases, tables & calculators by subject.* Washington, DC: U.S. Department of Labor. Accessed at http://data.bls.gov/timeseries/CES7071000001 ?data_tool=XGtable on March 23, 2015.

Voigt, K. (2014, June 12). FIFA World Cup: Breakdown of viewership statistics. *Christian Science Monitor.* Accessed at www.csmonitor.com/Business/Saving-Money/2014/0612/FIFA -World-Cup-Breakdown-of-viewership-statistics on January 1, 2015.

Wagner, T. (2008). *The global achievement gap: Why even our best schools don't teach the new survival skills our children need—and what we can do about it.* New York: Basic Books.

West, T. G. (2005). The gifts of dyslexia: Talents among dyslexics and their families. *Hong Kong Journal of Paediatrics, 10*(2), 153–158.

Yao Ming. (n.d.). Accessed at www.basketball-reference.com/players/m/mingya01.html on July 12, 2015.

Zhao, Y. (2012). *World class learners: Educating creative and entrepreneurial students.* Thousand Oaks, CA: Corwin Press.

Dr. Daisy Zhang-Negrerie, PhD, received her bachelor's degree in mathematics from Calvin College, and PhD in physical organic chemistry from the University of Chicago.

After being a university professor for fifteen years, during which she received tenure, multiple awards for teaching excellence, and the Fulbright Scholar Award, Dr. Zhang-Negrerie switched her research efforts to education in the areas of teaching methodology and curriculum development. She decided to implement what she believed should be taught, as well as how it should be taught, in a high school setting. Currently, Dr. Zhang-Negrerie teaches at Concordia International School Shanghai. There, she developed special classes such as Origami and Math, Learn to Design (where students produced innovative products including a nonconventional 3D, spiral-shaped periodic table), and a unique AP Calculus curriculum incorporating interdisciplinary exercises such as poetry, design, and art. Some of her students' poetry and artwork can be found in her most recent books, *From Tangency to Truth: An Intersection of Math, Poetry, and Art* and *Metaphorical Poems from a Calculus Classroom.*

Dr. Zhang-Negrerie has published over seventy journal papers and is a contributing author in more than ten editorial books in the fields of organic synthesis and quantum mechanical computations. She holds a professorship position at Tianjin University as a visiting professor and remains active in these areas of research.

To book Daisy Zhang-Negrerie for professional development, contact pd@solution-tree.com.

CHAPTER 3

Personal Matter: Personality Traits

DAISY ZHANG-NEGRERIE

"He is to the atom what Darwin is to evolution, Newton to mechanics, Faraday to electricity and Einstein to relativity. His pathway from rural child to immortality is a fascinating one" (Campbell, n.d.). This is how John Campbell (1999), author of the 515-page biography *Rutherford: Scientist Supreme*, describes New Zealand–born chemist Ernest Rutherford. Yes, Rutherford's works earned and ensured his immortality. He is one of the greatest scientists of all time, who has arguably received the highest number of awards and honors. After his death in 1937, he was honored by being interred with the greatest scientists of the United Kingdom, near Sir Isaac Newton's tomb in Westminster Abbey.

After being awarded the Nobel Prize in 1908, Rutherford continued to perform the most elegant experiments at the Cavendish Laboratory in Canada and further trained numerous future Nobel Prize winners, including James Chadwick, Patrick Blackett, G. P. Thomson, and Ernest Walton, toward their great achievements. He is the only scientist who conducted his most famous experiment—the "gold foil experiment"—after being awarded the Nobel Prize.

But Rutherford was not a born genius. He was not always successful in his attempts. In 1886, fifteen-year-old Ernest applied for the Marlborough Education Board scholarship to Nelson College, the only scholarship that was available to assist a local boy to attend secondary school, but was rejected. On his second attempt the following year, he was awarded the scholarship. At age seventeen when he applied for one of the ten scholarships given out by the University of New Zealand, he was, again, rejected; on his second attempt the following year, he succeeded. After college, Rutherford became a schoolteacher at Christchurch Boys' High School but failed to obtain a permanent position there after three rounds of applications, after which he tried his chances to go abroad to England for a research job. His application for the research job made it to the two finalists, but the university's examiners in England recommended the other candidate, James Maclaurin of Auckland University College; fortunately, Maclaurin turned down the offer, and the job was then awarded to Rutherford.

Personality Traits and Lifelong Success

We don't know how young Ernest dealt with the rejections time after time, but we can, without too much effort, picture a person who does not give up easily—a second attempt, a third try—Rutherford's story tells us that without his perseverance, the world would have lost one of the most accomplished scientists.

Not just Rutherford's but the life stories of almost every successful person reveal to us an undeniable truth: personality traits, such as perseverance, decisively contribute to extraordinary accomplishments. An interesting example was given by Malcolm Gladwell (2008) in his book *Outliers: The Story of Success*, in which he listed the colleges and universities where the last twenty-five Americans who won the Nobel Prize in medicine or chemistry got their undergraduate degrees. Perhaps surprisingly, small colleges such as Antioch College, Hamilton College, Amherst College, Gettysburg College, Hunter College, Berea College, and Augsburg College are spotted on the list. As we might surmise, even at the age of eighteen, the Nobel laureates were not necessarily the absolutely best high school students in the United States. This fact signifies that lifelong achievement should not be considered a direct product of an individual's innate ability or special talents, but an outcome of a lifelong journey of perseverance in efforts and hard work.

Why should personality traits contribute to a person's success? Academic research interests in the relation between personality traits and success have persisted throughout the 20th century. One explanation for why personality is important—if not more important than what were traditionally considered the main factors for success, such as cognitive ability, or IQ—is that intelligence "refers to what a person *can* do, whereas personality traits may provide information on *what* a person *will* do" (Furnham & Chamorro-Premuzic, 2004, p. 944).

Statistical research has shown that the contribution of IQ to academic success consistently diminishes from primary school to secondary school, then to postsecondary school (Furnham & Monsen, 2009), and research findings suggest that long-term academic performance would probably be more accurately predicted by a measure of personality traits rather than cognitive ability (Goff & Ackerman, 1992). Phillip L. Ackerman (1996) and colleagues found that domain knowledge (for example, music or astronomy) is logically and statistically related to general intelligence, verbal abilities, the personality trait of openness, typical intellectual engagement, and vocational interests. The PPIK (process, personality, interest, knowledge) theory proposed by Ackerman delineates the development of intellectual ability in solving real-life problems as an integration of four factors: (1) intelligence-as-process, which primarily refers to an individual's memory capacity, spatial orientation ability, and the abilities to reason and apply logic; (2) the individual's personality; (3) interest; and (4) domain knowledge, which refers to specific knowledge as well as the domain knowledge structure that allows one to perform certain specific tasks. The theory points out that personality traits influence the individual's knowledge-acquiring process, and interest serves as a motivational factor to allow the individual to invest cognitive resources, effort, and time to acquire knowledge. Through empirical research, Ackerman and coworkers found evidence of significant overlap and commonalities among the factors and argue that intelligence, personality, and interest development possibly occur in tandem, as the factors intertwine and influence each other during the course of knowledge acquisition (Ackerman & Heggestad, 1997).

The Definition and the Big Five Model of Personality Traits

There are several definitions of personality. Personality "is a complex blend of a constantly evolving and changing pattern of one's unique behavior, emerged as a result of one's interaction with one's environment and directed towards some specific ends" (Mangal, 2002, p. 396). It is "a person's complex set of traits that has an effect on behavior across time and situation" (Zimbardo & Gerrig, 1996, p. 508). It refers to internal factors such as "dispositions and interpersonal strategies that explain individual behaviors and the unique and relatively stable patterns of behaviors, thoughts, and emotions shown by individuals" (Hogan, Hogan, & Roberts, 1996, p. 470). It is "an individual's characteristic patterns of thought, emotion, and behavior, together with the psychological mechanisms—hidden or not—behind those patterns" (Funder, 1997, pp. 1–2).

The most popular theory about personality traits is the Big Five model of personality (Costa & McCrae, 1992). It has been considered as a "robust" and "parsimonious" model for understanding the relationships between personality and various academic behaviors (Poropat, 2009). The model identifies five distinctive factors: (1) neuroticism, (2) extraversion, (3) openness to experience, (4) agreeableness, and (5) conscientiousness. It is considered robust because the five factors—sometimes referred to as the *super traits*—are believed to encompass the entire domain of all specific personality traits, which are regarded as lower levels of the hierarchy and are sometimes referred to as *narrow traits* or *facets*. The model is said to be parsimonious to convey the belief that there is no need to take on a sixth factor, as any additional factor, if invented, would be conceivably sorted into a combination of the existing five factors.

Much empirical research to investigate the correlations between each of the Big Five personality factors and academic as well as workplace performance has been conducted, the results of which are summarized in table 3.1. (For a listing of this research, please see the empirical research section at the end of this chapter.)

Table 3.1: Summary of Research Findings on the Correlations Between Big Five Factors and Academic and Workforce Success

Big Five Traits	Academic Achievement	Workforce Performance
Conscientiousness	Conscientiousness is a trait that has been drawn upon as a main psychological resource in learning and education. Among the five traits, conscientiousness is found to be the most strongly associated with academic success. It is consistently related to achievement from preschool through high school, postsecondary level, and adulthood, even though there are exceptions in certain case studies. Narrow traits or facets associated with conscientiousness that positively affect academic achievement are persistence, dutifulness, self-discipline, and motivation in achievement-attainment.	Of the five factors, conscientiousness has been shown to be the most consistent and significant predictor of workplace performance across a wide range of job types. Valued workplace behaviors such as leadership and organizational citizenship and lack of undesired behaviors such as procrastination are connected to this factor, and contribute positively to the overall job performance.
Openness/Intellect	Among the five factors, openness is the next strongest trait related to academic achievement after conscientiousness. It is positively correlated to knowledge and achievement. It may facilitate the use of efficient learning strategies, which in turn affects academic success. The studies on foreign language conducted by Furnham (Furnham & Monsen, 2009) report openness to be the most significant predictor followed by conscientiousness to a lesser extent degree; however, Heaven and Ciarrochi (2012) predict this trait to be important only to those with high ability but not in low ability. Some studies show no statistically significant correlation between openness and academic achievement, and some even predict a negative correlation, arguing that the creative and imaginative nature of open individuals may sometimes be a disadvantage in academic settings.	Openness is found to be positively related to successful training activities. Openness is also connected to creativity and an optimistic attitude toward learning, therefore positively contributing to job performance.

Big Five Traits	Academic Achievement	Workforce Performance
Extraversion	There does not seem to be a relationship between extraversion and college performance, although some studies have found evidence for a small, negative correlation. The detrimental effect of extraversion on educational attainment begins at the university level. Extraverted children before grade 7 outperform introverted children; however, among adolescents and adults, some research has shown that introverts show higher achievement than extraverts, as avoidance of intensive socializing becomes advantageous. Extraversion correlates the most significantly to learning a foreign language for university students. Extraversion is positively related with elaborative processing.	Decisively different from the academic achievement result of this factor, extraversion is found to be strongly and positively correlated with occupations that require social interactions, training proficiency, and leadership abilities. It is also related to an individual's job satisfaction. High levels of satisfaction for extraverted people are in part due to their ability to connect and enjoy the interactions in the social environment with their colleagues, while introverts often report less satisfaction for these very reasons.
Neuroticism	Neuroticism is shown to predict poorer academic performance among school-aged children. Analysis of thirteen-year-old students suggests a negative correlation between neuroticism and academic achievement, particularly for the anxiety and impulsiveness facets, although some studies of both school children and university students have failed to find any significant correlations. The negative emotionality might be compensated by other moderating factors such as self-control and motivation.	Those who exhibit neurotic behaviors tend to be less happy and experience low job satisfaction, both of which influence the ability to perform well in tasks. On the other hand, neuroticism is helpful in jobs that require the formation of creative and novel ideas.
Agreeableness	Research data have shown that the correlation between agreeableness and academic achievement is consistently insignificant. But this factor is important for character training.	Agreeableness has been shown to predict performance in interpersonal-oriented jobs, but negatively correlated with leadership abilities or within occupations that require a certain degree of disagreeableness for success.

In addition, the narrow traits of self-control, perseverance, self-confidence, being proactive, tolerance, self-efficacy, and grit were found to have a more direct correlation with academic and workplace success (Duckworth, Peterson, Matthews, & Kelly, 2007; Gough, 1996; Middleton & Guthrie, 1959; Oakland, 1969; Rutkowski & Domino, 1975; Schmit & Ryan, 1993; Strayhorn, 2013). Other narrow traits mediated by the motivational factors such as goal orientation, work drive, and self-regulated learning strategy, as well as optimism, learning style, and thinking style, have also confirmed their roles as predictors of academic success (please see the sources in the empirical research section at the end of this chapter for more information on these topics). Even though most of the narrow traits studies conclude that the more specific subfacets are stronger predictors of academic and workplace performance than the broad Big Five super traits, the relevant narrow traits all revolve around the super traits of conscientiousness, openness, and emotional stability (which is the opposite pole of neuroticism), supporting the primary research results of the super traits.

Table 3.2 (page 54) displays a collection of ninety personality trait adjectives based on the Abridged Big Five–Dimensional Circumplex (AB5C) model, developed by De Raad and Schouwenburg (1996), as blends of two factors of the Big Five model. The table consists of a ten-by-ten matrix, with each Big Five factor comprising two columns, one representing the positive factor pole and the other representing the negative pole. For example, I+ represents the extraverted traits and I– the introverted traits; IV+ high emotional stability (or low neuroticism), and IV– low emotional stability (or high neuroticism). The exact same entries constitute the ten rows of the table. Adjectives in each cell represent a blend of the two super traits from the corresponding column and row. For instance, entries at the crossing of III+/I+ (column/row), namely, *industrious*, *diligent*, and *practical*, refer to an extraverted way of showing conscientiousness, while those at I+/III+, *energetic*, *busy*, and *firm*, refer to a conscientious person's style of being extraverted. This mapping is helpful in identifying the different sorts of constructs under the umbrella of the Big Five personality traits.

Key Personality Traits for Lifelong Achievement

The definition of personality—behavioral patterns as a result of "one's interaction with one's environment" (Mangal, 2002, p. 287)—implies that personality is subject to constant changes and modifications as long as there is interaction with the environment. Empirical studies reveal that educational experiences have a profound effect on students' personality development (Jackson, 2011). Based on the data from empirical research on the correlations between personality traits—both within the frame of the Big Five model and the more specific narrow constructs—and lifelong achievement, five personality facets have emerged as the most relevant to one's success in today's world: grit, self-control, self-confidence, empathy, and a service mindset.

Grit

University of Pennsylvania psychology professor Angela Duckworth and colleagues are often credited as being among the first to use *grit* as a noun and *gritty* as an adjective to describe a person's noncognitive trait. It is defined as

> perseverance and passion for long-term goals. Grit entails working strenuously toward challenges, maintaining effort and interest over years despite failure, adversity, and plateaus in progress. The gritty individual approaches achievement as a marathon; his or her advantage is stamina. Whereas disappointment or boredom signals to others that it is time to change trajectory and cut losses, the gritty individual stays in the course. (Duckworth et al., 2007, pp. 1087–1088)

Commonly associated personality traits in a gritty person are perseverance, hard work, tenacity, passion, and strong will. In fact, the word *grit* was already used as early as 1911 to mean what the current definition embodies. A letter was sent to the editor of a small New Zealand newspaper in Rutherford's hometown, which complained that the selection procedure for the science honors society in England was biased by the social connection and the social status of the ancestors: "I have in mind one who by his brain-power, grit, and perseverance has forced his way to the top rung of the ladder, until he now ranks amongst the highest, if not the highest, in the scientific world" (Rutherford.org.nz, n.d.). Three years later, Rutherford was knighted in the New Year's Honors List for 1914.

In a series of six case studies, Duckworth and colleagues (2007) found that grit is strongly connected to long-term success. A self-reported survey, consisting of a series of simple questions that measures on a five-point scale, consistency of passion, such as "I have been obsessed with a certain idea or project for a short time but later lost interest," and consistency of effort over time, such as "Setbacks don't discourage me," was used to collect data during these studies. Embedded in the survey questions was the grit scale, also developed by Duckworth and colleagues (2007) and used to establish the correlations between grit and success (p. 1090). The survey is self-reported. Duckworth and her colleagues studied 190 participants in the Scripps National Spelling Bee, a competition that requires thousands of hours of practice (Duckworth, Kirby, Tsukayama, Berstein, & Ericsson, 2011). They found that grittier spellers, those who scored high on the grit scale and engaged in long hours of deliberate practice, did visibly well in the spelling performance. Other studies have also found a positive correlation between grit and achievement. Strayhorn (2013), for example, reports a positive and unique correlation between grit and college retention rate of black male students in a predominantly white college. Such studies indicate that grit may be a key factor for success in academics and in life.

The predictive validity of grit should not come as a surprise, as it has a strong component of conscientiousness, consistent with all the previous findings in literature concerning the Big Five model. The other component that carries equal weight in the definition of grit is *passion*, which finds no direct entry in table 3.2 (page 54). The closest adjective connected to this quality is found at the crossing of III– and V–, namely, *indifferent* as its opposite. The portrayed combination of *indifferent* at the negative poles of conscientiousness and openness to experience would logically place *passion* at the crossing of the positive poles of conscientiousness and openness, which is in complete agreement with the positive

Table 3.2: Narrow Traits Derived From the Abridged Big Five–Dimensional Circumplex (AB5C)

	Extraversion		Agreeableness		Conscientiousness		Emotional Stability		Openness to Experience	
	I+	I−	II+	II−	III+	III−	IV+	IV−	V+	V−
I+	spontaneous talkative extraverted		cordial amiable friendly	domineering bossy hotheaded	industrious diligent practical	reckless lawless careless	self-assured certain decisive	excitable uncontrolled romantic	imaginative original strong-minded	chauvinistic reactionary
I−		silent introverted closed	modest meek patient	cunning selfish aloof	careful perfectionistic cautious	lax work-shy absentminded	sober-minded controlled rational	insecure depressed unbalanced	philosophical analytic contemplative	conservative slavish unimaginative
II+	cheerful sociable jovial	tranquil composed	mild peaceful obliging		responsible tidy well-mannered	nonchalant unsuspecting	stable calm even-tempered	sensitive emotional tender	freedom-loving subtle broad-minded	obedient docile credulous
II−	fierce explosive wild	unsociable suspicious inscrutable		unaccommodating stubborn irreconcilable	stern choosy	headstrong abnormal unmannered	tough despotic insensitive	irritable changeable moody	provocative ironical radical	stingy materialistic narrow-minded
III+	energetic busy firm	reserved serious thoughtful	caring polite fair	ambitious thrusting	orderly precise punctual		balanced resolute realistic	worrisome troubled	constructive interested full of character	conventional dogmatic law-abiding
III−	rash uninhibited loud	apathetic dull uninterested	flexible pliable	egotistical recalcitrant arrogant		disorderly irresponsible lazy	laconic	unstable irrational capricious	nonconforming disobedient undogmatic	uncritical superficial hypocritical
IV+	vigorous optimistic enterprising	unexcitable	tolerant kind honest	autocratic heartless inflexible	consistent tenacious purposeful	carefree unobstructed opportunistic	imperturbable cool-headed		critical inventive versatile	old-fashioned presumptuous
IV−	impulsive gossipy indiscreet	somber withdrawn shy	gentle sensitive permissive	ill-tempered quarrelsome snarly	finicky	chaotic inaccurate scatterbrained		panicky nervous vulnerable	poetic idealistic artistic	small-minded shortsighted vacuous
V+	temperamental enthusiastic dynamic	individualistic	humane loyal unselfish	rebellious demanding self-willed	observant inquisitive scrupulous	undisciplined extravagant eccentric	independent fearless self-confident	sensitive affected perceptible	creative reflective	
V−	chatty	timid moderate insincere	willing indulgent good-natured	intolerant malicious greedy	dutiful disciplined respectable	indifferent unreliable deceitful	unemotional callous	anxious fearful dependent		obsequious overpolite

Source: De Raad & Schouwenburg, 1996, p. 323.

correlations consistently reported in the empirical research on these topics (please see the empirical research section at the end of this chapter for representative sources).

Though not specifically studied as a narrow trait to correlate with academic or work-place success, passion is the inner motor behind perseverant people. It empowers them to move forward in spite of severe drawbacks. Almost all accomplished people staunchly believe passion plays a central role in their success. In every interview and nearly all public addresses, Steve Jobs brought up the word *passion* or *love*—"you have to have a lot of passion in what you do," and "you got to do what you love," because "you can't do great work if you don't love it" (Jobs, 2005).

Self-Control

Self-control has been found as one of the most consistent and reliable predictors of performance in school, workplace, social life, and health issues, beyond that of intelligence or the conscientiousness super trait (O'Connor & Paunonen, 2007). It is defined as "the ability to suppress proponent responses in the service of a higher goal" (Duckworth & Seligman, 2006, p. 199), or "the ability to control one's behavior and desires and delay gratification for later rewards" (Myers, 2012, p. 403). Behavioral aspects of the self-control trait can be found scattered throughout the column of *conscientiousness* as *disciplined*, *purposeful*, and *responsible*, which makes it a valid narrow trait that positively relates to success.

If passion is the inner motor for a gritty person, self-control is the muscle behind that person's perseverant character. A study conducted in the early 1990s by the psychologist K. Anders Ericsson suggests that talent is really about deliberate practice, about putting in those ten thousand hours of intense training. In their article, "The Role of Deliberate Practice in the Acquisition of Expert Performance," Ericsson and coworkers write,

> The differences between expert performers and normal adults are not immutable, that is, due to genetically prescribed talent. Instead, these differences reflect a life-long period of deliberate effort to improve performance. (Ericsson, Krampe, & Tesch-Romer, 1993, p. 400)

According to Ericsson, the most relevant talent is the capability of deliberate practice, concurring with what Thomas Edison said: "Genius is one percent inspiration, ninety-nine percent perspiration."

The famous "marshmallow test," invented by Stanford psychologist Walter Mischel and colleagues (Mischel, Ebbesen, & Raskoff Zeiss, 1972), has proven that the ability to delay gratification is critical for a successful life. The test presented children with the choice of receiving one marshmallow to eat immediately or waiting fifteen minutes and then receiving two marshmallows. Decades later, those who took the choice of "wait for fifteen minutes and get two" ended up with higher SAT scores, higher educational attainment, a greater self-esteem, and a healthier lifestyle. More recent research on correlation between self-control, measured by asking participants to rate the frequency with which they performed an array of tasks indicative of the self-control level, and academic achievements, usually measured by grade point average (GPA) of college or university students, shows positive relationships (Muammar, 2011). Self-control can be learned, acquired, and mastered. Strategies include drawing upon the mediating role of motivational factors by restating the awaited reward or finding meaning in the "higher goal," and distracting oneself from the temptations in order to better control one's behavior and desires (Rotter, 1966).

Self-Confidence

Self-confidence refers to the assuredness in one's own worth, abilities, and power, regardless of the situation he or she is in. Someone who is self-confident has a strong sense of self-belief. He or she exudes calmness and composure. This assuredness is linked with possessing certain knowledge, skill sets, or abilities, whether it is acquired or innate. Self-confidence is based on three factors: (1) one's own opinion of the personal inventory of skills, abilities, and achievements; (2) the reflections of the opinions of others concerning one's competencies; and (3) one's internal assessment of the opinions of others. All three factors work together to influence one's self-confidence index in any situation or circumstance and at any given point in time.

In the personality scheme, self-confidence falls at the crossing of the positive poles of emotional stability and openness to experience. Established positive and negative correlations between openness and neuroticism, respectively, to academic and workplace success suggest the importance of this trait to success. Studies on the correlations between the direct measure of self-confidence and academic achievements further prove the role of self-confidence in achievement (Ahmad, Zeb, Ullah, & Ali, 2013; Al-Hebaish, 2012; Harris, 2009). People with low self-confidence most often give up a task prematurely not for the reasons of limited resources or adverse circumstances, but for the doubt in their own ability or competence.

General self-confidence is developed during the age of childhood and emerges from the accumulation of inter- and intrapersonal experiences. It is derived from several factors, with the most important ones being personal experiences and social messages received from others. Even though childhood experiences are important, self-confidence can be learned, built on, and developed.

The process of developing self-confidence involves two basic steps (Edberg, 2009): (1) learning and improving skills required for a task, and (2) facing fear of failure. In regard to the first step, recall from chapter 2 that everyone can be exceptionally good at something with sufficient time and effort. Research also suggests that a person's intelligence is malleable. Thus, one should have confidence in his or her capacity for acquiring the desired skills and developing the required abilities. As author of longtime bestseller, *How to Win Friends and Influence People*, Dale Carnegie (1937) famously noted about the decisive role of taking action, "Inaction breeds doubt and fear. Action breeds confidence and courage. If you want to conquer fear, do not sit home and think about it. Go out and get busy" ("Dale Carnegie quotes," n.d.).

The second step requires one to face fear courageously by adjusting one's perception of failure. Fear of failure often impedes and mentally inhibits one from taking action. New Zealand artist Peter McIntyre says that "confidence comes not from always being right but from not fearing to be wrong" ("Peter McIntyre quotes," n.d.). The best way to develop self-confidence is to overcome fear and gain energy from small-scale successes built on learning from failure. As 19th century Scottish historian Thomas Carlyle observed about the power of successes, "Nothing builds self-esteem and self-confidence like accomplishment" ("Thomas Carlyle quotes," n.d.). This experience of accomplishment, as well as gained appreciation of failure, will help one take the next round of action, and the two steps will work together to help build one's self-confidence.

Empathy

The *Merriam-Webster's Online Dictionary* definition of *empathy* is "the imaginative projection of a subjective state into an object so that the object appears to be infused with it" ("Empathy," n.d.). The academic definition of the empathic trait typically includes (1) the affective capacity to share in another's feelings" (Vreeke & van der Mark, 2003); (2) the cognitive ability to understand another's feelings and perspective, "a response to a specific demand occurring in a specific content (Caselman, 2007); and sometimes (3) the ability to communicate one's empathetic feelings and understanding to another by verbal or nonverbal means (Decety & Meyer, 2008). An empathic response is one that contains both an affective and a cognitive dimension, which requires both critical thinking/reasoning and applying imagination—what Gallo (1989) calls "creative thinking"—both convergent, critical processes and divergent, imaginative processes.

Consulting the personality scheme (table 3.2, page 54), we see that *imaginative, creative,* and *critical* all fall in the column of the positive pole of openness to experience (column V+), making this facet a desired trait to develop for its correlation to success as supported by empirical research. Other than the more obvious understanding that empathy can make people more productive in work environments, especially in those that require cooperation, empathy training can enhance learning ability. Research shows that empathy positively correlates to scores on measures of critical and higher-order thinking (Bonner & Aspy, 1984; Kohn, 1991). In addition to knowledge retention, self-determination, and strategy utilization, empathy is a key attribute of a successful learner, and many advocate that empathy enhancement should be adopted as an important education goal (Elias, 2003; Goleman, 1995; Nail, 2007).

In today's world of abundance, empathy has become one of the most vital skills for successful business because people buy on emotion rather than on justified logic, and empathy is key to understanding these emotional triggers. In the book *The Art of Innovation: Lessons in Creativity From IDEO, America's Leading Design Firm* (Kelley, 2001), the author emphasizes the importance of empathy in designing a new product. Innovation is born out of "focused observation," diving deeper under the superficial "nuances of human behavior but also [striving] to infer *motivation* and *emotion*" (p. 37), as "to make better products and services, you've got to care about the person actually using it" (p. 34).

The ability to imagine and gain insight into another person's point of view does not come easily, but sustained practice is an effective means to increasing levels of empathy. Empathy training programs, designed to enhance empathetic feelings and understanding and to increase prosocial behavior, lead to increased personal openness, mindfulness of others' needs in conflict situations, improved teamwork ability, and greater job satisfaction. In addition, these programs help to lay the groundwork for the growth of other positive traits, including skills in reasoning, critical thinking, imagination, and communication (Payton et al., 2008).

A Service Mindset

If developing empathy is an intellectual endeavor, developing a service mindset is putting this intellectual ability into action. Research shows that in order to live a truly fulfilled life, one ought to satisfy one's most fundamental needs. Self-determination theory (Deci & Ryan, 2002) argues that all human beings seek relatedness, competence, and autonomy, with the first of the three referring to the desire to care about, the feeling to be connected to, and the sense of being appreciated by others (Ryan & Deci, 2000).

Serving and being appreciated by others not only fulfills one's fundamental needs, but also improves one's learning ability through improved cognitive engagement. One movement that recognizes the value of service is service learning, a relatively new teaching and learning strategy that "integrates meaningful community service with instruction and reflection to enrich the learning experience, teach civic responsibility, and strengthen communities" (Fayetteville State University, n.d.). About a dozen studies conducted in the 2000s have found a positive impact of service learning on students' academic achievement. Research shows that service-learning students in grades K–12 improved their academic performance and school engagement (Davila & Mora, 2007). Low socioeconomic-status students who participated in service scored higher in achievement, motivation, grades, bonding to school, and attendance than similar students who did not participate in service (Scales, Roehlkepartain, Neal, Kielsmeier, & Benson, 2006). Of course, the quality of the programs matters; it is closely associated with the program's impact on academic outcomes, including students' attachment to school, school engagement, and motivation to learn (Billig, Root, & Jesse, 2005; Scales, Blyth, Berkas, & Kielsmeier, 2000).

Where Do We Go From Here?

Personality traits clearly matter to students' academic achievement, but more importantly, they play a critical role in a person's lifelong achievement. Up until recently, personality traits have been studied in school settings only as an enabling or disabling factor to student learning, but they should be an outcome of schooling in their own right because of their importance to life's success. In other words, developing desired personality traits should be viewed as an important part of the overall educational goal rather than a mere factor that helps or hinders student performance in school, which further suggests that the measurement of personality development in students should contribute to the evaluation system of the quality and effectiveness of a school.

Teaching desired personality traits is important, as

> Education is charged with the development of essential human competences: a facility for dealing meaningfully with complexity and a capacity for effective personal response. The manifestation of these competencies rests upon possession of a broad knowledge base, clear and resourceful thinking, and the will to act. (Gallo, 1989, p. 98)

A number of issues, however, arise immediately. First, we do not know enough yet about the shaping forces of personality traits. How much are personality traits determined genetically, and to what extent can they be influenced by education, life experience, and environment?

Second, we do not know whether personality traits are malleable throughout our lifetime or rather become frozen at a certain age. Are there critical periods for personality development?

Third, what kinds of experiences are the most effective in causing personality changes? Is one's educational experience among the most effective influences over personality development?

Finally, are personality traits stable across all contents and situations? Or do they perhaps have different expressions in different contexts? Is it possible that certain personality traits become more salient in one context over another, in dealing with one type of task over others, or in one social setting over others?

These questions require more research. But they should not stop schools and teachers from purposefully incorporating exercises to cultivate desirable personality traits into their routine educational practices.

Empirical Research

1. For review of empirical research and meta-analysis on the correlations between conscientiousness and academic achievement, see Shiner, R. L., & Masten, A. S. (2002); and Noftle, E. E., & Robins, R. W. (2007).

2. For empirical studies and reviews on correlations between conscientiousness and job performance, see Barrick, M. R., & Mount, M. K. (1991); Dudley, N. M., Orvis, K. A., Lebiecki, J. E., & Cortina, J. M. (2006); Hurtz, G. M., & Donovan, J. J. (2000); and Barrick, M. R., Mount, M. K., & Judge, T. A. (2001).

3. For review of empirical research on correlations between openness and academic achievement, see Farsides, T., & Woodfield, R. (2003); Mumford, M. D., & Gustafson, S. B. (1988); and Busato, V. V., Prins, F. J., Elshout, J. J., & Hamaker, C. (2000).

4. For a review on correlations between openness and workforce performance, see Neubert, S. P. (2004); and Barrick, M. R., & Mount, M. K. (1991).

5. For empirical studies and meta-analytic reviews on correlations between extraversion and academic achievement, see Noftle, E. E., & Robins, R. W. (2007); Entwistle, N. J., & Entwistle, D. (1970); Zeidner, M., & Matthews, G. (2000); Furnham, A., & Chamorro-Premuzic, T. (2004); Furnham, A., & Medhurst, S. (1995); Barrick, M. R., Mount, M. K., & Strauss, J. P. (1993); Gough, H. G. (1996); Oakland, J. A. (1969); Rutkowski, K., & Domino, G. (1975); Middleton, G., Jr., & Guthrie, G. M. (1959); Schmit, M. J., & Ryan, A. M. (1993); and Schmeck, R. R. (1988).

6. For empirical studies on correlations between extraversion and workforce outcome, see Louis, M. R. (1980); Lim, B.-C., & Ployhart, R. E. (2004); Judge, T. A., Heller, D., & Mount, M. K. (2002); Barrick, M. R., & Mount, M. K. (1991); Tett, R. P., Jackson, D. N., & Rothstein, M. (1991); and Neubert, S. P. (2004).

7. For empirical studies on correlations between neuroticism and academic achievement, see Shiner, R. L., & Masten, A. S. (2002); Busato, V. V., Prins, F. J., Elshout, J. J., & Hamaker, C. (2000); Crede, M., & Kuncel, N. R. (2008); and Heaven, P. C. L., Mak, A., Barry, J., & Ciarrochi, J. (2002).

8. For empirical studies on correlations between neuroticism and workplace performance, see Watson, D., & Clark, L. A. (1984); and Weiss, H. M., & Cropanzano, R. (1996).

9. For empirical studies on the correlation between agreeableness and academic achievement, see Shiner, R. L., & Masten, A. S. (2002).

10. For empirical studies on the correlation between agreeableness and workforce outcome, see Meyer, J. P., & Allen, N. J. (1991).

11. For studies on correlations between narrow traits and academic and workplace success, see Zweig, D., & Webster, J. (2004); Komarraju, M., Karau, S. J., Schmeck, R. R., & Avdic, A. (2011); Pornsakulvanich, V., Dumrongsiri, N., Sajampun, P., Sornsri, S., John, S. P., Sriyabhand, T., et al. (2012); Shams, F., Mooghali, A. R., Tabebordbar, F., & Soleimanpour, N. (2011); Zhang, L.-F. (2002); Zhang, L.-F. (2006); Bidjerano, T., & Dai, D. Y. (2007); Cupani, M., & Pautassi, R. M. (2013); and Fuller, B., Jr., & Marler, L. E. (2009).

12. For tips on building self-confidence, see Edberg, H. (2009); Babauta, L. (2007); Mind Tools (n.d.); and Chua, C. (2009).

References and Resources

Ackerman, P. L. (1996). A theory of adult intellectual development: Process, personality, interests, and knowledge. *Intelligence*, *22*(2), 227–257.

Ackerman, P. L., & Heggestad, E. D. (1997). Intelligence, personality, and interests: Evidence for overlapping traits. *Psychological Bulletin*, *121*(2), 219–245.

Ahmad, I., Zeb, A., Ullah, S., & Ali, A. (2013). Relationship between self-esteem and academic achievements of students: A case of government secondary schools in District Swabi, KPK, Pakistan. *International Journal of Social Sciences and Education*, *3*(2), 361–369.

Al-Hebaish, S. M. (2012). The correlation between general self-confidence and academic achievement in the oral presentation course. *Theory and Practice in Language Studies*, *2*(1), 60–65.

Babauta, L. (2007, December 9). *25 killer actions to boost your self-confidence*. Accessed at http://zenhabits.net/25-killer-actions-to-boost-your-self-confidence on March 23, 2015.

Barrick, M. R., & Mount, M. K. (1991). The Big Five personality dimensions and job performance: A meta-analysis. *Personnel Psychology*, *44*(1), 1–26.

Barrick, M. R., Mount, M. K., & Judge, T. A. (2001). Personality and performance at the beginning of the new millennium: What do we know and where do we go next? *International Journal of Selection and Assessment*, *9*(1–2), 9–30.

Barrick, M. R., Mount, M. K., & Strauss, J. P. (1993). Conscientiousness and performance of sales representatives: Test of the mediating effects of goal setting. *Journal of Applied Psychology*, *78*(5), 715–722.

Bidjerano, T., & Dai, D. Y. (2007). The relationship between the Big-Five model of personality and self-regulated learning strategies. *Learning and Individual Differences*, *17*(1), 69–81.

Billig, S. H. (2000). *Research on K–12 school-based service-learning: The evidence builds*. Denver, CO: RMC Research. Accessed at www.civicyouth.org/PopUps/Billig_Service_Learning.pdf on March 23, 2015.

Billig, S. H., Root, S., & Jesse, D. (2005, May). *The impact of participation in service-learning on high school students' civic engagement* (Circle Working Paper No. 33). Denver, CO: RMC Research.

Billig, S. H., & Sandel, K. (2003). *Colorado learn and serve: An evaluation report*. Denver, CO: RMC Research.

Bonner, T. D., & Aspy, D. N. (1984). A study of the relationship between student empathy and GPA. *Journal of Humanistic Education and Development*, *22*(4), 149–154.

Brunello, G., & Schlotter, M. (2011). *Non-cognitive skills and personality traits: Labour market relevance and their development in education and training systems* (IZA Discussion Paper No. 5743). Bonn, Germany: Institute for the Study of Labor.

Busato, V. V., Prins, F. J., Elshout, J. J., & Hamaker, C. (2000). Intellectual ability, learning style, personality, achievement motivation and academic success of psychology students in higher education. *Personality and Individual Differences*, *29*(6), 1057–1068.

Campbell, J. (1999). *Rutherford: Scientist supreme*. Ann Arbor, MI: Association for Asian Studies.

Campbell, J. (n.d.). *Rutherford—A brief biography*. Accessed at www.rutherford.org.nz/biography.htm on March 23, 2015.

Carnegie, D. (1937). *How to win friends and influence people*. New York: Simon & Schuster.

Caselman, T. (2007). *Teaching children empathy, the social emotion: Lessons, activities and reproducible worksheets (K–6) that teach how to "step into others' shoes"*. Chapin, SC: YouthLight, Inc.

Caspi, A., & Moffitt, T. E. (1993). When do individual differences matter? A paradoxical theory of personality coherence. *Psychological Inquiry, 4*(4), 247–271.

Chamorro-Premuzic, T., & Furnham, A. (2003). Personality traits and academic examination performance. *European Journal of Personality, 17*(3), 237–250.

Chavez-Eakle, R. A., Eakle, A. J., & Cruz-Fuentes, C. (2012). The multiple relations between creativity and personality. *Creativity Research Journal, 24*(1), 76–82.

Chen, I. (2014, September 15). *Measuring students' self-control: A "marshmallow test" for the digital age*. Accessed at ww2.kqed.org/mindshift/2014/09/15/measuring-self-control-a-marshmallow-test-for-the-digital-age on March 23, 2015.

Chowdhury, M. (2006). Students' personality traits and academic performance: A five-factor model perspective. *College Quarterly, 9*(3), 1–9.

Chua, C. (2009, February 26). *How to be the most confident person in the world*. Accessed at http://personalexcellence.co/blog/self-confidence on March 23, 2015.

Conard, M. A. (2006). Aptitude is not enough: How personality and behavior predict academic performance. *Journal of Research in Personality, 40*(3), 339–346.

Costa, P. T., & McCrae, R. R. (1992). *Revised NEO Personality Inventory (NEO-PI-R) and NEO Five-Factor Inventory (NEO-FFI) professional manual*. Odessa, FL: Psychological Assessment Resources.

Crede, M., & Kuncel, N. R. (2008). Study habits, skills, and attitudes: The third pillar supporting collegiate academic performance. *Perspectives on Psychological Science, 3*(6), 425–453.

Cupani, M., & Pautassi, R. M. (2013). Predictive contribution of personality traits in a sociocognitive model of academic performance in mathematics. *Journal of Career Assessment, 21*(3), 395–413.

"Dale Carnegie quotes." (n.d.) *Thinkexist*. Accessed at http://thinkexist.com/quotes/dale_carnegie/3.html on August 5, 2015.

Davila, A., & Mora, M. T. (2007, January). *Civic engagement and high school academic progress: An analysis using NELS data* (Circle Working Paper No. 52). College Park, MD: Center for Information and Research on Civic Learning and Engagement.

Decety, J., & Meyer, M. (2008). From emotion resonance to empathic understanding: A social developmental neuroscience account. *Development and Psychopathology, 20*(4), 1053–1080.

Deci, E. L., & Ryan, R. M. (Eds.). (2002). *Handbook of self-determination research*. Rochester, NY: University of Rochester Press.

De Raad, B., & Schouwenburg, H. C. (1996). Personality in learning and education: A review. *European Journal of Personality, 10*(5), 303–336.

Duckworth, A. L., Kirby, T. A., Tsukayama, E., Berstein, H., & Ericsson, K. A. (2011). Deliberate practice spells success: Why grittier competitors triumph at the National Spelling Bee. *Social Psychological and Personality Science*, *2*(2), 174–181.

Duckworth, A. L., Peterson, C., Matthews, M. D., & Kelly, D. R. (2007). Grit: Perseverance and passion for long-term goals. *Journal of Personality and Social Psychology*, *92*(6), 1087–1101.

Duckworth, A. L., & Seligman, M. E. (2006). Self-discipline gives girls the edge: Gender in self-discipline, grades, and achievement test scores. *Journal of Educational Psychology*, *98*(1), 198–208.

Dudley, N. M., Orvis, K. A., Lebiecki, J. E., & Cortina, J. M. (2006). A meta-analytic investigation of conscientiousness in the prediction of job performance: Examining the intercorrelations and the incremental validity of narrow traits. *Journal of Applied Psychology*, *91*(1), 40–57.

Dweck, C. S. (2008). *Mindset: The new psychology of success*. New York: Ballantine Books.

Edberg, H. (2009, February 20). *How to build self confidence: 6 essential and timeless tips*. Accessed at www.positivityblog.com/index.php/2009/02/20/how-to-build-self-confidence on March 23, 2015.

Elias, M. (2003). Academic and social emotional learning [Educational practices series, 11]. *International Academy of Education; International Bureau of Education*, 1–31.

Empathy. (n.d.). In *Merriam-Webster's online dictionary*. Accessed at www.merriam-webster.com/dictionary/empathy on March 23, 2015.

Entwistle, N. J., & Entwistle, D. (1970). The relationships between personality, study methods and academic performance. *British Journal of Educational Psychology*, *40*(2), 132–143.

Ericsson, K. A., Krampe, R. T., & Tesch-Romer, C. (1993). The role of deliberate practice in the acquisition of expert performance. *Psychological Review*, *100*(3), 363–406.

Farsides, T., & Woodfield, R. (2003). Individual differences and undergraduate academic success: The roles of personality, intelligence, and application. *Personality and Individual Differences*, *34*(7), 1225–1243.

Fayetteville State University. (n.d.). *Definition of service learning*. Accessed at www.uncfsu.edu/civic-engagement/service-learning/definition-of-service-learning on March 23, 2015.

Fuller, B., Jr., & Marler, L. E. (2009). Change driven by nature: A meta-analytic review of the proactive personality literature. *Journal of Vocational Behavior*, *75*(3), 329–345.

Funder, D. C. (1997). *The personality puzzle*. New York: Norton.

Furnham, A., & Chamorro-Premuzic, T. (2004). Personality and intelligence as predictors of statistics examination grades. *Personality and Individual Differences*, *37*(5), 943–955.

Furnham, A., & Medhurst, S. (1995). Personality correlates of academic seminar behaviour: A study of four instruments. *Personality and Individual Differences*, *19*(2), 197–208.

Furnham, A., & Monsen, J. (2009). Personality traits and intelligence predict academic school grades. *Learning and Individual Differences*, *19*(1), 28–33.

Gallo, D. (1989). Educating for empathy, reason and imagination. *Journal of Creative Behavior*, *23*(2), 98–115.

Gladwell, M. (2008). *Outliers: The story of success.* New York: Little, Brown.

Goel, M. G., & Aggarwal, P. A. (2012). A comparative study of self-confidence of single child and child with sibling. *International Journal of Research in Social Sciences, 2*(3), 89–98.

Goff, M., & Ackerman, P. L. (1992). Personality-intelligence relations: Assessment of typical intellectual engagement. *Journal of Educational Psychology, 84*(4), 537–552.

Goleman, D. (1995). *Emotional intelligence.* New York: Bantam Books.

Goodwin, B., & Miller, K. (2013). Grit plus talent equals student success. *Resilience and Learning, 71*(1), 4–76.

Gottfredson, L. S. (2001). Review of *Practical Intelligence in Everyday Life*. *Intelligence, 29*(4), 363–365.

Gough, H. G. (1996). Graduation from high school as predicted from the California Psychological Inventory. *Psychology in the Schools, 3*(3), 208–216.

Halvorson, H. G. (2011). *Succeed: How we can reach our goals.* New York: Plume.

Harris, S. L. (2009). *The relationship between self-esteem and academic success among African American students in the minority engineering program at a research extensive university in the southern portion of the United States.* Unpublished doctoral dissertation, Louisiana State University, Baton Rouge.

Haynes, L. A., & Avery, A. W. (1979). Training adolescents in self-disclosure and empathy skills. *Journal of Community Psychology, 26*(6), 526–530.

Heaven, P. C. L., & Ciarrochi, J. (2012). When IQ is not everything: Intelligence, personality and academic performance at school. *Personality and Individual Differences, 53*(4), 518–522.

Heaven, P. C. L., Mak, A., Barry, J., & Ciarrochi, J. (2002). Personality and family influences on adolescent attitudes to school and self-related academic performance. *Personality and Individual Differences, 32*(3), 453–462.

Hofstee, W. K. B., De Raad, B., & Goldberg, L. R. (1992). Integration of the Big Five and circumplex approaches to trait structure. *Journal of Personality and Social Psychology, 63*(1), 146–163.

Hogan, R., Hogan, J., & Roberts, B. W. (1996). Personality measurement and employment decisions: Questions and answers. *American Psychologist, 51*(5), 469–477.

Homayouni, A. (2011). Personality traits and emotional intelligence as predictors of learning English and math. *Procedia—Social and Behavioral Sciences, 30*, 839–843.

Hurtz, G. M., & Donovan, J. J. (2000). Personality and job performance: The Big Five revisited. *Journal of Applied Psychology, 85*(6), 869–879.

Jackson, J. J. (2011). *The effects of educational experiences on personality trait development.* Unpublished doctoral dissertation, University of Illinois, Urbana.

Jobs, S. (2005, June 12). *You've got to find what you love.* Commencement address presented at Stanford University, Stanford, CA.

Judge, T. A., Heller, D., & Mount, M. K. (2002). Five-factor model of personality and job satisfaction: A meta-analysis. *Journal of Applied Psychology, 87*(3), 530–541.

Kaslow, F. W. (1997). On the nature of empathy. *Intellect, 105*, 273–277.

Kelley, T. (2001). *The art of innovation: Lessons in creativity from IDEO, America's leading design firm*. New York: Currency/Doubleday.

Kohn, A. (1991). Caring kids: The role of the school. *Phi Delta Kappan, 72*(7), 496–506.

Komarraju, M., Karau, S. J., Schmeck, R. R., & Avdic, A. (2011). The Big Five personality traits, learning styles, and academic achievement. *Personality and Individual Differences, 51*(4), 472–477.

Kyllonen, P. C. (2005). The case for noncognitive assessments. *R&D Connections, 3*, 1–7. Accessed at www.ets.org/Media/Research/pdf/RD_Connections3.pdf on March 23, 2015.

Liff, S. B. (2003). Social and emotional intelligence: Applications for developmental education. *Journal of Developmental Education, 26*(3), 28–34.

Lim, B.-C., & Ployhart, R. E. (2004). Transformational leadership: Relations to the five-factor model and team performance in typical and maximum contexts. *Journal of Applied Psychology, 89*(4), 610–621.

Louis, M. R. (1980). Surprise and sense making: What newcomers experience in entering unfamiliar organizational settings. *Administrative Science Quarterly, 25*(2), 226–251.

Lounsbury, J. W., Welsh, D. P., Gibson, L. W., & Sundstrom, E. (2005). Broad and narrow personality traits in relation to cognitive ability in adolescents. *Personality and Individual Differences, 38*(5), 1009–1019.

Lubbers, M. J., Van Der Werf, M. P. C., Kuyper, H., & Hendriks, A. A. J. (2010). Does homework behavior mediate the relation between personality and academic performance? *Learning and Individual Differences, 20*(3), 203–208.

Ludtke, O., Trautwein, U., & Husemann, N. (2009). Goal and personality trait development in a transitional period: Assessing change and stability in personality development. *Personality and Social Psychology Bulletin, 35*(4), 428–441.

MacCann, C., Duckworth, A. L., & Roberts, R. D. (2009). Empirical identification of the major facets of conscientiousness. *Learning and Individual Differences, 19*(4), 451–458.

Mangal, S. K. (2002). *Advanced educational psychology* (2nd ed.). New Delhi, India: PHI Learning Private.

Meyer, J. P., & Allen, N. J. (1991). A three-component conceptualization of organizational commitment. *Human Resource Management Review, 1*(1), 61–89.

Middleton, G., Jr., & Guthrie, G. M. (1959). Personality syndromes and academic achievement. *Journal of Educational Psychology, 50*(2), 66–69.

Mind Tools. (n.d.). *Building self-confidence: Preparing yourself for success!* Accessed at www.mind tools.com/selfconf.html on March 23, 2015.

Mischel, W., Ebbesen, E. B., & Raskoff Zeiss, A. (1972). Cognitive and attentional mechanisms in delay of gratification. *Journal of Personality and Social Psychology, 21*(2), 204–218.

Muammar, O. M. (2011). Intelligence and self-control predict academic performance of gifted and non-gifted students. *Asia-Pacific Journal of Gifted and Talented Education*, *3*(1), 18–32.

Mumford, M. D., & Gustafson, S. B. (1988). Creativity syndrome: Integration, application, and innovation. *Psychological Bulletin*, *103*(1), 27–43.

Myers, D. G. (2012). *Exploring psychology* (9th ed.). New York: Worth Publisher.

Nail, T. (2007). *Evaluation of life effectiveness and leadership development in a Challenge Day Program for high school students.* Unpublished manuscript, Union Institute and University, Cincinnati, Ohio.

Neubert, S. P. (2004). *The five-factor model of personality in the workplace.* Accessed at www .personalityresearch.org/papers/neubert.html on March 23, 2015.

Noftle, E. E., & Robins, R. W. (2007). Personality predictors of academic outcomes: Big Five correlates of GPA and SAT scores. *Journal of Personality and Social Psychology*, *93*(1), 116–130.

Nye, J. V., Orel, E., & Kochergina, E. (2013). *Big Five personality traits and academic performance in Russian universities* (Higher School of Economics Research Paper No. WP BRP 10/PSY/2013). Moscow, Russia: National Research University Higher School of Economics. Accessed at http://papers.ssrn.com/sol3/papers.cfm?abstract_id=2265395 on March 23, 2015.

Oakland, J. A. (1969). Measurement of personality correlates of academic achievement in high school students. *Journal of Counseling Psychology*, *16*(5), 452–457.

O'Connor, M. C., & Paunonen, S. V. (2007). Big Five personality predictors of post-secondary academic performance. *Personality and Individual Differences*, *43*(5), 971–990.

Payton, J., Weissberg, R. P., Durlak, J. A., Dymnicki, A. B., Taylor, R. D., Schellinger, K. B., et al. (2008). *The positive impact of social and emotional learning for kindergarten to eighth-grade students.* Chicago: Collaborative for Academic, Social, and Emotional Learning.

"Peter T. Mcintyre quotes." (n.d.). *Thinkexist.* Accessed at http://thinkexist.com/quotes/Peter _T._Mcintyre/ on August 5, 2015.

Pornsakulvanich, V., Dumrongsiri, N., Sajampun, P., Sornsri, S., John, S. P., Sriyabhand, T., et al. (2012). An analysis of personality traits and learning styles as predictors of academic performance. *ABAC Journal*, *32*(3), 1–19.

Poropat, A. E. (2009). A meta-analysis of the five-factor model of personality and academic performance. *Psychological Bulletin*, *135*(2), 322–338.

Poundstone, W. (2012). *Are you smart enough to work at Google? Trick questions, Zen-like riddles, insanely difficult puzzles, and other devious interviewing techniques you need to know to get a job anywhere in the new economy.* New York: Little, Brown.

Roberts, B. W., & Jackson, J. J. (2008). Sociogenomic personality psychology. *Journal of Personality*, *76*(6), 1523–1544.

Roberts, B. W., Kuncel, N. R., Shiner, R., Caspi, A., & Goldberg, L. R. (2007). The power of personality: The comparative validity of personality traits, socioeconomic status, and cognitive ability for predicting important life outcomes. *Perspectives on Psychological Science*, *2*(4), 313–345.

Rotter, J. B. (1966). Generalized expectancies for internal versus external control of reinforcement. *Psychological Monographs: General and Applied, 80*(1), 609–636.

Rutherford.org.nz. (n.d.). *Rutherford's awards.* Accessed at www.rutherford.org.nz/awards.htm on March 23, 2015.

Rutkowski, K., & Domino, G. (1975). Interrelationship of study skills and personality variables in college students. *Journal of Educational Psychology, 67*(6), 784–789.

Ryan, R. M., & Deci, E. L. (2000). Self-determination theory and the facilitation of intrinsic motivation, social development, and well-being. *American Psychologist, 55*(1), 68–78.

Sakofsky, M. J. (2009). *The impact of empathy skills training on middle school children.* Unpublished master's thesis, State University of New York, Brockport.

Scales, P. C., Blyth, D. A., Berkas, T. H., & Kielsmeier, J. C. (2000). The effects of service-learning on middle school students' social responsibility and academic success. *Journal of Early Adolescence, 20*(3), 332–358.

Scales, P. C., & Roehlkepartain, E. C. (2005). *Can service-learning help reduce the achievement gap? New research points toward the potential of service-learning for low-income students.* Saint Paul, MN: New Youth Leadership Council. Accessed at http://msde.maryland.gov/NR /rdonlyres/CEFD2869-9129-46A3-91CE-443928D1ED6C/24873/CanServiceLearning HelpReducetheAchievementGap.pdf on March 23, 2015.

Scales, P. C., Roehlkepartain, E. C., Neal, M., Kielsmeier, J. C., & Benson, P. L. (2006). Reducing academic achievement gaps: The role of community service and service learning. *Journal of Experiential Education, 29*(1), 38–60.

Schmit, M. J., & Ryan, A. M. (1993). The Big Five in personnel selection: Factor structure in applicant and nonapplicant populations. *Journal of Applied Psychology, 78*(6), 966–974.

Shams, F., Mooghali, A. R., Tabebordbar, F., & Soleimanpour, N. (2011). The mediating role of academic self-efficacy in the relationship between personality traits and mathematics performance. *Procedia—Social and Behavioral Sciences, 29*, 1689–1692.

Shiner, R. L., & Masten, A. S. (2002). Transactional links between personality and adaptation from childhood through adulthood. *Journal of Research in Personality, 36*(6), 580–588.

Sternberg, R. J. (Ed.). (1990). *Wisdom: Its nature, origins, and development.* New York: Cambridge University Press.

Sternberg, R. J. (Ed.). (2000). *Handbook of intelligence.* New York: Cambridge University Press.

St. John, R. (2010). *The 8 traits successful people have in common: 8 to be great.* Toronto, Ontario, Canada: Train of Thought Arts.

Strayhorn, T. L. (2013). What role does grit play in the academic success of black male collegians at predominantly white institutions? *Journal of African American Studies, 18*(1), 1–10.

Tenaw, Y. A. (2013). Relationship between self-efficacy, academic achievement and gender in analytical chemistry at Debre Markos College of Teacher Education. *African Journal of Chemical Education, 3*(1), 3–28.

Tett, R. P., Jackson, D. N., & Rothstein, M. (1991). Personality measures as predictors of job performance: A meta-analytic review. *Personnel Psychology, 44*(4), 703–742.

"Thomas Carlyle quotes." (n.d.) *Thinkexist*. Accessed at http://thinkexist.com/quotes/thomas_carlyle/2.html on August 5, 2015.

Tough, P. (2012). *How children succeed: Grit, curiosity and the hidden power of character*. Boston: Houghton Mifflin Harcourt.

Townsend, J. C. (2012, September 26). Why we should teach empathy to improve education (and test scores). *Forbes*. Accessed at www.forbes.com/sites/ashoka/2012/09/26/why-we-should-teach-empathy-to-improve-education-and-test-scores on March 23, 2015.

Vreeke, G. J., & van der Mark, I. L. (2003). Empathy, an integrative model. *New Ideas in Psychology, 21*(3), 177–207.

Walter, M., Ebbesen, E. B., & Raskoff Zeiss, A. (1972). Cognitive and attentional mechanisms in delay of gratification. *Journal of Personality and Social Psychology, 21*(2), 204–218.

Watson, D., & Clark, L. A. (1984). Negative affectivity: The disposition to experience aversive emotional states. *Psychological Bulletin, 96*(3), 465–490.

Weiss, H. M., & Cropanzano, R. (1996). Affective events theory: A theoretical discussion of the structure, causes and consequences of affective experiences at work. *Research in Organizational Behavior, 18*, 1–74.

Zeidner, M., & Matthews, G. (2000). Intelligence and personality. In R. J. Sternberg (Ed.), *Handbook of intelligence* (pp. 581–610). New York: Cambridge University Press.

Zettler, I. (2011). Self-control and academic performance: Two field studies on university citizenship behavior and counterproductive academic behavior. *Learning and Individual Differences, 21*(1), 119–123.

Zhang, L.-F. (2002). Measuring thinking styles in addition to measuring personality traits? *Personality and Individual Differences, 33*(3), 445–458.

Zhang, L.-F. (2006). Thinking styles and the Big Five personality traits revisited. *Personality and Individual Differences, 40*(6), 1177–1187.

Zimbardo, P. G., & Gerrig, R. J. (1996). *Psychology and life* (14th ed.). New York: HarperCollins.

Zweig, D., & Webster, J. (2004). What are we measuring? An examination of the relationships between the Big-Five personality traits, goal orientation, and performance intentions. *Personality and Individual Differences, 36*(7), 1693–1708.

Kendra Coates, MAT, MS, is Director of PreK–3rd Education with the High Desert Education Service District in Oregon, where she designs, leads, and evaluates a regional preK–3rd initiative funded by the Oregon Department of Education's Early Learning Division. Her work includes designing, implementing, and evaluating districtwide preK–3rd approaches in growth mindsets, social and emotional learning, family engagement, and professional learning in elementary schools. She co-led a preK–3rd standards alignment workgroup aimed at developing approaches to learning and social and emotional development standards for the state of Oregon. Kendra has been an educator since the mid-1990s with a background as a teacher and administrator at multiple levels across the P–20 continuum and in a variety of settings, including abroad. She has taught literacy courses for the Oregon State University–Cascades reading endorsement and MA in teaching programs.

Kendra's educational passion focuses on noncognitive competencies. She is an early learning curriculum developer and professional development specialist with Mindset Works, a company founded by psychologist Carol Dweck and colleagues. Kendra authored their literacy-based preK–3rd curriculum. In addition, she leads professional learning for schools, districts, and organizations as an independent consultant in the areas of preK–3rd education, growth mindset and social and emotional learning, and family engagement.

Kendra received a bachelor's degree in political science from Pacific Lutheran University, a master's degree in Special Education from Pacific University, and a master's degree in curriculum and instruction from Portland State University. She holds educational licenses in literacy, preK–12 special education, early childhood and elementary education, and school administration in the state of Oregon. She is currently a doctoral candidate with the University of Oregon's Educational Methodology, Policy, and Leadership program.

Kendra can be reached at kendrajcoates@gmail.com.

To book Kendra Coates for professional development, contact pd@solution-tree.com.

CHAPTER 4

Dreams and Nightmares: Motivational Factors

KENDRA COATES

The "I Have a Dream" speech delivered by Martin Luther King Jr. on August 28, 1963, on the steps of the Lincoln Memorial in Washington, DC, has been sealed as one of the finest speeches in American history. King was sharing his own dream with the crowd. The dream so eloquently painted by King moved over 250,000 people on site and throughout the United States to demand equal rights for African Americans. It is impossible to measure the full broad impact of the speech on the world, but it undoubtedly facilitated the passage of the landmark Civil Rights Act of 1964, which outlawed discrimination based on race, color, religion, sex, or national origin in the United States.

Dreams are powerful motivators. King's dream for social justice and equal rights for all led him on a courageous journey through obstacles and dangers. His dream motivated not only him but also millions of others to initiate, participate in, and persist in civil rights activities under extremely adverse conditions. But what is motivation, and how does it develop? How do we encourage the development of qualities that positively affect motivation, and how do we measure the growth of these factors? This chapter will explore the mindset that influences people to act and the implications these factors may have.

What Is Motivation?

The reason to initiate, participate in, and persist in certain activities has been the subject of motivational psychology. Motivation is a psychological construct used to explain why human beings do certain things: "Motives are reasons people hold for initiating and performing voluntary behavior. They indicate the meaning of human behavior, and they may reveal a person's values. Motives often affect a person's perception, cognition, emotion, and behavior" (Reiss, 2004, p. 179).

Motivation is critical to learning and accomplishment of any sort, because without it, one would not even begin to engage in activities that lead to accomplishment. Thus, understanding why people choose to do certain things and not others has been a topic of interest of philosophers and psychologists for a long time. For example, Aristotle (in a translation by J. A. K. Thomson, 1953) distinguished ends and means according to the reasons one performs the behavior. When a person does something for no apparent reason other than the behavior itself, it indicates an end motive. That is, the behavior itself is the end. When a person engages in behaviors in order to achieve something else, the behavior is a means to other ends. The motivation is thus a means. This distinction is the origin of the modern-day distinction between intrinsic and extrinsic motivation.

In the thousands of years following Aristotle, human beings have developed increasingly sophisticated understandings, models, and theories of motivation to explain human and animal behaviors. Given the purpose of this book, I can only focus on a very narrow set of ideas pertinent to education. Specifically, I am interested in motivational theories and concepts that research shows to have implications for human learning and achievement: mindsets, possible selves, hope, curiosity, and passion. What I selected to examine in this chapter is by no means exhaustive. Instead, I treat these concepts as a sample of motivational factors that schools should attend to as valuable educational outcomes that have been traditionally neglected. Moreover, these factors may have different names, and some may overlap with psychological traits discussed under personality.

Mindsets

Beliefs about intelligence and abilities begin to develop at a very early age and are passed down from generation to generation. One such vehicle through which children learn their parents' beliefs and values is praise. The type of praise (process vs. person) a toddler receives influences his or her adopted mindsets later on in childhood (Gunderson, Gripshover, Romero, Dweck, Goldin-Meadow, & Levine, 2013). Mindsets are beliefs, attitudes, and perceptions people have about themselves, specifically about their intelligence, abilities, skills, and talents. Mindsets exist along a continuum and are developed, nurtured, and refined over a lifetime. At one end of the continuum is a fixed mindset. Individuals holding a fixed mindset believe their intelligence, abilities, and skills are static, unchanging qualities. At the other end is a growth mindset. Those holding a growth mindset believe their intelligence, abilities, and skills are malleable and can be developed through effort, hard work, and learning. Stanford University psychologist Carol Dweck (2006) discovered the constructs of growth and fixed mindset and has been a leading scholar exploring the relationship between our mindset and our motivation and achievement.

An individual's mindset exists within his or her goal orientation. There are two types of goals: learning and performance. Learning goals are based on an individual's desire to increase his or her knowledge and skills (improve ability), while performance goals are based on an individual's desire to gain positive judgments of his or her performance (prove ability). Both lead to different outcomes impacting mindset and motivation levels. For example, individuals with a growth mindset tend to focus on learning goals. As a result, they enjoy learning; embrace challenges and persist through obstacles and setbacks; view mistakes and failures as opportunities to learn and grow; have higher levels of motivation; and employ a wide variety of effective learning techniques. They are motivated to learn for learning's sake. On the other hand, individuals who have a fixed mindset tend to focus on performance goals. They spend their time worrying about their level of intelligence and how much ability they have in a given area; avoid challenges and give up easily in the face of setbacks and obstacles; view mistakes and failures as part of their identity, even going to such extremes as lying about their mistakes or trying to hide them; and employ minimal learning techniques. They are motivated by looking smart rather than becoming smarter (Dweck, 2006). Dweck (2006) reminds us that "becoming is better than being" (p. 25). In other words, a growth mindset opens up possibilities, while a fixed mindset is limiting.

Mindsets are learned, teachable, and measurable, and they interact with and influence the development of other motivational factors outlined in this chapter. Multiple studies demonstrate that mindsets have a direct influence on grades, and that teaching a growth mindset predicts motivation and raises overall achievement, especially for students operating under stereotype threat (Aronson, Fried, & Good, 2002; Blackwell, Trzesniewski, & Dweck, 2007; Good, Aronson, & Inzlicht, 2003; Paunesku, Walton, Romero, Smith, Yeager, & Dweck, 2015). Dweck and her colleagues concluded that "educational interventions and initiatives that target these psychological factors can transform students' experience and achievement in school, improving core academic outcomes such as GPA and test scores months and even years later" (Dweck, Walton, & Cohen, 2014, p. 2). Farrington and her colleagues concluded in their literature review on noncognitive factors that "the extensive body of research on mindsets further suggests that a psycho-social approach could have major implications for reform efforts aimed at closing racial/ethnic gaps in student performance and educational attainment" (Farrington et al., 2012, p. 28).

In many ways, motivational factors like *possible selves*, *hope*, *curiosity*, and *passion* are influenced by our beliefs and perceptions. They are often identified as outcomes of a growth mindset. First of all, people with a growth mindset love to learn and can be characterized as enthusiastic and curious learners. They view effort and hard work as essential components to learning and success (Dweck, 2006); embrace change and believe in the ability to change for the better (Dweck, 2006); persist and persevere in the face of obstacles, setbacks, and challenges (Dweck, 2006); demonstrate grit in goal setting and attainment (Duckworth, Peterson, Matthews, & Kelly, 2007); tend to be more hopeful and understand how intentional thought leads to adaptive action (Snyder, 1994); and view mistakes and failure as opportunities to learn and grow (Dweck, 2006). Overall, a growth mindset has a positive influence on motivation, efficacy, agency, and learning.

Starting with individuals' beliefs about themselves, their intelligence, abilities, skills, talents, and learning is a logical starting place for the development of their motivation. According to Dweck (2007),

> The most motivated and resilient students are *not* the ones who think they have a lot of fixed or innate intelligence [like those with a fixed mindset]. Instead, the most motivated and resilient students [those with a growth mindset] are the ones who believe that their abilities can be developed through their effort and learning. (p. 6)

Students, teachers, administrators, and parents all benefit from building growth mindset learning communities. Schools can adopt a proactive approach to developing a growth mindset by teaching children key growth mindset principles and practices early and consistently across their educational continuum. Growth mindset principles and practices include the basics of neuroscience (neuroplasticity), learning goals, learning as a process (effort, the power of *yet*), praising engagement and effort in the process, growth-oriented feedback, taking on challenges, persistence, and learning from mistakes. By doing so, parents and educators are practicing key growth mindset principles and practices for themselves while building the foundation of a child's motivational framework.

Parents and educators must remember that actions speak louder than words. When adults' actions do not align with their identified growth mindset, the development of students' growth mindsets is significantly compromised and the benefits of a growth mindset are not fully realized. Students receive mixed messages when adults talk about the importance of a growth mindset while still engaging in fixed mindset practices (labeling, praising the person instead of the process, grouping by ability, setting performance goals, emphasizing grades and test scores). Students need to see and feel a growth mindset in action; otherwise, it is reduced to lip service. With all its positive side effects, the world needs heavy doses of a growth mindset. Mindset Works, a company founded by Dweck and colleagues, provides a variety of resources to help parents and educators teach and support the development of a growth mindset.

Possible Selves

The concept of possible selves complements and extends mindsets, motivation, affect, and cognition. Possible selves was first introduced by Hazel Markus, a social psychologist and pioneer in cultural psychology (Markus & Nurius, 1986). There are three main constructs of the theory: (1) hope (what we hope to become), (2) fears (what we are afraid of becoming), and (3) expectations (what we think we might become). The theory of possible selves has woven its way into the discourse of visions for innovation, effort, and improvement. As Rosabeth Moss Kanter states, "A vision is not just a picture of what could be; it is an appeal to our better selves, a call to become something more" ("Rosabeth Moss Kanter quotes," n.d.). In education, envisioning the future has become an important tool for leveraging students' engagement, motivation, and persistence in learning.

Possible selves as a motivating factor for student learning was specifically explored by Martin Lamb, a professor at the University of Leeds in England. He was particularly interested in the relationship between possible selves, motivation, and second-language acquisition and conducted much of his research in Indonesia focused on adolescents learning English. In a longitudinal study, he explored the relationship between future-oriented components of the self and motivated learning behavior, and proposed that a major part of the motivation to learn a second language is derived from a person's view of his or her own possible future self (Lamb, 2011). The study found that the presence of future-oriented components of the self was a key motivator for learning English.

Daphna Oyserman, a research professor at the University of Michigan Institute for Social Research, developed an identity-based motivation model based on integrating research on the future-oriented aspects of self-concept, including possible selves, with research on social and personal identities, specifically racial-ethnic identities and cultural psychological research on cultural mindsets (Oyserman, Bybee, Terry, & Hart-Johnson, 2004). Built on her identity-based motivation model, she developed a nine-week, after-school, small group, activities-based intervention. The intervention was grounded in a social cognitive approach (Bandura, 1986; Dweck & Leggett, 1988; Elliott & Dweck, 1988), a foundational component of mindset theory. She found that students who participated in her nine-week intervention demonstrated improved academic possible selves and engagement (Oyserman, Terry, & Bybee, 2002). These outcomes were a result of facilitating change in possible selves as well as strategies to attain them. Specifically, the intervention focused on helping students:

- articulate specific academically oriented possible selves;
- connect possible selves for the coming year to specific strategies to attain these selves;
- connect these short-term possible selves and strategies to adult possible selves;
- and develop skills to effectively interact with others in order to attain these possible selves. (Oyserman, et al, 2002, p. 324)

In addition to its impact on student achievement, imagining possible selves plays an important role in parenthood, especially parents' involvement and engagement in their child's education. New parents wonder, What kind of parent do I want to be? (hoped-for selves), What kind of parent do I not want to be? (feared selves), and What kind of parent will I be? (expected selves). Specifically, possible selves plays a role in the parent-child relationship and the types of strategies parents use to support their children. A study exploring African American mothers' and daughters' beliefs about possible selves and their strategies for reaching goals found that possible selves influenced the types of strategies the mothers and daughters used to help the daughters reach their goals (Kerpelman, Shoffner, & Ross-Griffin, 2002). For example, a mother's college experience influenced her strategies for how she supported her daughter reaching her academic and career goals. Oyserman and colleagues (2004) examined the role of parental support on adolescents' possible selves, strategies, and the likelihood of attaining possible selves. Their study of over three thousand Hong Kong secondary students found that practical parental support provided students a foundation to engage in strategies to attain their possible selves. For example, if students felt like they could ask their parent about something they needed to know about the world, they were more likely to believe they could attain their hoped-for possible self and avoid their feared-for possible self.

The role of possible selves could even play a valuable role in the types of interventions targeting parents in prison. A study exploring the role of possible selves of young fathers in prison as it relates to life after prison found that their hoped-for and expected selves were most related to parenting and employment (Meek, 2011). Young fathers were very concerned about their present and future identity as a parent. These findings suggest that parenthood and possible selves could play an important role in developing positive interventions to support young fathers in prison.

Possible selves as a recognized motivational strategy is evident in the University of Kansas Center for Research on Learning's Strategic Instruction Model (SIM), an integrated model aimed at meeting the needs of diverse learners by promoting effective teaching and learning practices. It is also a focus of FutureSelves, a New Zealand company that provides software and skills to promote the concept of possible selves.

Possible selves is future-oriented and holds significant implications for student achievement and success, instructional improvement, and parent involvement and engagement. Promoting the concept of possible selves is promoting the future of each individual and increases the overall well-being of a community. When engaging in practices that support possible selves (for example, metacognition, implementing strategies to set and attain goals), students, teachers, and parents can see their better selves in the future. These practices, combined with a growth mindset, will increase the likelihood of individuals taking action to realize their possible selves because they view their abilities and talents as something they have control over, the basis for student ownership of learning and teacher ownership of teaching. In this way, possible selves plays a promising role in building a better educational community as each member moves closer to their hoped-for possible self. A motivational strategy like possible selves helps to develop students' identities as learners. When students identify as *learners*, they feel a sense of belonging to their learning community and therefore are more engaged and motivated.

Hope

Another motivational factor arising from a growth mindset is hope. Psychologist C. R. Snyder (1994) first introduced Hope Theory as a new motivational model for use in educational research in the early 1990s. He characterized hope as the capacity to engage in goals thinking (capacity to conceptualize goals), pathways thinking (capacity to develop specific strategies to reach those goals), and agency thinking (capacity to initiate and sustain the motivation to employ those strategies).

Building on Snyder's Hope Theory, Mark Van Ryzin conducted a study assessing school environments from the student's perspective using the ABCs (autonomy, belongingness, and competence) of development. The study became known as the Hope Study and is summarized in the book *Assessing What Really Matters in Schools: Creating Hope for the Future* (Newell & Van Ryzin, 2009). The Hope Study found that students with high levels of hope get better grades and graduate at higher rates than those with lower levels and that the presence of hope in a student is a better predictor of grades and class ranking than standardized test scores (Newell & Van Ryzin, 2009). This model is central to EdVisions Schools, an educational model aimed at building hope in students.

In addition to the Hope Study, others have demonstrated the positive relationship between hope, academic achievement, and overall well-being, and have observed hope as a motivational factor (Marques, Lopez, & Pais-Ribeiro, 2011). In a longitudinal study of entering college freshmen, hopeful thinking, as measured by the Hope Scale, predicted better overall grade point averages (Snyder et al., 2002). Hope was also a predictor of positive affect and the best predictor of grades in a study that examined the role of three positive thinking variables (self-esteem, trait hope, and positive attributional style) in predicting future high school grades (Ciarrochi, Heaven, & Davies, 2007).

Findings from these studies support the importance of integrating hope and positive thinking in education programs aimed at supporting the development of perseverance and resiliency. Positive thinking that takes into consideration the reality of obstacles and setbacks produces the greatest effects (Oettingen, 2014). This scientifically founded approach to positive thinking can enhance the process of possible selves and reinforce the growth mindset principle and practice of taking on challenges and persisting through obstacles and setbacks. Obstacles and setbacks are not to be feared but rather to be embraced as valuable learning opportunities. Based on the reciprocal relationship between goal orientation within mindset theory and goals thinking within hope theory, those with a growth mindset tend to be more hopeful and those who are more hopeful tend to have a growth mindset. Over time, a hopeful outlook reinforces a growth mindset, and a growth mindset promotes a hopeful outlook. Lu Xun, a Chinese essayist, likens hope in this way to "a path in the countryside. Originally, there is nothing—but as people walk this way again and again, a path appears" (Kristof & WuDunn, 2014, p. i). Higher levels of hope lead to the desire to seek change and excellence in life because hope increases the capacity to imagine a better possible self in the future and take purposeful action to move closer to that better self.

Curiosity

A growth mindset gives rise to a third factor that influences motivation. Curiosity, or the desire for truth, is one of the greatest motivators in life, according to Plato (Reiss, 2000). Walt Disney notes that "we keep moving forward, opening new doors, and doing new things, because we're curious and curiosity keeps leading us down new paths" (Williams & Denney, 2004, p. 350). From ancient philosophers to innovative 20th century animators, curiosity is regarded as one basic need that drives learning. Curiosity is the desire to learn for learning's own sake, according to Ohio State University psychologist Steven Reiss (2000), who suggests that curiosity is born, an evolutionary instinct. It gives animals advantage for survival:

> It prods animals both to explore environments and to learn from experience. By exploring environments, animals can find food, water, and other essential materials. Learned habits help animals gather food more efficiently and avoid danger. In human beings, curiosity includes the desires to read, write, and think, in addition to the primal desire to explore new places. (Reiss, 2000, p. 41)

Others believe it is learned. For example, Carnegie Mellon University psychologist George Loewenstein's (1994) information gap theory suggests that our perception of a gap in our knowledge and understanding creates curiosity. If knowledge and understanding were a sidewalk, curiosity would grow where there were cracks in the sidewalk. Loewenstein's information gap theory was born from his desire to address the gaps that he found in previous theories and approaches on curiosity. These include drive theories, incongruity theories, and the competence and intrinsic motivation approach. Drive theories include Freud's view of curiosity as internally stimulated (Aronoff, 1962) and Daniel Berlyne's (1954) view of curiosity as externally stimulated, which was the basis of epistemic curiosity, or the desire to know.

This desire is a part of Kagan's (1972) four basic human motives: (1) the motive to resolve uncertainty (epistemic curiosity), (2) sensory motives, (3) anger and hostility, and (4) the motive for mastery. Another incongruity theorist, Jean Piaget (1952), viewed curiosity as the child's need to make sense of the world and a product of cognitive disequilibrium, the imbalance between new knowledge and prior knowledge.

The competence and intrinsic motivation approach was based on Robert White's (1959) theory that curiosity stemmed from the motivation to master one's environment, what he referred to as competence. Deci (1975) further enhanced the relationship between curiosity and competence when he included competence as one of our psychological needs. A study of Hong Kong university students identified a link between curiosity and higher levels of intrinsic motivation in its investigation of factors affecting intrinsic motivation (Hon-Keung, Man-Shan, & Lai-Fong, 2012).

Multiple studies have also linked curiosity with better health and relationships and higher levels of intelligence, happiness, and overall well-being. Todd Kashdan (2009), professor of psychology at George Mason University and author of *Curious? Discover the Missing Ingredient to a Fulfilling Life*, found that higher levels of curiosity predicted more frequent growth-oriented behaviors and a greater presence of meaning and life satisfaction (Kashdan & Steger, 2007). Ultimately, the study supported curiosity as a key ingredient in the development of well-being and a meaningful life.

The role of curiosity in learning cannot be overstated. Educators can nurture curiosity in themselves and their students by understanding how the levels of curiosity (diversive, epistemic, and empathic) align with higher-order thinking skills and learning experiences and organizing them accordingly. In this way, educators can better understand students' needs to develop their curiosity and to create a space for optimal curiosity growth, and teach students how to organize their lives in ways that nurture their curiosity. Educators can use Bloom's Revised Taxonomy and Webb's Depth of Knowledge (DOK) to help them design learning experiences that align with students' curiosity needs. For example, engaging students in question asking and refinement nurtures their epistemic curiosity and aligns with Webb's level of strategic thinking and Bloom's level of analysis.

The future wants and needs curious learners. New products, new companies, new educational models, new organizational structures and systems, and other new innovations will be created by those who have high levels of curiosity and motivation. The growth and well-being of ourselves, those with whom we interact, and our global community demand we create learning communities that foster curiosity, exploration and investigation, question-asking and refinement, and divergent thinking. The absence of these types of learning communities fosters a very narrow right-question/right-answer mentality that suppresses curiosity growth, question asking, creative problem thinking and solving, learning, and idea making—the ingredients of innovation. Innovation is insurance for a sustaining, productive, and healthy future.

Passion

The growth mindset produces a fourth effect, passion, which can significantly impact motivation. Psychologist Robert Vallerand (2010) at Université du Québec à Montréal proposed the Dualistic Model of Passion (DMP) to explain the relationship between motivation and passion. DMP helps explain why something that you love can be good or bad for you. According to DMP, some people experience harmonious passion while others experience obsessive passion. Harmonious passion encompasses a sense of choice in that individuals feel they have chosen a given endeavor or career path. As a result, they feel they can choose to engage or disengage in their passion at any time and ultimately have a healthier relationship with their passion. On the other hand, obsessive passion encompasses a sense of obligation in that individuals feel they have to engage their passion or else they experience some type of negative consequence like the loss of status or self-esteem. Ultimately, they do not feel like they can choose to disengage from their passion, and they may be negatively affected by these feelings.

Based on DMP, individuals are motivated to explore their environment and engage in various activities to foster individual growth. Through engagement in a variety of activities, individuals will discover a preference for a few based on the perception that the activity is enjoyable and important for one reason or another. An interesting aspect of passion comes from the notion that passionate activities become self-defining and part of an individual's identity. They are not simply something one values or enjoys doing. For example, one who has a passion for drawing sees him- or herself as an artist.

Interestingly, few studies have investigated the impact of passion on academic development and long-term success. In two studies that investigated dramatic arts students' and psychology undergraduates' passion for studying (Vallerand et al., 2007), researchers demonstrated that both harmonious and obsessive passion predicted deliberate practice (that is, the amount of free time spent practicing). Consequently, deliberate practice predicted increased objective performance in both samples of students. However, students whose passion was obsessive were most at risk for stress, dissatisfaction, and burnout.

Another facet of passion is grit, what Angela Duckworth defines as the perseverance and passion for long-term goals (Duckworth et al., 2007). Duckworth conducted a series of studies aimed at finding out what characteristics beyond IQ led to a person's success in a given field and discovered that grit significantly contributed to successful outcomes. She concluded that the combination of passion and perseverance may be as important as intelligence in contributing to an individual's success. (The combination of grit, curiosity, and other noncognitive competencies and their impact on achievement and success were explored by Paul Tough [2012] in his book, *How Children Succeed: Grit, Curiosity, and the Hidden Power of Character*.)

Passion, especially a passion for learning, is a highly desirable ingredient for motivation, achievement, and success. A passion for learning is a combination of curiosity and persistence and results in high levels of achievement and success. However, high levels of achievement and success do not necessarily guarantee a genuine passion for learning. Developing a passion for learning ensures students and educators continue to grow and discover new ways to explore and deepen their capacity, a process for sustaining and enhancing motivation. A passion for learning moves beyond school learning to lifelong learning that encompasses the combination of a growth mindset, a better possible self, hope, curiosity, and passion.

Measuring Motivation

From the second children are born, they are measured—height, weight, circumference of their head, skin color (for jaundice)—and compared to their peers. The measurement of their qualities and comparison to their peers continue throughout their lifetimes. When a child declares "I'm taller than you" to his or her younger brother at a well check, he or she is expressing sense-making of the world by reflecting the beliefs and values of that world. What, how, and why a child's qualities are measured influence his or her emerging beliefs and values, and in turn, these beliefs and values shape his or her motivational framework.

Mindset, possible selves, hope, curiosity, and passion are beliefs, values, and qualities that together create a robust motivational framework. By measuring each of these elements, individuals can better understand how each element acts and reacts to the others in given situations and contexts; how each element changes and develops over time; and how each element contributes to the development of motivation, productivity, achievement, success, and overall well-being. With this understanding, individuals improve their ability and power to change, manipulate, and enhance the space for increasing their motivational levels.

Motivation is a social construct and therefore it is not directly observable. How it is defined informs how it is measured. It also means that once it is defined, the manifestations of motivation, or the five motivational factors explored in this chapter, are actually being measured. The five factors are also social constructs and are measured according to various tools, most commonly self-reports, designed exclusively within each domain. We must remember that measurement tools are for learning, not for judging and labeling, and no test can measure an individual's potential. As Dweck (2006) reminds us, an individual's "true potential is unknown (and unknowable)" (p. 7).

Table 4.1 (page 82) presents examples of the types of measures currently used to measure each of the motivational factors outlined in this chapter.

Each motivational factor develops along a continuum. Therefore, a measurement tool only measures a given point in time along this developmental continuum. Furthermore, motivation is dynamic and there is much to learn about it. Due to the complementary and reciprocal nature of the five factors, there is a significant opportunity to connect and integrate the various tools into one comprehensive motivational framework assessment. Collectively, the tools can be used to help educators and students learn about, develop, and nurture their motivational frameworks—a motivational portfolio.

Measure of Mindset

To measure an individual's mindset or theory of intelligence, Dweck developed the theory of intelligence scale, also known as the Mindset Survey (Dweck, Chiu, & Hong,

Table 4.1: Motivational Factors, Name of Measure, Reliability Coefficients, and Sample Items

Factor	Name of Measure	Items	Reliability	Sample Item
Mindset	Theory of Intelligences Survey	8	.80–.82	No matter how much intelligence you have, you can always change it a good amount.
Possible Selves	Possible Selves Questionnaire	6	N/A	Next year I expect to be . . .
Hope	Children's Hope Scale	6	.72–.86	I am doing just as well as other kids my age.
	Adult Dispositional Hope Scale (ADHS)	12	.74–.84	I energetically pursue my goals.
Curiosity	Need for Cognition (NFC) Scale	18	+.90	Thinking is not my idea of fun.
Passion	Passion Scale	34	.79–.89	This activity allows me to live a variety of experiences.
	Grit-S	8	.73–.83	New ideas and projects sometimes distract me from previous ones.

1995). The survey is an eight-item self-report that measures students' perception of their intelligence and how they approach new learning opportunities, challenges, and mistakes. The survey is designed for eight-year-olds and older. Items are rated on a six-point Likert scale ranging from 1 = *disagree a lot* to 6 = *agree a lot*. Educators can use the Mindset Survey at the individual, classroom, or school level in the following ways:

* Pre- and post-survey
* Opportunity to compare and contrast student mindsets in different content areas
* Formative assessment to inform and guide growth mindset instruction
* Reflection opportunity for students (such as in discussions and writing exercises)
* Opportunity to engage students in discussion about growth and fixed mindsets
* Tool to measure the impact of instruction, a given program, or intervention on mindsets
* Opportunity to better understand how beliefs translate into behaviors

Specifically, parents and educators can learn to identify behaviors that demonstrate a growth mindset and motivation (for example, asking questions, learning something new, taking on challenges and persisting through difficulty, appropriate risk-taking, learning from mistakes, trying different strategies to solve a problem, expression of self-efficacy and agency); provide process praise (focused on effort, strategies, choices, and actions) in place of person praise (focused on fixed qualities); and engage in active observation of these growth mindset behaviors to create environments that support and enhance them. The Mindset Survey can also serve as a catalyst for engaging educators and parents in work to improve their growth mindset practices. What practices support elements of a growth mindset? What practices support elements of a fixed mindset? What steps can be taken to replace fixed mindset practices with growth mindset practices? Here, measuring and developing possible selves complement the effort to move from fixed mindset to growth mindset practices.

Measure of Possible Selves

To examine how individuals imagine their possible selves, Oyserman developed the Possible Selves Questionnaire, an open-ended questionnaire for adolescents (Oyserman et al., 2004). The questionnaire measures how individuals view themselves in the future by asking them to imagine who they will be in the future and what they are doing to realize their possible selves. Educators can use the Possible Selves Questionnaire as a stand-alone tool for goal setting or as a component of a comprehensive goal-setting process within the context of cultivating self-awareness, self-management, and a growth mindset. For example, educators can use the tool to reflect on their future selves as teachers, to engage parents in reflecting on their role in supporting their child's education, and to engage students in metacognitive practices, goal setting, and implementing strategies to attain their goals.

Additionally, the tool can be a starting point for a more comprehensive exploration of possible selves, including writing or self-authoring, a simple but powerful exercise. Self-authoring is a term used by Jordan Peterson, a professor in the department of psychology at the University of Toronto who wanted to explore whether writing could affect student motivation. He designed an undergraduate course that combined expressive writing with goal setting, and it is the intersection of these two processes that he calls self-authoring. The method was found to nearly eliminate the gender and ethnic minority achievement gap for students engaging in the writing exercises (Schippers, Scheepers, & Peterson, 2015). This suggests that in the quest to find silver bullets in education, simple exercises like expressive writing combined with goal setting may hold more power than they were previously given credit for. Performing such exercises with a growth mindset holds great potential for improving motivation and learning.

Measure of Hope

To measure elements of hopeful thinking, Snyder (1991) and colleagues first developed the Adult Dispositional Hope Scale (ADHS) that targets adults fifteen years and older. It is a self-report questionnaire that measures agency thinking and pathways thinking. Items are scored on an eight-point Likert scale. They later developed the Children's Hope Scale, a dispositional self-report scale that targets children and adolescents ages eight to sixteen (Snyder et al., 1997). The scale measures hope, the combination of agency thinking and pathways thinking toward goals. Items are rated on a six-point Likert scale ranging from 1 = *none of the time* to 6 = *all of the time.*

Educators can use the Children's Hope Scale at the individual, classroom, and school level to measure students' levels of hope, to understand their goal-directed thinking, and to measure the growth of students' positive thinking as it relates to the attainment of their goals. If an individual student, group of students, class, or school has high levels of hope, what behaviors do they exhibit? By studying the behaviors of students with high hope levels, educators can learn what skills and practices may benefit others. The tool can help identify students who may benefit from improving their hopeful thinking. Like the Possible Selves Questionnaire, the scale can be used as a stand-alone tool or as a component of a comprehensive goal-setting process within the context of cultivating hope, self-awareness, self-management, and a growth mindset.

The tool can be used by educators to learn how students feel about their classroom and school climate. Do students feel a sense of hope in your classroom? In your school? Are some learning communities more hopeful than others? Why or why not? In this way, educators can use the tool to better understand the impact of their classroom and school environments on students' hopeful thinking and to inform and guide the development of learning communities that foster hope. Students can reflect on the content and results of the tool through discussions and writing exercises. They can use the information to examine and imagine possible selves. Overall, the tool is an opportunity for educators and students to learn about, develop, and nurture their motivation.

Educators can use the Adult Dispositional Hope Scale to measure their own hopeful thinking within the context of professional learning and well-being. High hope levels are associated with positive outcomes while low hope levels are associated with negative outcomes. Increasing individuals' hopeful thinking can help meet the universal educational goal of increasing positive outcomes.

Measure of Curiosity

To measure intellectual curiosity, John T. Cacioppo and Richard E. Petty (1982) developed the Need for Cognition (NFC) Scale for adolescents and adults. Specifically, the scale measures "the tendency for an individual to engage in and enjoy thinking" (Cacioppo & Petty, 1982, p. 116). The scale includes eighteen statements individuals rate on a five-point Likert scale to reflect how characteristic the statement is of themselves. Educators can use the NFC at the individual, classroom, and school level to measure levels of curiosity and curiosity growth, as well as to provide students the opportunity to reflect on their need for cognition (to understand and make sense of their experiences) and monitor their own curiosity growth. Students can reflect on the content and results of the tool through discussions and writing exercises. Individuals high in NFC are inquisitive, seek out new learning experiences, and enjoy challenges and effortful learning (Cacioppo, Petty, & Kao, 1984), all outcomes of a growth mindset.

The NFC can be used to better understand the behaviors of curious learners, helping educators learn what skills and practices cultivate curiosity growth and learning. Raising curiosity increases the desire to explore, investigate and discover, to take learning risks, and to learn new things. The NFC is strongly associated with intellectual engagement, epistemic curiosity (need to know), and openness to ideas (Cacioppo et al., 1984). Curiosity opens doors of opportunity otherwise closed and grows into a passion for learning, an essential element for increasing motivation, productivity, and achievement.

Educators can use the NFC to learn how their classroom and school environments are spaces for curiosity growth and to examine and explore ways to improve them. Do students have high levels of curiosity in your classroom? In your school? The tool provides educators valuable information so that they can make meaningful improvements in their practices and ability to create spaces that encourage curiosity. In addition, educators can use the NFC within professional learning opportunities to measure their curiosity, curiosity growth, and thus openness to ideas, often a goal of professional learning. Understanding how their own curiosity develops will help educators support students' curiosity growth. Overall, the tool is an opportunity for educators to better understand their own and students' curiosity growth for the purpose of meeting students' curiosity needs as they learn and increase their potential.

Measure of Passion

Two tools, the Passion Scale and the Grit Scale, can help educators assess students' levels of passion. Robert Vallerand developed the Passion Scale, a scale that measures harmonious and obsessive passion (Vallerand et al., 2003). The survey is designed for adolescents and adults. Items are rated on a seven-point Likert scale ranging from 1 = *do not agree at all* to 7 = *completely agree*.

Educators can use the Passion Scale at the individual, classroom, or school level to measure students' attitudes toward a given activity that they identify as something they are passionate about. For example, educators can use the tool to understand students' attitudes toward learning and whether or not students have a harmonious passion or obsessive passion for learning. Individuals who are obsessively passionate are threatened by failure because their identity is related to their performance. In this sense, obsessive passion aligns with fixed mindset outcomes (focus on performance goals, negative view of failure), while harmonious passion aligns with growth mindset outcomes (focus on learning goals, strong sense of autonomy and self-direction). Helping students develop a harmonious passion toward learning nurtures their growth mindsets and their identity as learners. When an individual identifies as a learner, he or she has a strong passion for learning, which leads to greater motivation to engage in learning activities. Passion leads to greater motivation to engage in activities congruent with one's identity.

The Passion Scale can be used by educators within professional learning opportunities to measure their attitudes toward teaching and whether they are holding a harmonious passion or obsessive passion for teaching. In this way, the Passion Scale serves as a metacognitive opportunity for teachers to reflect on their psychological well-being within their professional work. It's a tool to raise teachers' awareness of their attitudes toward teaching and how those attitudes impact their stress levels that can lead to burnout and ultimately teacher shortages.

The second tool educators can use to gauge students' passion is the Grit Scale. Developed by Angela Duckworth, it measures passion within the context of grit (Duckworth & Quinn, 2009). The Grit-S is a shorter version of the original twelve-item scale and targets adolescents and adults. Responses range from *very much like me* to *not like me at all* and are assigned points based on reverse scoring. Educators can use the Grit Scale at the individual, classroom, or school level to measure students' levels of grit. Combined with the Mindset Survey, educators can better understand how students are manifesting grit as an outcome of a growth mindset. The recognition of the importance of measuring elements of motivation like mindset and grit is demonstrated by the inclusion of mindset, grit, and motivation measures in the National Assessment of Educational Progress (NAEP), the Nation's Report Card, beginning in 2017.

Together, these instruments can assist educators in nurturing students' passion for learning. A passion for learning can lead to a passion for creativity and innovation, which is a powerful vehicle to ensure that learners in today's classrooms can effectively take on the global challenges of tomorrow. In classrooms and schools around the world, seeds of innovation are planted every day. The individual holding the cure for cancer cultivates his or her passion and potential in today's classrooms.

Where Do We Go From Here?

As our understanding of human practices like thinking, feeling, and doing continues to evolve, so does our understanding of motivation. At the core of studying motivation lies our own learning; our desire to know (epistemic curiosity); our desire to understand the *why* behind thinking, feeling, and doing (empathic curiosity); and ironically, our own motivation that dictates the level to which we continue to explore and investigate motivation. There are many new questions to examine and many more to ask.

For example, how do the five motivational factors consistently interact with each other? Do the factors influence motivation equally? How do the United States' rapid growth and low rate of job creation impact motivation? More and more students are graduating from college in debt and ready for a job that does not exist for them. This reality has the potential to decrease motivation, especially for those who already struggle to develop their growth mindsets, possible selves, hope, curiosity, and passion. On the other hand, this reality is motivating for those who are actively developing a robust motivational framework because it calls into action the very thing they are cultivating—their motivation. It calls for students to engage their growth mindsets and take ownership of their future as well as invest in the future of others by becoming job and career creators. It also calls for a reexamination of what it means to hold a traditional job.

How does the Information Era impact curiosity and thus motivation? Curiosity, especially diverse curiosity (need for novelty), can be satisfied instantaneously by the Internet. Due to this instant gratification, levels of diverse curiosity may be altered in such a way that negatively impacts epistemic (need to know) and empathic curiosity (need to know and understand why), which in turn negatively impacts motivation. However, this change could increase epistemic and empathic curiosity levels because more learning is accessible to more people and more people are readily able to share their new thinking, questions, learning, and ideas. Every time people on the other side of the world learn something new and share it on a global platform like the Internet, their learning potentially increases the learning of others. More knowledge and understanding create more gaps to fill. The Information Era creates cracks in a longer sidewalk where curiosity can flourish.

How do globalization and technological advances impact motivation? Our technology is so advanced the world does not need that many people doing the things that needed to be done before. Simply, the world does not need as many people working as in times before the Information Era. What does this mean for future motivation and productivity levels? What does this mean for individuals creating and sustaining meaningful lives for themselves and seeking change and excellence in their lives? The role of motivation in the future will increase in value as the world grows more complicated and dynamic. As the value increases, so will the demand to measure, develop, and monitor motivational levels in ourselves and others. The factors outlined in this chapter and their respective measures serve as a starting place for measuring, developing, and monitoring motivational outcomes in education. They are ingredients for an individual's motivational framework; however, this does not mean there is one way to mix the ingredients together or that more or different ingredients are not needed in different situations and contexts. An individual's motivational framework is malleable and adaptive to various elements, and each individual must cultivate his or her ability to change, manipulate, and enhance their framework to best serve their most productive, meaningful, and healthy life.

While an abundance of theories and approaches attempt to make sense of motivation, is it possible to account for all contributing factors? What role does rethinking play in our understanding of motivation? To answer these questions, we might reconsider the role of positive thinking and its impact on motivation. (*Rethinking Positive Thinking: Inside the New Science of Motivation* by Gabriele Oettingen [2014] provides more information on this topic.) Each contributing motivational factor outlined in this chapter would benefit from rethinking, more question asking, and deeper and wider study. We learn more by asking questions and realizing there are better questions to ask. We just don't know the better questions to ask *yet*.

References and Resources

Aristotle. (1953). *Ethics: The Nicomachean ethics* (J. A. K. Thomson, Trans.). London: Allen & Unwin.

Aronoff, J. (1962). Freud's conception of the origin of curiosity. *The Journal of Psychology: Interdisciplinary and Applied, 54*(1), 39–45.

Aronson, J., Fried, C., & Good, C. (2002). Reducing the effects of stereotype threat on African American college students by shaping theories of intelligence. *Journal of Experimental Social Psychology, 38*(2), 113–125.

Bandura, A. (1977). *Social learning theory*. Englewood Cliffs, NJ: Prentice Hall.

Bandura, A. (1986). From thought to action: Mechanisms of personal agency. *New Zealand Journal of Psychology, 15*(1), 1–17.

Bandura, A. (1989). Human agency in social cognitive theory. *American Psychologist, 44*(9), 1175–1184.

Berlyne, D. E. (1954). A theory of human curiosity. *British Journal of Psychology, 45*(3), 180–191.

Blackwell, L. S., Trzesniewski, K. H., & Dweck, C. S. (2007). Implicit theories of intelligence predict achievement across an adolescent transition: A longitudinal study and an intervention. *Child Development, 78*(1), 246–263.

Cacioppo, J. T., & Petty, R. E. (1982). The need for cognition. *Journal of Personality and Social Psychology, 42*(1), 116–131.

Cacioppo, J. T., Petty, R. E., & Kao, C. F. (1984). The efficient assessment of need for cognition. *Journal of Personality Assessment, 48*(3), 306–307.

Ciarrochi, J., Heaven, P. C. L., & Davies, F. (2007). The impact of hope, self-esteem, and attributional style on adolescents' school grades and emotional well-being: A longitudinal study. *Journal of Research in Personality, 41*(6), 1161–1178.

Costa, A. L., & Kallick, B. (2014). *Dispositions: Reframing teaching and learning*. Thousand Oaks, CA: Corwin Press.

Deci, E. L. (1975). *Intrinsic motivation*. New York: Plenum Press.

Deci, E. L. (1995). *Why we do what we do: Understanding self-motivation*. New York: Penguin.

Deci, E. L., & Ryan, R. M. (2000). The "what" and "why" of goal pursuits: Human needs and the self-determination of behavior. *Psychological Inquiry, 11*(4), 227–268.

Duckworth, A. L., Peterson, C., Matthews, M. D., & Kelly, D. R. (2007). Grit: Perseverance and passion for long-term goals. *Journal of Personality and Social Psychology*, *92*(6), 1087–1101.

Duckworth, A. L., & Quinn, P. D. (2009). Development and validation of the Short Grit Scale (GRIT-S). *Journal of Personality Assessment*, *91*(2), 166–174.

Dweck, C. S. (2006). *Mindset: The new psychology of success*. New York: Random House.

Dweck, C. S. (2007). Boosting achievement with messages that motivate. *Education Canada*, *47*(2), 6–10.

Dweck, C. S., Chiu, C.-Y., & Hong, Y.-Y. (1995). Implicit theories and their role in judgments and reactions: A world from two perspectives. *Psychological Inquiry*, *6*(4), 267–285.

Dweck, C. S. & Leggett, E. L. (1988). A social-cognitive approach to motivation and personality. *Psychological Review, 95*(2), 256–273.

Dweck, C. S., Walton, G. M., & Cohen, G. L. (2014). *Academic tenacity: Mindsets and skills that promote long-term learning*. Seattle, WA: Bill and Melinda Gates Foundation. Accessed at https://web.stanford.edu/~gwalton/home/Welcome_files/DweckWaltonCohen_2014.pdf on March 23, 2015.

Elliott, E. S. and Dweck, C. S. (1988). Goals: An approach to motivation and achievement. *Journal of Personality and Social Psychology*, *54*(1), 5–12.

Farrington, C. A., Roderick, M., Allensworth, E., Nagaoka, J., Keyes, T. S., Johnson, D. W., et al. (2012). *Teaching adolescents to become learners: The role of noncognitive factors in shaping school performance: A critical literature review*. Chicago: University of Chicago Consortium on Chicago School Research.

Good, C., Aronson, J., & Inzlicht, M. (2003). Improving adolescents' standardized test performance: An intervention to reduce the effects of stereotype threat. *Journal of Applied Developmental Psychology*, *24*(6), 645–662.

Gunderson, E., Gripshover, J., Romero, C., Dweck, C., Goldin-Meadow, S., & Levine, S. (2013). Parent praise to 1 to 3-year-olds predicts children's motivational frameworks 5 years later. *Child Development*, *84*(5), 1526–1541.

Headden, S., & McKay, S. (2015). *Motivation matters: How new research can help teachers boost student achievement*. Stanford, CA: Carnegie Foundation.

Hon-Keung, Y., Man-Shan, K., & Lai-Fong, C. A. (2012). The impact of curiosity and external regulation on intrinsic motivation: An empirical study in Hong Kong education. *Psychology Research*, *2*(5), 295–307.

Kagan, J. (1972). Motives and development. *Journal of Personality and Social Psychology*, *22*(1), 51–66.

Kashdan, T. B. (2009). *Curious? Discover the missing ingredient to a fulfilling life*. New York: HarperCollins.

Kashdan, T. B., & Steger, M. F. (2007). Curiosity and pathways to well-being and meaning in life: Traits, states, and everyday behaviors. *Motivation and Emotion*, *31*(3), 159–173.

Kerpelman, J. L., Shoffner, M. F., & Ross-Griffin, S. (2002). African American mothers' and daughters' beliefs about possible selves and their strategies for reaching the adolescents' future academic and career goals. *Journal of Youth and Adolescence, 31*(4), 289–302.

Kristof, N. D., & WuDunn, S. (2014). *A path appears: Transforming lives, creating opportunity.* New York: Alfred A. Knopf.

Lamb, M. (2011). Future selves, motivation and autonomy in long-term EFL learning trajectories. In G. Murray, X. Gao, & T. Lamb (Eds.), *Identity, motivation and autonomy in language learning* (pp. 177–194). Tonawanda, NY: Multilingual Matters.

Loewenstein, G. (1994). The psychology of curiosity: A review and reinterpretation. *Psychological Bulletin, 116*(1), 75–98.

Markus, H., & Nurius, P. (1986). Possible selves. *American Psychologist, 41*(9), 954–969.

Marques, S. C., Lopez, S. J., & Pais-Ribeiro, J. L. (2011). "Building hope for the future": A program to foster strengths in middle-school students. *Journal of Happiness Studies, 12*(1), 139–152.

Meek, R. (2011). The possible selves of young fathers in prison. *Journal of Adolescence, 34*(5), 941–949.

Nagaoka, J., Farrington, C. A., Ehrlich, S. B., & Heath, R. D. (2015). *Foundations for young adult success: A developmental framework* [Report]. Chicago: University of Chicago Consortium on Chicago School Research. Accessed at http://ccsr.uchicago.edu/sites/default/files/publications/Wallace%20Report.pdf on September 16, 2015.

Newell, R. J., & Van Ryzin, M. J. (2009). *Assessing what really matters in schools: Creating hope for the future.* Lanham, MD: Rowman & Littlefield.

Oettingen, G. (2014). *Rethinking positive thinking: Inside the new science of motivation.* New York: Current.

Oyserman, D., Brickman, D., & Rhodes, M. (2007). School success, possible selves, and parent school involvement. *Family Relations, 56*(5), 479–489.

Oyserman, D., Bybee, D., Terry, K., & Hart-Johnson, T. (2004). Possible selves as roadmaps. *Journal of Research in Personality, 38*(2), 130–149.

Oyserman, D., Terry, K., & Bybee, D. (2002). A possible selves intervention to enhance school involvement. *Journal of Adolescence, 25*(3), 313–326.

Paunesku, D., Walton, G., Romero, C., Smith, E. N., Yeager, D. S., & Dweck, C. S. (2015). Mind-set interventions are a scalable treatment for academic underachievement. *Psychological Science, 26*(6), 784–793.

Piaget, J. (1952). *The origins of intelligence in children* (M. Cook, Trans.). New York: International Universities Press.

Reiss, S. (2000). *Who am I? The 16 basic desires that motivate our actions and define our personalities.* New York: Berkley.

Reiss, S. (2004). Multifaceted nature of intrinsic motivation: The theory of 16 basic desires. *Review of General Psychology, 8*(3), 179–193.

Rosabeth Moss Kanter quotes. (n.d.). Accessed at www.brainyquote.com/quotes/authors /r/rosabeth_moss_kanter.html on August 11, 2015.

Schippers, M. C., Scheepers, A. W. A., & Peterson, J.B. (2015). A scalable goal-setting intervention closes both the gender and ethnic minority achievement gap. *Palgrave Communications*. doi.10.1057/palcomms.2015.14

Snyder, C. R. (1994). *The psychology of hope: You can get there from here*. New York: Free Press.

Snyder, C. R., Hoza, B., Pelham, W. E., Rapoff, M., Ware, L., Danovsky, M., et al. (1997). The development and validation of the Children's Hope Scale. *Journal of Pediatric Psychology*, *22*(3), 399–421.

Snyder, C. R., Harris, C., Anderson, J. R., Holleran, S. A., Irving, L. M., Sigmon, S. T., et al. (1991). The will and the ways: Development and validation of an individual-differences measure of hope. *Journal of Personality and Social Psychology*, *60*(4), 570–585.

Snyder, C. R., Shorey, H. S., Cheavens, J., Pulvers, K. M., Adams, V. H., III, & Wiklund, C. (2002). Hope and academic success in college. *Journal of Educational Psychology*, *94*(4), 820–826.

Tooley, M., & Bornfreund, L. (2014). *Skills for success: Supporting and assessing key habits, mindsets, and skills in PreK–12* [Report]. Washington, DC: New America Foundation. Accessed at www.newamerica.org/downloads/11212014_Skills_for_Success_Tooley _Bornfreund.pdf on September 16, 2015.

Tough, P. (2012). *How children succeed: Grit, curiosity, and the hidden power of character*. Boston: Houghton Mifflin Harcourt.

Vallerand, R. J. (2008). On the psychology of passion: In search of what makes people's lives most worth living. *Canadian Psychology*, *49*(1), 1–13.

Vallerand, R. J. (2010). On passion for life activities: The dualistic model of passion. In M. P. Zanna (Ed.), *Advances in experimental social psychology* (Vol. 42, pp. 97–193). New York: Academic Press.

Vallerand, R. J., Blanchard, C., Mageau, G. A., Koestner, R., Ratelle, C., Leonard, M., et al. (2003). Les passions de l'âme: On obsessive and harmonious passion. *Journal of Personality and Social Psychology*, *85*(4), 756–767.

Vallerand, R. J., Salvy, S.-J., Mageau, G. A., Elliot, A. J., Denis, P. L., Grouzet, F. M. E., et al. (2007). On the role of passion in performance. *Journal of Personality*, *75*(3), 505–534.

White, R. W. (1959). Motivation reconsidered: The concept of competence. *Psychological Review*, *66*(5), 297–333.

Williams, P., & Denney, J. (2004). *How to be like Walt: Capturing the Disney magic every day of your life*. Deerfield Beach, FL: Health Communications, Inc.

Zhu, S., Tse, S., Cheung, S.-H., & Oyserman, D. (2014). Will I get there? Effects of parental support on children's possible selves. *British Journal of Educational Psychology*, *84*(3), 435–453.

Ross C. Anderson is senior lead researcher at the Educational Policy Improvement Center in Eugene, Oregon. He is former Director of Strategic Initiatives in the Norwich School District in Connecticut, where he designed, led, and evaluated a wide range of projects focused on equitable opportunities for learners, community partnerships for creative engagement of students, and other district reform efforts. Over his career in the education field, he has led $10 million of grant-funded system design, innovation, and research work.

In recognition of his contributions in southeastern Connecticut, Anderson was named a 2013 awardee of the top forty community change agents under forty years old. Anderson's work builds from the belief that the creativity of educators and students, alongside an empowered community, holds great promise for sustained systemic improvements for equitable student outcomes. This belief guides his leadership of a federally funded, multi-year project, ArtCore, collaboratively developing and researching a middle school transformation model. This project investigates the effects of creative teaching and learning opportunities on student growth trajectories of metacognitive and noncognitive skills, such as creativity, growth mindset, self-efficacy, and engagement in learning. Anderson coauthored the *Skills and Dispositions Developmental Frameworks* published by the Center for Innovation in Education—a resource already supporting innovations in the next generation of state accountability systems. From state departments of education to classroom teachers, Anderson works across every level of the education system. He provides research-based guidance on innovative policies and practices, facilitates design thinking for educators, and investigates the effects of these efforts on meaningful outcomes of student success.

Anderson received a bachelor's degree in architecture from Yale University and is pursuing his PhD in the Department of Educational Methodology, Policy, and Leadership at the University of Oregon.

To book Ross C. Anderson for professional development, contact pd@solution-tree.com.

CHAPTER 5

The Makers: Creativity and Entrepreneurial Spirit

ROSS C. ANDERSON

Post-it Notes, the ubiquitous, sticky office staple produced by 3M, came to be by accident. In 1968, while attempting to create a strong adhesive for the aerospace industry, Spencer Silver instead made a mistake and discovered the tacky adhesive, now used on Post-it Notes (Glass & Hume, 2013). Rather than making the incredibly strong glue appropriate for airplane parts, he had created weak glue that could peel away without leaving a residue. It took over five years of imagining novel but impractical possibilities before Silver came up with the best use for the new substance. Notably, he did not think of the Post-it Note on his own. It took the combination of his imagination and a real-world problem, posed by 3M colleague Art Fry.

Silver's low-tack adhesive presented a possible solution to an annoying problem that plagued Fry when he sung with his church choir—losing his page between hymns. To find the right use for his adhesive, Silver needed a real-life, practical problem to solve. Silver and Fry went through a great deal of iterative prototyping and sought input and the expertise of others before getting the solution just right. As Silver remembers, "I got to be known as 'Mr. Persistent,' because I wouldn't give up" (Glass & Hume, 2013). It took even more time to convince 3M company leaders to consider the Post-it Note a marketable product that could turn a profit. Ten years after Silver's first accidental discovery of the low-tack adhesive and following an initial marketing flop, his persistence paid off, and the Post-it Note began its rapid ascent into the consciousness of people worldwide.

What Are Creativity and Entrepreneurial Spirit?

As the story of the Post-it Note illustrates, creativity and the entrepreneurial spirit have become intertwined sets of ideas, skills, and mindsets. Developing new artistic pursuits, product ideas, or market niches requires seeing the world through alert eyes by making fresh connections constantly (Ward, 2004). Both creativity and entrepreneurial spirit share a common attitude and approach: *just because it isn't broken doesn't mean you can't try to fix it.* The will to pursue an idea, before others believe or understand it, is at the core of both creativity and the entrepreneurial spirit.

Creativity

There is no consensus on a precise definition for such a culturally and contextually malleable skill as creativity, though most agree on two non-negotiable components: originality and effectiveness. Originality describes something novel, unique, unusual, and distinct from what we expect to experience or have experienced. Effectiveness describes the usefulness, fit, appropriateness, and value of the creative act, product, or idea (Runco & Jaeger, 2012). Creativity can also reflect a personally meaningful interpretation for an individual in a specific context (Beghetto & Kaufman, 2007).

Creativity experts Ronald Beghetto and James Kaufman (2007) explain creativity in a way that builds from the past century of research while incorporating the power that creativity plays in thinking, learning, and creating at all levels of development. Their Four-C Model identifies eminent creative contributions to the world as *big-C* Creativity—Steve Jobs's iPhone, for example. The vast majority of less impactful creative contributions is termed *little-C* creativity—think of a student's best work of art that gets framed and hung on the wall. *Mini-C* classifies the everyday creativity in learning, the seeds that grow into creative contributions appreciated by others. Between little-C and big-C is *pro-C*, which describes expert-level creativity that has yet to gain historical eminence. The Four-C creativity classification recognizes the factors of time, knowledge, and growth that are required to advance from doodling to worldwide acclaim. Though not all scholars agree that a categorical distinction between levels of creativity is meaningful (Runco, 2014), the Four-C model at least demonstrates that creativity is accessible to all of us.

Entrepreneurial Spirit

Along with originality and effectiveness, entrepreneurial spirit requires at least two other important components—the improvement of the human experience and impact on others. Entrepreneurial spirit necessitates the personal motive and choice to pursue personal betterment, to further a cause, to support the development of others, or to create a new product. This effort takes guts, grit, and a strong belief in oneself (de la Fuente, Vera, & Cardelle-Elawar, 2012). Like creativity, entrepreneurial spirit builds on an attitude, a perspective, and an intention that depend largely on the social and cultural context; this is the value proposition of one's ideas and work. Qualities of entrepreneurial spirit overlap with noncognitive attributes that researchers have tied to labor market success across fields, including openness to experience, agreeableness, extraversion, conscientiousness, and emotional stability (Kuhn & Weinberger, 2002; Mueller & Plug,

2006; Nyhus & Pons, 2005). Though creativity is at the heart of entrepreneurial spirit, the main distinction lies in the motivational origins of an idea—self-improvement, the improvement for others, and the creation of economic profit to propel the idea, sustain further impact, and support future innovation. Creativity and entrepreneurial spirit do merge in many ways. For instance, the ability and self-confidence to approach a challenge with flexible thinking are essential to both. The ability to formulate the right question to answer or problem to solve spans the two domains as well (Ward, 2004).

The Rising Value of Creativity and Entrepreneurial Spirit: The Creativity Age

Thanks to technological development, we have entered a new economy in which traditional lines of jobs have been, and continue to be, replaced by machines at an accelerating rate, as Massachusetts Institute of Technology (MIT) professor Erik Brynjolfsson and Andrew McAfee (2014), a research scientist at the MIT Center for Digital Business, write in their book *The Second Machine Age: Work, Progress, and Prosperity in a Time of Brilliant Technologies.* If jobs cannot be automated, they can move to other countries with cheaper labor. Alan S. Blinder, a professor of economics at Princeton University and former vice chairman of the Federal Reserve, estimated in 2009 that "22% to 29% of all U.S. jobs are or will be potentially offshorable within a decade or two" (p. 69). Furthermore, some traditional lines of jobs disappear simply because the products or services they make are no longer in demand or have been replaced by technology. For instance, we don't have nearly as many blacksmiths who make horseshoes or telephone switchboard operators today as we did at the turn of the 20th century.

As a result, the American economy is going through a hollowing-out process that results in bipolar growth of jobs. With the disappearance of midlevel jobs comes growth in jobs at the extreme high end and low end. "We are getting more and more people at the very top and the very bottom and the middle has been shrinking," observed Alan Krueger, chairman of the Council of Economic Advisers, at the Aspen Ideas Festival in 2012 (Aspen Institute, 2012, 5:46).

At the high end are creative, entrepreneurial knowledge workers like Mark Zuckerberg, cofounder of Facebook. At the extreme low end are the workers in grocery stores, restaurants, and Starbucks, who might be serving the coffee and mopping the restaurant floor for the Zuckerbergs. "Highly skilled, highly educated workers do increasingly well in an increasingly specialized economy driven by knowledge work," Marcus Wohlsen (2012) explains. "Their prosperity feeds demand for low-paying service work. But when tech companies grow, they no longer create the kind of medium-skilled, middle-class jobs they did in the past."

We have already seen the impact of this new economy. As traditional lines of jobs disappear, so does the middle class that these jobs used to support in the United States and other developed countries. The disappearance of the middle class has become a grave concern in the United States and other Western developed nations. This is bad news for the United States, a country that has thrived on the middle class. Short of taking unrealistic actions such as destroying the machines or bringing back the lost jobs, what can we do to create the new middle class?

Economist Richard Florida (2002, 2012) provides an answer in his international bestseller, *The Rise of the Creative Class*. Florida suggests that we accept the fact that we have gone through the Agricultural Age and Industrial Age and entered the Creativity Age. Creativity has risen to become a fundamental economic force shaping a new social class, the creative class—that is, individuals "whose economic function is to create new ideas, new technology and/or creative content" (Florida, 2002, p. 8). While the working class has been shrinking, the creative class has grown to include some forty million individuals, comprising about one-third of the U.S. workforce since the 1980s.

During the recession in the 2000s, the creative class fared better than others. The rate of unemployment for the creative class was below 5 percent when the overall unemployment rate in the United States was over 10 percent, according to Florida (2012). Nearly three million jobs were added to the creative class between 2001 and 2010, while the working class, from manufacturing to construction and transportation, lost over six million jobs during the same period. Moreover, creative class workers saw their wages grow by 4.4 percent while the wages of blue-collar workers declined by 4.6 percent during the recession. This is because "creative class workers, even in the hardest hit fields, have the skills, education and human capital that allows them to switch jobs, fields and careers when required, an option that is largely unavailable to blue-collar workers," writes Florida in a 2011 *Atlantic* article.

Philip Auerswald, senior fellow in entrepreneurship of the Kauffman Foundation, adds entrepreneurship to the answer. In his book *The Coming Prosperity: How Entrepreneurs Are Transforming the Global Economy*, Auerswald (2012) argues "the vast majority of alleged threats to humanity are, in fact, dwarfed by the magnitude of opportunities that exist in the twenty-first century" (p. 8). These opportunities will be harnessed by entrepreneurs or "black-collar workers," a term inspired by Steve Jobs's black turtleneck (Freeman & Auerswald, 2012). And as such, entrepreneurs will rule the future. Anticipating questions of doubt that the entire world will be built of entrepreneurs, Freeman and Auerswald (2012) share:

> From where we sit now, it seems improbable that an entire economy could be built of such workers. Where are the drones in this picture? Where are the undifferentiated masses of the unfulfilled? Try asking yourself this question instead: from the standpoint of a 15th-century peasant, how likely is the reality of the present day? . . . Just as former farmers were compelled to convert themselves into blue-collar workers

> to realize their potential in the economy of the 20th century, so will former factory workers (and retooling economic drones of all types) convert themselves into black-collar workers to realize their potential in the economy of the 21st century.

Lending support to Auerswald, LinkedIn cofounder and chairman Reid Hoffman and author Ben Casnocha (2012) argue in their best-selling book, *The Start-Up of You*, that the United States is in a new world where everyone has to think like an entrepreneur and an innovator.

It seems apparent that the United States' future lies with the creative class and the entrepreneurs. Human societies have always benefited from great innovators and entrepreneurs who have brought scientific discoveries, technological advancements, arts, music, literature, wealth, and prosperity, but they constituted only a small portion of the entire population. In fact, in the Agricultural and Industrial Ages, we needed a lot more people to suppress their creativity so they could follow orders to complete their repetitive and routine tasks that called for only a limited number of skills and talents. We needed lots of people with similar skills, in other words.

But today, human societies have arrived at a point when creativity and entrepreneurship have become a necessity for all individuals if we are to continue to prosper in the future. Arts and music are no longer something nice to have as enrichment; they have become a major force for economic development collectively as well as individual fulfillment and prosperity (Florida, 2002, 2012; Kelley & Kelley, 2013). Creativity is no longer a choice for a select few; it has become an essential quality for all. Entrepreneurship is no longer required of a few who can start businesses and employ thousands of people; it has become fundamental to everyone because we all need to become job creators instead of job seekers when rewarding jobs are not created by others (Zhao, 2012). Today, creativity and entrepreneurial thinking mean job stability (Florida, 2012).

At a time when creativity and entrepreneurial spirit are in the highest demand ever, there is startling evidence that the next generation, that we need to become creative entrepreneurs in the future, may be losing its creative potential. Using data from tests of divergent thinking, a proxy to creative potential, a 2011 longitudinal study provides evidence of an American public waning in this important ability (Kim, 2011). The comparison of results from five normative samples over forty years revealed alarming decreases, especially for children (Bronson & Merryman, 2010; Kim, 2011). Past studies revealed that tests of creative potential were much more powerful at predicting future creative accomplishments than IQ tests (Bronson & Merryman, 2010). Given this strong predictive power, it should be worrisome that students in kindergarten through sixth grade showed the greatest decrease. As the need for creativity is upon us, this research signals a potential threat to the United States' current dominant position.

Measuring Creativity and Entrepreneurial Spirit

Hundreds of tests, instruments, rating scales, and surveys have been created to measure different aspects of creativity with the assumption that creative potential, behaviors, and production can be evaluated and placed on a developmental, growth-oriented scale (Treffinger, 2009). Measurement of entrepreneurial spirit, however, is relatively lacking. Most instruments are surveys or assessments created for specific entrepreneurship education programs and research studies. Fortunately, they overlap in content with many of the creativity assessments on the market.

Most creativity assessment tools were originally designed to create reliable and valid procedures to monitor creativity growth for all students. Historically, these assessments have been used most frequently to identify highly creative individuals and select young people for specialized programs. The most widely used assessments evaluate the originality and relevance of a product or the fluency and elaboration of process, but there are others that include personality traits, behaviors, and experiences that theoretically lead to creativity. Still others are meant to provide criteria from which to evaluate creative work as well as learning habits within a specific context. Table 5.1 describes the elements of creativity defined by these three types of creativity assessment tools, which can focus on one of the three aspects of creativity most easily measured and attributable to an individual: creative thinking and creative process, creative behaviors and experiences, and creative acts and products.

Table 5.1: Elements of Creativity Defined by Assessment Types

Creative Thinking and Creative Process (Range of Internal Reliability .70–.90+)	Creative Behaviors and Experiences (Range of Internal Reliability .45–.90+)	Creative Acts and Products (Range of Internal Reliability .70–.90+)
• Information encoding • Idea fluency, flexibility, and originality expressed verbally and visually • Problem construction • Conceptual combination • Recognizing solutions • Elaboration of ideas • Self-evaluation of ideas • Boundary breaking	• Motivation to ask questions and be unconventional • Motivation to take risks • Imaginative, curious, flexible, and open • Abstracting from the concrete • Restructuring problems • Tolerating ambiguity • Independence • Experimenting with media and technique	• Originality and novelty • Relevance • Effectiveness • Technical quality • Aesthetic appeal • Expression • Complexity and balance • Evidence of effort • Richness of imagery • Emotionality—"wow" factor

Sources: Amabile, 1996; Cropley, 2000.

Creative Thinking and Processes

A sample of measures of creative thinking and creative process is listed in table 5.2 (pages 99–100). Divergent or original thinking, a required part of the creative process,

Table 5.2: Creative Thinking and Creative Process Tests

Selected Measures		
Author(s) and Year	**Assessment Name**	**Pros, Cons, and Content**
Torrance (1999)	Torrance Tests of Creative Thinking	**Pros:** Many age levels; high interrater reliability; high predictive ability for future creative achievement; widely available; proven to avoid bias due to race or socioeconomic status; other versions are available that use action and movement or sounds as stimuli requiring less drawing skill; great normative data for research
		Cons: Expensive for large quantities; requires training or expense to score reliably
		Content: Picture construction and completion; written response to divergent cues such as unusual questions, product improvement, or unusual uses of stimuli
Doolittle (1990)	Creative Reasoning Test	**Pros:** Requires associative and divergent thinking using riddles
		Cons: Limited depth to creative thinking and interpretation
		Content: Twenty items presented in the form of riddles
Urban & Jellen (1996)	Test for Creative Thinking—Drawing Production (TCT-DP)	**Pros:** Many age levels; ratings of work include breaking boundaries, humor, and affectivity; high interrater reliability; results of measure align with creative pursuits of individuals tested; minimal time required to test and score responses; based on a more general theory of creativity than just divergent ideas; encompasses both thinking and personality related to entrepreneurial spirit
		Cons: Must order from the Netherlands; lacks strong validation
		Content: Incomplete figures from which to elaborate graphically
Mumford, Supinski, Threlfall, & Baughman (1996)	Process-Based Measures of Creative Problem-Solving Skills	**Pros:** Five areas include problem construction, information encoding, category selection, category combination, and reorganization; moderate to high interrater reliability from trained judges; high correlations with outcomes of a simulated management and advertising task
		Cons: May require training and a degree of expertise to rate solutions and responses efficiently and reliably
		Content: Category combination provides sets of exemplars that need to be given a category title, then categorized under a single category, described in a sentence, added to with other exemplars from the category, and given linking features

Continued →

Selected Measures		
Author(s) and Year	**Assessment Name**	**Pros, Cons, and Content**
Runco (2015)	rCAB (Runco Creativity Assessment Battery)	**Pros:** Designed carefully over thirty-five years of research in multiple settings with strong reliability and validity statistics reported; available in multiple languages; comparative, normed scoring by geography and socioeconomic status; computer administration and scoring available; targets multiple dimensions of creativity in distinct assessments; can be adjusted to create domain-specific subscales; includes scales for ideational behavior attitude, verbal, figural, and entrepreneurial divergent thinking, and problem finding and solving; versions created and socially validated for teachers, parents, and students across educational levels
		Cons: May be costly and require expert assistance depending on needs; may require training to assess and score student responses
		Content: Ideational behavior questionnaire (for example, "I am reflective"); divergent thinking (for example, "Many Uses Game"); idea generation and idea recognition situational challenges; Runco evaluation of setting and climate to evaluate a classroom or the home; creative self-efficacy; teacher's practices; other questionnaires created or in development
Pullman & Martin (2014)	Mission Skills Assessment	**Pros:** Six different skills and dispositions assessed in battery help to detect associations and distinguish measurement between skills (teamwork, creativity, ethics, resilience, curiosity, and time management); collaboratively developed between Educational Testing Service and middle school teachers and administrators; efficient to administer schoolwide once per year; externally scored with other outcome data to include in report to school; a RAND Corporation report found it to be the most cost-effective, reliable assessment of 21st century skills (Soland, Stecher, & Hamilton, 2013)
		Cons: Only computer testing options available; may be costly to administer and requires waiting 6–8 months to get results
		Content: Creativity assessment triangulates between three data sources, self-report (for example, "I generate novel ideas"), fluency test (for example, "Write all the things that are round . . ."), and teacher rating (for example, "This student thinks 'outside the box'")

Sources: Cropley, 2000; M.A. Runco, 2014; Runco & Acar, 2012; Urban, 2005; Ward, 2004.

can be reliably assessed to show a person's flexibility of thinking, active imagination, curiosity, tolerance for ambiguity, and ability to abstract from the concrete (Cropley, 2000). Theoretically, if individuals perform well in divergent thinking, they have a high degree of creative potential (Runco & Acar, 2012). Exemplified by the Torrance Tests of Creative Thinking (TTCT, the test used in the longitudinal study showing Americans' decline in creative potential), divergent thinking or creative production tests use verbal or figural cues. While limitations exist, the scientific community trusts most divergent thinking tests, and, as discussed, they can be strong predictors. They also overlap conveniently with entrepreneurial spirit by incorporating the critical traits of evaluation of ideas and recognition of opportunity (Cropley, 2000; Ward, 2004). According to one available service on the market, some recently developed divergent thinking tests can be scored automatically and virtually using normative samples that tailor to specific needs (M. A. Runco, 2014).

The Test for Creative Thinking–Drawing Production (TCT-DP) incorporates originality but also calls out other *noncognitive* skills and dispositions that help creative thinking translate to real-world success (Cropley, 2000). The test begins with six sheets of white paper, each with a large framed box in the center. Filled mostly with empty negative space, the box on each sheet contains some kind of shape, line, or other stimuli meant to trigger creative thinking. Purposefully vague and suggestive, the shape might be geometric, curvy, or linear. The stimuli may include several distinct parts and form a composition, or they might be broken and lie outside the empty box. It could be common and natural or highly irregular. Intentionally open-ended, the task requires flexibility to elaborate a creative and cohesive response. The criteria used for judging a response include several dimensions of creativity, such as continuations of the stimuli, connections made to produce a theme, boundary breaking, three-dimensional perspective, humor, and unconventionality. To detect even nascent development of creative thinking and production, the evaluator rates a response on a scale of six stages from early imitation to advanced production (Urban, 2005). From Zulu children in South Africa to Turkish and Moroccan students, the TCT-DP has demonstrated cultural adaptability in reliably measuring creativity of children and even detecting growth. Several studies using the TCT-DP show that academically low-achieving students can demonstrate highly creative thought. Conversely, academically high-achieving students do not necessarily score very well in creativity production (Urban, 2005).

Measuring the Creator

Creativity inventories attempt to identify the common cognitive, emotional, behavioral, and personality factors that span creative disciplines. Research has identified the consistently common features of creative people, including openness, conscientiousness, self-acceptance, curiosity, hostility, drive, and impulsivity (Plucker & Makel, 2010). Inventory-type instruments try to zero in on experiences and behaviors that demonstrate these characteristics. They range from exceedingly long biographical scales to brief checklists that vary widely in validity and reliability (Cropley, 2000). Table 5.3 (page 102) shows a sample of several measures and their pros and cons. In contrast to these lengthy

Table 5.3: Creative Behaviors and Abilities Inventories

Selected Measures		
Author(s) and Year	**Assessment Name and Domains of Measurement**	**Pros, Cons, and Content**
Byrd (1986)	Creatrix Inventory (creativity and risk-taking)	**Pros:** Integrates cognitive and noncognitive aspects of creativity; rates risk-taking behavior and innovation (entrepreneurial spirit); generates data
		Cons: Large, nine-point scale; focus on older youth and adults; costly
		Content: Twenty-eight statements in two dimensions (creativity and risk taking); matrix score provides overall orientation of person; sample statement such as "Daydreaming is a useful activity"
Runco (2015)	Creative Activity and Achievement Checklist (creative activities and accomplishments)	**Pros:** Grades 5–8; high inter-rater reliability
		Cons: Originally did not include a broad enough selection to reflect current domains of creativity using technology, but has been updated in the rCAB
		Content: Original areas included literature, music, drama, arts, crafts, and science
Colangelo, Kerr, Huesman, Hallowell, & Gaeth (1992)	Iowa Inventiveness Inventory (inventiveness)	**Pros:** Self-reported ratings matched characteristics of people in real life (such as actual inventors); appears to get at what constitutes an inventor; five-point scale
		Cons: Low internal consistency; only readily available to researchers
		Content: Sixty-one statements aimed at how an inventor approaches the world
Kumar, Kemmler, & Holman (1997)	Creativity Styles Questionnaire (CSQ) (creative types)	**Pros:** Self-rating; available free online; easy scoring on five-point scale
		Cons: Inconsistent reliability; appropriate for older youth only
		Content: Use of senses, belief in unconscious processes, collaboration, superstition, and environmental control; sample questions such as "I am secretive about my new ideas" and "I am at my creative best when I work with one other person"
Khatena & Torrance (1998)	Khatena-Torrance Creative Perception Inventory (creative selves)	**Pros:** Self-report model; widely available; strong validation procedures; strong reliability
		Cons: Expensive for quantity; authors do not provide information about implications of results
		Content: Acceptance of authority, self-confidence, inquisitiveness, awareness of others, disciplined imagination, environmental sensitivity, initiative, self-strength, intellectuality, individuality, artistry

Sources: Beghetto, 2006; Cropley, 2000, Plucker & Makel, 2010.

inventories, a three-item creative self-efficacy survey has been used reliably in research and could easily apply to practice. The following three items are answered on a four-part Likert scale: *I am good at coming up with new ideas; I have a lot of good ideas;* and *I have a good imagination* (Beghetto, 2006).

Measuring Acts and Creations

Tests and inventories can assess the process and behaviors but are no replacement for feedback on the product and process of creative work provided by an authentic audience. Table 5.4 (page 104) identifies two similar instruments designed to judge the quality of a creative product. The instruments list criteria and prompt the assessor to judge these qualities compared to other similar products rather than against some artificial exemplar. Generally, the criteria include a product's originality and effectiveness, its elegance and coherence, its *wow* factor, and its elaboration (Amabile, 1996; Cropley, 2000).

Assessing Entrepreneurial Spirit

Some components of entrepreneurial spirit, such as idea generation, persistence, and risk taking, are captured by many of the creativity and divergent thinking assessment formats. Researchers have investigated aspects of entrepreneurial spirit that distinguish it from creativity, including entrepreneurial knowledge, activities, and attitude, entrepreneurial self-efficacy, and intention. Self-assessments developed by researchers include dimensions of solving problems, managing money, convincing others, leadership, decision making, interest in starting a business, and understanding of profit and regulation (Kourilsky & Walstad, 1998; Nakkula, Luytens, Pineda, Dray, Gaytan, & Hugulay, 2004; Wilson, Kickul, & Marlino, 2007). Middle and high school entrepreneurship competitions run by organizations such as Students for the Advancement of Global Entrepreneurship (SAGE) give students feedback through expert judges who use a standard evaluation rubric (DeBerg, 2013). Table 5.5 (page 105) provides greater detail about the entrepreneurial assessments and rubrics used in research and practice to date.

Limitations of Measuring Creativity

Experts are clear that no single assessment format will capture an individual's creative behavior or creative potential fully (Plucker & Makel, 2010). A divergent thinking assessment, like the TCT-DP, complemented by a self-reporting or observation tool, such as those provided by the rCAB (Runco, 2015), does get much closer. Together, these tools portray a more comprehensive picture within a specific context. Evaluating student creations and creative process with specific criteria adds a third layer of rich feedback. The three formats complement one another in practice, ensuring that different creative strengths are recognized and that feedback is useful. Inevitably, there are dangers of oversimplifying a student's creativity by attempting to measure it within the narrow context

Table 5.4: Creative Products

	Selected Measures	
Author(s) and Year	**Assessment Name**	**Pros, Cons, and Content**
Besemer & O'Quin (1987)	Creative Product Semantic Scale	**Pros:** Confirmed empirically to be valid with good reliability; flexible for many types of products
		Cons: Research shows that just providing basic categories by which to judge a work (for example, usefulness, complexity, effectiveness) proves just as reliable without training
		Content: Forty-three items; three dimensions include novelty, resolution, and elaboration and synthesis
Amabile (1996) & Hennessey (1994)	Consensual Assessment Technique	**Pros:** Identifies level of creativity based on consensus of observers; does not necessarily require experts but benefits from the perspectives of creators familiar with a discipline; used across broad range of products; allows for cultural and contextual specificity
		Cons: Depending on context and raters, reliability can range
		Content: Examples of dimensions include overall creativity, novel use of materials, novel idea, personal liking, aesthetic appeal, technical goodness, organization, expression, silliness, movement complexity, and effort evident

Sources: Amabile, 1996; Cropley, 2000.

of a classroom (Lucas, Claxton, & Spencer, 2013). Most importantly, to actually help a learner and nurture their creativity, assessments of any type must define growth in terms of individual mastery goals rather than performance goals that only compare progress to others (Beghetto, 2005)—a limitation of several existing measures listed.

The Five Creative Dispositions formative assessment tool, created and piloted in the United Kingdom in collaboration with the Creativity, Culture, and Education and the OECD Centre for Educational Research and Innovation, is meant to provide this type of individualized feedback to students using a common language (Lucas et al., 2013). For students, the development of self-awareness and effective self-monitoring toward mastery are critically important to both cognitive and creative growth (Conley, 2014; Hattie, 2009). Another recently published tool defines creativity on a developmental framework from beginner-level skills to emerging expertise and identifies the milestones and developmental markers that a learner progresses through over extensive practice, exposure, and experience (Lench, Fukuda, & Anderson, 2015). These new resources provide opportunities for educators to develop local assessments that inform classroom practices in support of creative development of diverse learners.

Table 5.5: Entrepreneurial Knowledge, Attitude, Self-Efficacy, Aspiration, and Quality of Enterprise

Selected Measures Used in Research and Program Evaluation		
Author(s) and Year	**Assessment Name**	**Pros, Cons, and Content**
Gallup & Operation HOPE (2013)	Gallup-HOPE Index	**Pros:** Developed by experts; rates knowledge, self-perception, and optimism; interest and aspiration to start a business; connection between education and success
		Cons: Limited in scope; used as a measurement of trends nationally, not to evaluate an individual program or student
		Content: Entrepreneurial knowledge (for example, purpose of profits, supply and demand, purpose of regulations, description of entrepreneur); attitudes and aspirations (for example, "I plan to start my own business" or "I will invent something that changes the world")
Nakkula, Luytens, Pineda, Dray, Gaytan, & Hugulay (2004)	Entrepreneurial Activities Checklist	**Pros:** Designed through focus groups with students; includes a broad range of activities that students can engage in; targets the development of nonbusiness entrepreneurial attitude and behavior
		Cons: Available activities may need to be modified to be relevant to specific contexts
		Content: Includes forty-nine different activities in different domains (that is, business, general, sports, social, and arts) and three levels of engagement (that is, starter, leader, or joiner); students are scored based on their level of activity in each domain (for example, organizing a social event, serving as team captain on a sports team, or participating in a theater group)
DeBerg (2013)	SAGE Social Enterprise Business Evaluation	**Pros:** Refined during the 2000s for use in both national and global competitions; targets measurable impact, community assets used, sustainable business practices, development of a succession plan, and the use of mass media for publicity; uses a point system for each criterion to create a scale score; judges the quality of presentation as well as content to help students improve their pitch
		Cons: No research available testing the inter-rater reliability among panel judges
		Content: Rubrics available for both social enterprise business (SEB) and socially responsible business (SRB); SEB rubric asks if the "organization succinctly defined exactly what change it is trying to achieve" and "does the business meet the needs of the present without compromising the ability of future generations to meet their own needs?"

Emerging Trends and Issues

Today, there is widespread acceptance that creativity and entrepreneurial spirit should be important educational outcomes. Almost invariably across all versions of proposals for essential skills for the 21st century, creativity is included, and entrepreneurship is included in most. Many education systems and schools aim to cultivate creativity and entrepreneurial thinking as part of their vision or mission. However, very few formal, if any, education systems include creativity and entrepreneurial thinking as an integrated part of their assessment of student learning or evaluation of teacher effectiveness and school quality. As a result, these two critical 21st century skills have mostly remained great wishes and strong desires rather than actual practices.

It is expected, though, that creativity and entrepreneurial thinking will be included as educational outcomes to be assessed more regularly and hold greater stake in teacher and school evaluation, as well as student progress. But before that can happen, a number of issues need to be addressed.

Creating and Teaching

The general view is that we are all born creative and entrepreneurial, but our genetic endowment may not be exactly the same. In other words, some people may be born more creative and entrepreneurial than others (Shane, 2010). There is also general agreement that nurture plays a significant role in suppressing or enhancing creativity and entrepreneurial abilities. For example, there is evidence that certain cultures treat the creativity of individuals differently (Kaufman & Beghetto, 2008) and may produce more entrepreneurial thinkers than others (Zhao, 2014). International studies also show a negative correlation between test scores and entrepreneurial confidence (Zhao, 2012). Some research indicates that certain classroom environments and teaching practices may either stifle or promote creativity (Beghetto, 2013; Beghetto & Kaufman, 2010; Zhao, 2012, 2014). However, it is unclear if creativity and entrepreneurship can be explicitly taught or if these skills and mindsets simply need the right conditions and space to grow and thrive. Despite the many efforts and programs to teach creativity and entrepreneurship, evidence of their effectiveness is mixed (Zhao, 2012).

A further question is how changeable an individual's creativity and entrepreneurial spirit are. While we know schools and teachers can affect creativity and entrepreneurial spirit, we know little about the degree of their impact. Moreover, can existing creativity measures capture the changes within a short period of time, and are they sensitive to natural developmental growth? These questions are important because if we are to hold teachers and schools accountable for cultivating creativity and entrepreneurial thinking, we must be able to capture the change in these skills within a relatively short time frame such as a year or two.

A related question involves the process and trajectory of growth in creativity and entrepreneurial thinking. Do students become more creative and entrepreneurial bit by bit, or do they jump from one stage to another stage? Or perhaps they have great creativity inside all the time, just waiting for the right moment, and their creative potentials are suddenly triggered by some learning event.

Creativity and Motivation

So far, most of the creativity measures treat creativity and entrepreneurial thinking as cognitive skills, but we know they are also closely related to psychological factors, particularly motivation and self-efficacy. It would be surprising to find that people can be creative but that they do not want to be creative. While much research has affirmed the value of intrinsic motivation in promoting creativity, recent analysis suggests that external reward for creativity can make people more creative. But if the reward is for being compliant or doing conventional tasks, people stay compliant and conventional (Eisenberger & Shanock, 2003). This finding has a number of implications for assessing creativity and entrepreneurial thinking as necessary educational outcomes. First, in addition to or in place of creativity measures, we may measure students' perception about the teacher or school in terms of support for creativity. For example, we can ask students if they are often rewarded or punished for being creative and entrepreneurial. Second, we can measure students' motivation to create. That is, we can ask how much they want to engage in creative and entrepreneurial tasks as a proxy of creativity measurement. Third, we could also measure creativity and entrepreneurial thinking through examining students' authentic learning processes and products because often motivation is task-specific. In other words, students may be motivated to create in one domain but not others, including isolated, generic divergent thinking tasks. Thus, by allowing students to choose the domain in which they wish to create, we can more accurately assess their creativity skill.

Individual Creativity and Social Creativity

Available measures of creativity assume creativity resides in individuals. Based on this notion, the development and growth of creativity happens inside the individual, and creation is the action of individual creators. Research shows that creativity grows out of interactions between an individual and the world he or she works and plays in. It also grows from relationships between the individual and other human beings. In other words, "creativity does not happen inside a person's head, but in the interaction between a person's thoughts and a socio-cultural context" (Fischer, Giaccardi, Eden, Sugimoto, & Ye, 2005, p. 485). The affordances of the medium and context and the engagement with an audience are essential components of creativity (Glăveanu, 2013). Entrepreneurial activities are no different; they need an audience of potential investors or consumers whose own ideas, needs, and interests shape the creation. Both creativity and entrepreneurial spirit are deeply social and relational, often emerging from awareness of the needs or desires of others.

Thus, to accurately measure creativity and entrepreneurial skills, we have to consider the social nature of creativity and entrepreneurship. In addition to the measures of creativity as an individual attribute and generic cognitive ability, we may need to *measure creativity and entrepreneurship in action*. That is, we may have to create authentic social contexts in order to accurately measure students' creativity and entrepreneurial skills. By cultivating authentic opportunities for the purpose of assessment, we naturally shift the emphasis of teaching and learning toward the explicit modeling and practice of these skills.

Where Do We Go From Here?

In summary, creativity and entrepreneurial thinking are beginning to be accepted as important education outcomes, but most of the measures of creativity and entrepreneurial thinking were not designed for mainstream schools or for a context of accountability. Our understanding of how to explicitly teach strategies and nurture habits of creativity and entrepreneurial thinking is improving. Yet, issues remain if we are to treat creativity and entrepreneurial thinking as an essential part of educational assessment. Nonetheless, the urgency for cultivating creative and entrepreneurial citizens makes it imperative that we begin to regard creativity and entrepreneurial skills as part of what counts in education today and well into the future.

References and Resources

Amabile, T. M. (1996). *Creativity in context.* Boulder, CO: Westview Press.

Aspen Institute. (2012). *Reversing the middle-class jobs deficit* [Audio clip]. Washington, DC: Author. Accessed at www.aspenideas.org/session/reversing-middle-class-jobs-deficit-0 on March 23, 2015.

Auerswald, P. E. (2012). *The coming prosperity: How entrepreneurs are transforming the global economy.* New York: Oxford University Press.

Beghetto, R. A. (2005). Does assessment kill student creativity? *Educational Forum, 69*(3), 254–263.

Beghetto, R. A. (2006). Creative self-efficacy: Correlates in middle and secondary students. *Creativity Research Journal, 18*(4), 447–457.

Beghetto, R. A. (2013). *Killing ideas softly? The promise and perils of creativity in the classroom.* Charlotte, NC: Information Age.

Beghetto, R. A., & Kaufman, J. C. (2007). Toward a broader conception of creativity: A case for "mini-C" creativity. *Psychology of Aesthetics, Creativity, and the Arts, 1*(2), 73–79.

Beghetto, R. A., & Kaufman, J. C. (Eds.). (2010). *Nurturing creativity in the classroom.* New York: Cambridge University Press.

Besemer, S. P., & O'Quin, K. (1987). Creative product analysis: Testing a model by developing a judging instrument. In S. G. Isaksen (Ed.), *Frontiers of creativity research: Beyond the basics* (pp. 341–357). Buffalo, NY: Bearly.

Blinder, A. S. (2009). How many US jobs might be offshorable? *World Economics, 10*(2), 41–78.

Bronson, P., & Merryman, A. (2010, July 10). The creativity crisis. *Newsweek.* Accessed at www.newsweek.com/creativity-crisis-74665 on March 23, 2015.

Brynjolfsson, E., & McAfee, A. (2014). *The second machine age: Work, progress, and prosperity in a time of brilliant technologies.* New York: Norton.

Byrd, R. (1986). *Creativity and risk-taking.* San Diego, CA: Pfeiffer International Publishers.

Colangelo, N., Kerr, B., Huesman, R., Hallowell, K., & Gaeth, J. (1992). The Iowa Inventiveness Inventory: Toward a measure of mechanical inventiveness. *Creativity Research Journal, 5*(2), 157–163.

Conley, D. T. (2014). *Getting ready for college, careers, and the Common Core: What every educator needs to know.* San Francisco: Jossey-Bass.

Cropley, A. J. (2000). Defining and measuring creativity: Are creativity tests worth using? *Roeper Review, 23*(2), 72–79.

DeBerg, C. (2013). *SAGE information handbook.* Roseville, CA: SAGEGLOBAL Publications.

DeHaan, R. L., & Venkat Narayan, K. M. (Eds.). (2008). *Education for innovation: Implications for India, China and America.* Rotterdam, the Netherlands: Sense.

de la Fuente, J., Vera, M. M., & Cardelle-Elawar, M. (2012). Contributions to education from the psychology of innovation and entrepreneurship, in today's knowledge society. *Electronic Journal of Research in Educational Psychology, 10*(3), 941–966.

Doolittle, J. (1990). *Creative Reasoning Test.* Pacific Grove, CA: Midwest Publications/Critical Thinking Press.

Dyer, J., Greersen, H. & Christensen, C. M. (2011). *The innovator's DNA.* Boston: Harvard Business Review Press.

Eisenberger, R., & Shanock, L. (2003). Rewards, intrinsic motivation, and creativity: A case study of conceptual and methodological isolation. *Creativity Research Journal, 15*(2–3), 121–130.

Fischer, G., Giaccardi, E., Eden, H., Sugimoto, M., & Ye, Y. (2005). Beyond binary choices: Integrating individual and social creativity. *International Journal of Human-Computer Studies, 63*(4–5), 482–512.

Florida, R. (2002). *The rise of the creative class and how it's transforming work, leisure, community and everyday life.* New York: Basic Books.

Florida, R. (2011, October 6). *The creative class is alive.* Accessed at www.theatlanticcities.com /jobs-and-economy/2011/10/creative-class-alive/252 on September 25, 2012.

Florida, R. (2012). *The rise of the creative class: Revisited.* New York: Basic Books.

Freeman, H., & Auerswald, P. (2012, March 13). Bliss is on the way: The case for economic optimism. *Good.* Accessed at http://magazine.good.is/articles/bliss-is-on-the-way-the-case -for-economic-optimism on March 23, 2015.

Gallup, & Operation HOPE (2013). *The 2013 Gallup-HOPE Index.* New York: Operation HOPE.

Glass, N., & Hume, T. (2013, April 4). *The "hallelujah moment" behind the invention of the Post-it note.* Accessed at www.cnn.com/2013/04/04/tech/post-it-note-history on March 23, 2015.

Glăveanu, V. P. (2013). Rewriting the language of creativity: The Five A's framework. *Review of General Psychology, 17*(1), 69–81.

Hattie, J. (2009). *Visible learning: A synthesis of over 800 meta-analyses relating to achievement.* New York: Routledge.

Hennessey, B. A. (1994). The consensual assessment technique: An examination of the relationship between ratings of product and process creativity. *Creativity Research Journal, 7*(2), 193–208.

Hoffman, R., & Casnocha, B. (2012). *The start-up of you: Adapt to the future, invest in yourself, and transform your career.* New York: Crown Business.

Isaksen, S. G. (Ed.). (1987). *Frontiers of creativity research: Beyond the basics.* Buffalo, NY: Bearly.

Kaufman, J. C., & Beghetto, R. A. (2008). Exploring "mini-C": Creativity across cultures. In R. L. DeHaan & K. M. Venkat Narayan (Eds.), *Education for innovation: Implications for India, China and America* (pp. 165–180). Rotterdam, the Netherlands: Sense.

Kaufman, J. C., & Sternberg, R. J. (Eds.). (2010). *The Cambridge handbook of creativity.* New York: Cambridge University Press.

Kelley, T., & Kelley, D. (2013). *Creative confidence: Unleashing the creative potential within us all.* New York: Crown Publishing Group.

Khatena, J., & Torrance, E. P. (1998). *Manual for Khatena-Torrance Creative Perception Inventory.* Bensenville, IL: Scholastic Testing Service.

Kim, K. H. (2011). The creativity crisis: The decrease in creative thinking scores on the Torrance Tests of Creative Thinking. *Creativity Research Journal, 23*(4), 285–295.

Kourilsky, M. L., & Walstad, W. B. (1998). Entrepreneurship and female youth: Knowledge, attitudes, gender differences, and educational practices. *Journal of Business Venturing, 13*(1), 77–88.

Kuhn, P., & Weinberger, C. (2002). *Leadership skills and wages* (IZA Discussion Paper No. 482). Bonn, Germany: Institute for the Study of Labor.

Kumar, V. K., Kemmler, D., & Holman, E. R. (1997). The Creativity Styles Questionnaire—revised. *Creativity Research Journal, 10*(1), 51–58.

Lench, S., Fukuda, E., & Anderson, R. (2015). *Essential skills and dispositions: Developmental frameworks for collaboration, creativity, communication, and self-direction.* Lexington, KY: Center for Innovation in Education at the University of Kentucky.

Lucas, B., Claxton, G., & Spencer, E. (2013, January). *Progression in student creativity in school: First steps towards new forms of formative assessments* (OECD Education Working Paper No. 86). Paris: Organisation for Economic Co-operation and Development.

Mueller, G., & Plug, E. J. S. (2006). Estimating the effect of personality on male and female earnings. *Industrial and Labor Relations Review, 60*(1), 3–22.

Mumford, M., Supinski, E., Threlfall, K., & Baughman, W. A. (1996). Process-based measures of creative problem-solving skills: III. Category selection. *Creativity Research Journal, 10,* 73–85.

Nakkula, M., Lutyens, M., Pineda, C., Dray, A., Gaytan, F., & Hugulay, J. (2004). *Initiating, leading and feeling in control of one's fate: Findings from the 2002–2003 study of NFTE in six Boston public high schools.* Cambridge, MA: Harvard University Graduate School of Education.

Nyhus, E. K., & Pons, E. (2005). The effects of personality on earnings. *Journal of Economic Psychology, 26*(3), 363–384.

Plucker, J. A., & Makel, M. C. (2010). Assessment of creativity. In J. C. Kaufman & R. J. Sternberg (Eds.), *The Cambridge handbook of creativity* (pp. 48–73). New York: Cambridge University Press.

Pullman, L., & Martin, J. E. (2014). *Mission skills assessment (MSA): User's guide and toolkit.* Accessed at http://indexgroups.org/msa/docs/MSA-Toolkit-Interactive.pdf on March 23, 2015.

Runco, M. (2014). "Big C, little c" creativity as a false dichotomy: Reality is not categorical. *Creativity Research Journal, 26*(1), 131–132.

Runco, M. (2015). *Runco Creativity Assessment Battery (rCAB).* Accessed at http://creativitytestingservices.com/ on August 11, 2015.

Runco, M. A. (1984). Teachers' judgments of creativity and social validation of divergent thinking tests. *Perceptual and Motor Skills, 59*(3), 711–717.

Runco, M. A. (2014). *Huge advance in creativity testing!* Accessed at http://creativitytestingservices.com/blog on January 5, 2015.

Runco, M. A., & Acar, S. (2012). Divergent thinking as an indicator of creative potential. *Creativity Research Journal, 24*(1), 66–75.

Runco, M. A., & Jaeger, G. J. (2012). The standard definition of creativity. *Creativity Research Journal, 24*(1), 92–96.

Runco, M. A., Walczyk, J. J., Acar, S., Cowger, E. L., Simundson, M., & Tripp, S. (2014). The incremental validity of a short form of the ideational behavior scale and usefulness of distractor, contraindicative, and lie scales. *Journal of Creative Behavior, 48*(3), 185–197.

Shane, S. (2010). *Born entrepreneurs, born leaders: How your genes affect your work life.* New York: Oxford University Press.

Soland, J., Stecher, B. M., & Hamilton, L. S. (2013). *Measuring 21st-century competencies: Guidance for educators.* New York: Asia Society.

Torrance, E. P. (1999). *Torrance Tests of Creative Thinking: Norms and technical manual.* Beaconville, IL: Scholastic Testing Service.

Treffinger, D. J. (2009). Myth 5: Creativity is too difficult to measure. *Gifted Child Quarterly, 53*(4), 245–247.

Urban, K. K. (2005). Assessing creativity: The Test for Creative Thinking–Drawing Production (TCT-DP). *International Education Journal, 6*(2), 272–280.

Urban, K. K., & Jellen, H. G. (1996). *Test for Creative Thinking–Drawing Production (TCT-DP).* Lisse, the Netherlands: Swets and Zeitlinger.

Ward, T. B. (2004). Cognition, creativity, and entrepreneurship. *Journal of Business Venturing, 19*(2), 173–188.

Wilson, F., Kickul, J., & Marlino, D. (2007). Gender, entrepreneurial self-efficacy, and entrepreneurial career intentions: Implications for entrepreneurship education. *Entrepreneurship Theory and Practice, 31*(3), 387–406.

Wohlsen, M. (2012, August 3). Silicon Valley creating jobs, but not for everyone. *Wired.* Accessed at www.wired.com/business/2012/08/silicon-valley-creates-jobs-but-not-for-everyone on September 23, 2012.

Zhao, Y. (2012). *World class learners: Educating creative and entrepreneurial students.* Thousand Oaks, CA: Corwin Press.

Zhao, Y. (2014). *Who's afraid of the big bad dragon? Why China has the best (and worst) education system in the world.* San Francisco: Jossey-Bass.

Michael Thier, MAT, is a research and policy fellow with a joint appointment at the Educational Policy Improvement Center and the University of Oregon's Center for Equity Promotion. Previously, he directed International Baccalaureate programs in North Carolina, where he was a National Board–certified teacher, after working as a journalist for *Newsday* in New York.

Using mixed methods, Thier seeks to understand globalization's role in K–12 education. He studies programs and policies that enable and constrain the development of global competence and citizenship, measurement of metacognitive skills, and the effects of school remoteness on students' opportunity to learn. He has research collaborators in Australia, Canada, China, the Netherlands, Qatar, Senegal, Spain, and the United States.

In 2013, his first scholarly publication won *English Journal*'s Paul and Kate Farmer Award for Excellence in Writing. He was named a Margret McBride Lehrman Fellow and received the first of his two Jean DuRette Awards in 2014. Additionally, he won a Sasakawa Young Leaders Foundation Fellowship for international research and was named Outstanding Graduate Student by the American Educational Research Association's special interest group on educational change.

Thier is a candidate for a concurrent PhD in Educational Methodology, Policy, and Leadership and MPA at the University of Oregon. He earned his BA in journalism from New York University, and his MAT (English 7–12) at the State University of New York at Stony Brook.

To book Michael Thier for professional development, contact pd@solution-tree.com.

CHAPTER 6

Globally Speaking: Global Competence

MICHAEL THIER

While many American college graduates struggle to find employment at home, Gavin Newton-Tanzer, a twenty-six-year-old American, has started several companies and nonprofit organizations that employ nearly thirty people, Americans and Chinese, transforming China's education system in the process. Newton-Tanzer graduated from Newtown High School in Connecticut in 2007 at age eighteen. Then he spent a year in China. He learned language and culture, made friends, and served as volunteer in the 2008 Beijing Olympic Games. Now, he speaks fluent Mandarin Chinese, with a Beijing accent, in addition to French and Spanish. More importantly, he spotted the need for better understanding about China. When he returned home to attend college at Columbia University, he started the Global China Connection (GCC), a student organization that now boasts more than sixty chapters in more than ten countries. GCC connects thousands of future youth leaders who have a desire and are willing to have a better understanding of China and the opportunities it offers.

While still a student at Columbia in 2010, Newton-Tanzer founded China Pathway, a company that provides consulting services for Chinese students intending to study abroad and Chinese educational institutions to develop study abroad programs. In 2011, he founded UExcel International Academy with Compass Education Group to bring international school programs to public schools in China. But Newton-Tanzer's new venture is most impressive as it transforms Chinese education. In 2012, he founded Sunrise International Education with its premier program in American-style high school debate for Chinese students. Already, Sunrise has trained more than one hundred thousand Chinese students and organized tournaments as large as ten thousand participants. In many ways, Gavin's programs are delivering more impact on Chinese students than many government reform efforts in terms of helping develop skills in independent, critical thinking and public speaking, in addition to broadening students' educational experiences.

Newton-Tanzer demonstrates both the challenges and the opportunities globalization has brought to humanity. On one hand, globalization has resulted in the movement of certain types of jobs out of developed countries. It has also created opportunities for new lines of jobs. But taking advantage of these opportunities requires us to be equipped with something called global competence. Once a set of skills reserved for specialists, global competence has become a "central capability for the 21st century" for everyone (Hammer, 2011, p. 474).

Defining Global Competence

Despite frequent use of the term, *global competence* does not have a consistently agreed-upon definition (Deardorff, 2004b, 2014; Hunter, 2004a; Katzarska-Miller, Reysen, Kamble, & Vithoji, 2012; Morais & Ogden, 2010; Perry & Southwell, 2011). Singh and Qi (2013) reviewed nearly 170 peer-reviewed articles, scholarly books, and published international curriculum guidelines. They found global competence interchanged frequently for eleven other terms: *common humanity, cosmopolitanism, cultural intelligence, global citizenship, global-mindedness, intercultural understanding, international-mindedness, omniculturalism, multiliteracies, peace and development,* and *world-mindedness.* Such variety reflects the continual evolution of the concept (Deardorff, 2004a) throughout more than ninety years of efforts from education, engineering, international business, government, and other sectors that have felt the impact of globalization (Hunter, White, & Godbey, 2006). In the discussion that follows, this chapter references related constructs for the purpose of explicating global competence fully. Where possible, this chapter uses *global competence* to avoid confusion. However, some instances require use of overlapping terms in this developing field of scholarship. In those instances, this chapter remains faithful to the terms the sources used originally.

The concept of global competence has gone through considerable changes even in the 21st century (see table 6.1). Newer definitions embrace local approaches (Hunter et al., 2006) and expect action taking on issues of global significance (for example, Brustein, 2009). Moreover, recent definitions are more likely to treat the construct as a capacity than as a competence, which suggests a continuum (for example, Mansilla & Jackson, 2011). Previous conceptions featured dichotomous thinking, depicting individuals as either globally competent or not (for example, Hunter, 2004b; Olson & Kroeger, 2001). Table 6.1 traces global competence definitions introduced since 2000, when the term began to narrow in meaning after two decades of various applications.

There is more agreement for the learning outcomes of global competence than there has been for its overall definitions. Table 6.2 (page 116) shows the convergence across the

Table 6.1: 21st Century Definitions of Global Competence

Author(s)	Year	Definition
Olson & Kroeger	2001	Enough substantive knowledge, perceptual understanding, and intercultural communication skills to effectively interact in our globally interdependent world
Hunter (2004b)	2004	Having an open mind while actively seeking to understand cultural norms and expectations of others; leveraging this gained knowledge to interact, communicate, and work effectively outside one's environment
American Council on Education and the Fund for Improvement of Postsecondary Education (ACE/ FIPSE)	n.d.	Knowledge, attitudes, and skills students need to be world citizens and to succeed in today's global workforce
Brustein	2009	Ability to work cooperatively in seeking and implementing solutions to challenges of global significance
Reimers	2010	Knowledge and skills that help people understand the flat world in which they live, the skills to integrate across disciplinary domains to comprehend global affairs and events and to create possibilities to address them; also, the attitudinal and ethical dispositions that make it possible to interact peacefully, respectfully, and productively with fellow human beings from diverse geographies
Falk, Moss, & Shapiro	2010	Possessing the knowledge, skills, and attitudes to be an engaged, responsible, and effective citizen of the United States, living in a globally interdependent society
National Education Association (NEA)	2010	Acquisition of in-depth knowledge and understanding of international issues, an appreciation of an ability to learn and work with people from diverse linguistic and cultural backgrounds, proficiency in a foreign language, and skills to function productively in an interdependent world community
Singmaster	n.d.	Knowledge of world regions, cultures, and global issues; skills in communicating and collaborating in cross-cultural environments in languages other than English and in using information from different sources around the world; values of respect and concern for other cultures, people, and places
Zhao	2010	Set of knowledge and skills that allows effective interaction with people who speak different languages, believe in different religions, and hold different values
Mansilla & Jackson	2011	Capacity and disposition to understand and act on issues of global significance
Young	2014	Ability to work on problems that cut across the world's geographical, cultural, and political boundaries; being prepared for life in our increasingly interconnected world

knowledge, skills, dispositions, and behaviors sought from individuals with high levels of global competence.

Defining global competence seems to depend on the need one has when seeking global competence. In turn, the definition informs how one should measure it. For example, Cisco (2008) approaches global competence for economic reasons, which is consistent with many multinational companies. With quarterly earnings over $12 billion and seventy-five

Table 6.2: Selected Learning Targets for Development of Global Competence

Domain	Learning Target	Citations
Knowledge	Understand current global issues, processes, trends, and systems; relationships between local and global issues; differences and similarities between one's culture and that of others; and how historical forces have shaped current world systems	ACE/FIPSE (n.d.); Brustein (2009); Hunter (2004b); Mansilla & Jackson (2011); National Education Association (NEA, 2010); Parkinson (2009); Reimers (2010); Willard (2006)
	Understand nuances of intercultural communication	Brustein (2009); Mansilla & Jackson (2011); Parkinson (2009); Willard (2006)
Skills	Use diverse cultural perspectives to think critically and solve problems	ACE/FIPSE (n.d.); Brustein (2009); Hunter (2004b); Mansilla & Jackson (2011); Reimers (2010); Zhao (2010)
	Adapt behavior to interact effectively with those who are different	Brustein (2009); Hunter (2004b); Mansilla & Jackson (2011); Willard (2006); Zhao (2010)
	Collaborate as a part of a multinational/multicultural team	Brustein (2009); Hunter (2004b); Parkinson (2009); Willard (2006)
	Speak, listen, read, and write in a language other than one's first language	ACE/FIPSE (n.d.); Brustein (2009); NEA (2010); Parkinson (2009); Zhao (2010)
Attitudes, Dispositions, or Values	Recognize that one's own worldview is not universal	Hunter (2004b); Mansilla & Jackson (2011); NEA (2010); Parkinson (2009); Reimers (2010); Zhao (2010)
	Demonstrate willingness to engage in/curiosity for diverse cultural situations	ACE/FIPSE (n.d.); Hunter (2004b); Mansilla & Jackson (2011); NEA (2010)
	Demonstrate comfort with cultural ambiguity/dissonance	ACE/FIPSE (n.d.); Hunter (2004b); Parkinson (2009); Willard (2006); Zhao (2010)
Behaviors	Resist cultural stereotyping	Hunter (2004b)
	Take action to improve conditions	Mansilla & Jackson (2011)
	Celebrate diversity	ACE/FIPSE (n.d.); Hunter (2004b)

Note. Hunter (2004b) defines "celebrating diversity" as an attitude (p. 69), but the act of celebration connotes a behavior as seen in ACE/FIPSE (n.d.).

thousand employees in 165 countries, it seems that Cisco would seek global competence when hiring because it estimates that 99 percent of the world is still not connected, making for billions of potential customers for its networking services. By contrast, Harvard University professor Fernando Reimers (2010) is more interested in solving global problems and populating the global village. Correspondingly, he propagates three *A*s of globalization: (1) an *affective* dimension that cultivates "positive disposition toward cultural difference;" (2) an *action* dimension that develops one's ability to speak, understand, and think in multiple languages; and (3) an *academic* dimension that instills deep knowledge and capacity to think critically about complex, global challenges (p. 184). Whichever version of the definition we choose, we can see that global competence is about holding a global perspective in life and work, having the skills and knowledge to live and learn across cultural and national boundaries, and having a positive disposition toward diversity.

The Importance of Global Competence

Gavin Newton-Tanzer exemplifies an individual whose high level of global competence enables him to spot and take action on opportunities in the age of globalization. The age of globalization means a globally interconnected and interdependent world in which every human being is affecting and affected by others despite distances that might be thousands of miles (or kilometers). For example, some Chinese festivals would affect deliveries of iPhones in the United States because when Chinese workers take time off, the phones are not being made.

In the age of globalization, everyone participates, voluntarily or not, in global affairs. Thus, as Yong Zhao identified in 2010, global competence—a skill set once reserved for soldiers, diplomats, and tour guides—became a universal need regardless of one's future profession or occupation. In the same year, the National Education Association (2010), the largest union in the United States, called global competence "a pressing concern for public education" due to economic interdependence, the diversification of the United States, increasing complexity of global challenges, and an opportunity to enhance academic achievement (p. 2). Four years later, the American Council on the Teaching of Foreign Languages (ACTFL, 2014) called global competence critical for a 21st century education and "vital to successful interactions among diverse groups of people locally, nationally, and internationally" (p. 1). ACTFL identified five American needs that acquiring global competence can address.

1. Employees who can compete economically in the age of globalization

2. Agents of diplomacy and national security

3. Problem solvers for dilemmas larger than nations can tackle in isolation

4. Inhabitants for a global village that trades discord for harmony

5. Opportunities for individuals to grow personally

Global Employees and Global Markets

In a globally interconnected and interdependent economy, workers, managers, and entrepreneurs need considerable levels of global competence to perform daily tasks. Today, most workplaces have global dimensions. Many companies employ workers worldwide; thus, many workplaces have workers from many different nations and cultures. Many workers interact daily, either online or face to face, with colleagues from different cultural and linguistic backgrounds. Managers often work with teams scattered around the globe. For business leaders and entrepreneurs, the global market represents tremendous potential for new products, services, investment capital, and talent.

As a result, individuals with high levels of global competence have much better job prospects than those without. Businesses that excel in global competence are much more successful overseas than those with staff lacking such skills. Entrepreneurs such as Newton-Tanzer have applied such skills to create more profitable enterprises. Even locally, businesses and individuals that demonstrate high levels of global competence will be better positioned to reap the benefits of ever-growing amounts of tourists, students, and other visitors from across the globe.

Diplomacy and National Security

Military conflicts are among the most costly, unproductive endeavors for humanity. James Madison (1795) provided this insight long ago:

> Of all the enemies to public liberty, war is, perhaps, the most to be dreaded, because it comprises and develops the germ of every other. War is the parent of armies; from these proceed debts and taxes; and armies, and debts, and taxes are the known instruments for bringing the many under the domination of the few ...No nation could preserve its freedom in the midst of continual warfare. (p. 491)

Although the scale of wars since World War II has diminished, the world continues to engage in smaller conflicts, spending fortunes in preparation for fighting with each other. In 2014, global military spending reached $1.55 trillion or about $220 per person for the seven billion people on earth (Wolfe, 2014). Not even counting the human casualties and emotional costs to all military families and civilians affected, the money is no small change, considering what it could do if spent on food, shelter, or clean water for the billion children living in poverty.

There may be no hope to end human military conflicts completely soon or ever, but global competence can certainly help alleviate the problem. Professional diplomats need global competence to engage in productive dialogues and prevent wars. More importantly, if we are successful in bringing global understanding to more, if not all, members of humanity, and helping people engage in global business and social exchanges, the chance of reducing military conflicts will be greatly improved. After all, as Thomas Friedman's Golden Arches Theory of Conflict Prevention suggests, when people are engaged in productive economic activities and understand their interests as interdependent, they are less likely to engage in hostile warfare against each other. Friedman (1999) developed the Golden Arches Theory by observing that "no two countries that both have McDonald's have ever fought a war against each other since they each got their McDonald's" in his book *The Lexus and the Olive Tree* (p. ix). After critics found a handful of examples to contradict the Golden Arches Theory, Friedman rebranded it the Dell Theory of Conflict Prevention. In his book *The World Is Flat* (2005), Friedman opined that the high costs of economic interdependence between two countries that share the same global supply chain would greatly reduce their likelihood of fighting military wars against each other. Whether connected by chains that serve fast food or produce personal computers, it seems clear that economically interdependent nations have too many incentives to avoid combat.

Thus, global competence is not only to prepare one for jobs in diplomatic and national security agencies, which do indeed need many more globally competent individuals. It can also prepare a generation of citizen diplomats, an essential outcome because true national security comes when people denationalize and envision themselves as citizens of the globe. Given these criteria, it is safe to say true national security has mostly eluded world civilizations to this point.

Problem Solvers for Global Problems

The Ebola scare and reactions experienced all over the world exemplify how local problems have gone global in this new age. So, too, are the many international negotiations and conferences on climate change and carbon dioxide emissions and the financial crisis of 2007–2008. Very few problems are entirely local, even when they happen in some of the most isolated parts of the world. Water shortage in North Africa, for example, can result in massive numbers of refugees fleeing to other countries.

Clearly, altruistic reasons exist to seek solutions for global problems, which Zhao (2009a) illustrated using a Chinese saying that describes the interdependence of two grasshoppers tied to one string. Neither grasshopper can jump without disturbing the other. This degree of interdependence has become the norm among nations. When one thinks of the world as a global village, it becomes "fairly dangerous to live as the only wealthy family in a poverty-stricken village" (Zhao, 2009a, p. 167). However, Zhao provided another compelling reason American educators should prepare students to tackle what Churchman (1967) would call *wicked problems*. Such problems are multilayered and often affect the entire globe or a substantial portion of it. Global problems require global solutions. And global solutions require globally competent individuals who can think and work with global mindsets and skills.

Global Villagers

Religious and political groups frequently assert harmony among their goals (Reimers, 2010; Zhao, 2009a, 2009b, 2010). Paradoxically, religion and politics have created substantial discord. Zhao (2009a) emphasizes the need to transcend socially constructed divides such as ethnicity, politics, race, and religion to create a new mindset in which we abandon subdividing as *us* and *them* and treat all human beings as *us*. For example, globally competent individuals are less likely to fear foreigners as "job robbers" who engender economic hardships (Zhao, 2009a, p. 168). Instead, globally competent individuals examine their own cultures critically as something learned and unconscious, not something "genetically transmitted" (Zhao, 2009a, p. 173). Ultimately, the global villager eschews zero-sum thinking, which assumes a person or nation must lose if another person or nation is to win.

Personal Growth

The previous four arguments in favor of global competence contain tangible outcomes: better-paying jobs, fewer wars, problems solved, or equity realized. But global competence could be pursued for self-actualization. As one of the earliest writers on the topic, 17th century Czech education pioneer John Comenius wanted "whole populations to emerge from ignorance by teaching 'everything to everyone' and from every point of view" (as quoted in Hill, 2012, pp. 246–247). Consistent with a Renaissance sensibility, Comenius did not articulate economic, political, or social outcomes. Instead, he conceptualized the abilities to think, interact, and live across cultures as having an intrinsic benefit, one that has not appeared much in literature on global competence. However, Bandura (1994) identified an element of self-efficacy in general that bears particular mention when viewed through a global competence lens. He described individuals who build efficacy successfully as likely to "measure success in terms of self-improvement rather than by triumphs over others" (Bandura, 1994, p. 72). Simultaneously, the pursuit of global competence allows one to target increasing both self-efficacy and the efficacy of others.

Measuring Global Competence

Assessing global competence is not easy because of the diversity in definitions. There are more than 140 instruments for assessing global competence. Two challenges attend measurement of global competence (Deardorff, 2014). First, as rationale for seeking global competence varies, so does definition. Therefore, so does the distinct learning goal one should measure. Furthermore, of the 140-plus instruments, all except Hunter's Global Competence Checklist are proxies rather than instruments that measure global competence holistically. Second, with the exception of measures that assess knowledge of global topics or foreign language capacity, almost all global competence proxy measures rely on self-report data, which fail to capture external perspectives (Deardorff, 2014), retain the possibilities of faking (Huws, Reddy, & Talcott, 2009), and invite social desirability bias (Braskamp, Braskamp, & Engberg, 2014; Hammer, 2011; Morais & Ogden, 2010). Deardorff (2004a, 2014) asserts measurement error can be reduced by collecting a portfolio of evidence through multimethod, multiperspective approaches that pair quantitative with qualitative methods, as well as self-report with observational approaches. Doing so captures both results and processes of globalized education. Braskamp et al. (2014) argue that social-desirability bias is less likely to be present when measures are not used as selection criteria.

This section presents descriptions, purposes, and strengths and weaknesses of the reliability and validity of measures that align to the five global competence rationales expressed previously. Table 6.3 reports measures that could be used in those approaches. It is noteworthy that no single measure encompasses all of the learning targets listed in table 6.3.

Table 6.3: Global Competence Measures by Selected Learning Targets

Measure	Understand current global issues, processes, trends, and systems; relationships between local/global issues; differences/similarities between one's culture and others'; and how historical forces have shaped current world systems	Understand nuances of intercultural communication	Adapt thinking/actions to collaborate across national or cultural groups	Recognize that one's own worldview is not universal	Willingness to engage in/curiosity for diverse cultural situations	Comfort with cultural ambiguity/dissonance	Take action to improve conditions
Cultural Intelligence Scale (Van Dyne, Ang, & Koh, 2008)	X	X	X	X	X		
Global Competence Checklist (Hunter, 2004a)	X	X	X	X	X	X	
Global Citizenship Scale (Morais & Ogden, 2010)	X	X	X				X
Global Perspective Inventory (Braskamp, Braskamp, & Engberg, 2014)	X	X	X	X	X	X	
Intercultural Development Inventory (Hammer, 2011)			X	X	X	X	

Cultural Intelligence Scale

If we are interested in measuring one's readiness to compete economically in the age of globalization, Linn Van Dyne, Soon Ang, and Christine Koh (2008) created a defensible choice. Table 6.4 reports reliability coefficients and four examples from the twenty-item instrument that captures the four subscales of the Cultural Intelligence Scale (CQS).

1. **Metacognitive**—Cultural consciousness and awareness during interactions with those from different cultural backgrounds

2. **Cognitive**—Knowledge of norms, practices, and conventions in different cultural settings

3. **Motivational**—Directing attention and energy toward cultural differences

4. **Behavioral**—Exhibiting appropriate verbal and nonverbal actions when interacting with people from different cultural backgrounds

Table 6.4: Domains, Reliability Coefficients, and Example Items for the Cultural Intelligence Scale (CQS)

Domain	Items	Reliability	Example Item
Metacognitive	4	.71—.77	I check the accuracy of my cultural knowledge as I interact with people from different cultures.
Cognitive	6	.84—.85	I know the cultural values and religious beliefs of other cultures.
Motivational	5	.75—.77	I am confident that I can socialize with locals in a culture that is unfamiliar to me.
Behavioral	5	.83—.84	I change my nonverbal behavior when a cross-cultural interaction requires it.

Note: All items are scaled *strongly disagree* (1) to *strongly agree* (7). Multiple reliability coefficients express the range from self-reports to peer observations.

Source: Van Dyne et al., 2008.

Van Dyne and colleagues (2008) conducted six reliability and validity studies, sampling more than 1,500 unique participants. Ironically, CQS is a rare global competence proxy measurement that has sampled in multiple countries with roughly two-thirds of the validation study participants being from Singapore. The rest are from the United States. CQS's authors studied the instrument's discriminant and incremental validity, plus its generalizability across time, as well as the Singaporean context. Furthermore, CQS represented the only global competence proxy measure to present reliability data between self-reports and peer observations, a distinct advantage of this instrument. However, when Van Dyne et al. (2008) developed the scale and studied its generalizability across time and the Singaporean context, it oversampled females often by a three-to-one ratio. Such oversampling could be problematic when viewed alongside findings that females present more positive attitudes toward global-mindedness and related constructs than males (Deng & Boatler, 1993; Hett, 1993; Pratto, Sidanius, Stallworth, & Malle, 1994; Zhai & Scheer, 2004). Furthermore, CQS might not be immediately accessible in K–12 schools in that its six validation studies featured undergraduate or master's students with mean ages from twenty to thirty-five and one to two years of work experience.

Global Competence Checklist

If we are interested in measuring one's readiness to employ global competencies for diplomatic or military purposes, William D. Hunter (2004b) might provide the most accessible instrument. Table 6.5 reports reliability coefficients and four examples from the eighteen-item instrument that captures the four subscales in the Global Competence Checklist (GCC).

Table 6.5: Domains, Reliability Coefficients, and Example Items of the Global Competence Checklist (GCC)

Domain	Items	Reliability	Example Item
Knowledge	5	.61	Understanding of the concept of globalization
Skills	4	.76	Ability to collaborate across cultures
Attitudes	7	.67	Willingness to step outside of one's own culture and experience life as "the other"
Experience	2	.78	Effective participation in social and business settings anywhere in the world
Note: All items are dichotomous (Yes/No).			

Source: Hunter, 2004b.

The GCC's advantages include its unique status of measuring global competence holistically and use of external observation rather than self-report. Also, it might best conform to military understandings of global competence. When establishing a conceptual foundation of cross-cultural competence among army leaders, Allison Abbe, Lisa M. V. Gulick, and Jeffrey L. Herman (2008) identified that the construct could be conceived as multidimensional, developmental, trait-based, or behavioral. Hunter's checklist provides a multidimensional approach that measures traits and behaviors. Unless the GCC was applied as a repeated measure that informed participant adaptation over time, however, a complementary measure would be needed to adopt a developmental approach.

Though Hunter's definition that includes leveraging and competition might be problematic in the global village, it might be particularly useful in diplomatic or military settings where consequences are often dire. Furthermore, Hunter's definition might be the result of fourteen members of his Delphi technique group being American, a potential bias toward Western cultural norms, which Hunter reported, but one that might resonate in diplomatic or military settings. Additionally, Hunter's intentional oversampling of transnational coporate human resource managers may explain the definition's tendency toward a competitive conceptualization. A small validation sample of fifty-four participants is one reason the GCC has weaker psychometric properties than other measures in this section. However, the GCC's subjective, external evaluation may make it most facile for K–12 settings, which already delegate broad powers that allow educators to assess subjectively. The dichotomous nature of the items makes the GCC an efficient measure to detect if a student does or does not have one of the eighteen competencies it includes.

Global Citizenship Scale

If we are interested in measuring one's readiness to contribute to solutions for problems of global significance, Duarte B. Morais and Anthony C. Ogden (2010) provide a unique global competence proxy measure for three reasons. The Global Citizenship Scale (GCS) is the lone measure to (1) measure global citizenship, (2) specify global competence as a domain, and (3) capture action taking. Table 6.6 reports reliability coefficients and seven examples from the thirty-item instrument that captures the three domains of the GCS:

1. **Social responsibility**—Perceived level of interdependence and social concern to others, society, and the environment

2. **Global competence**—Employs Hunter's definition and includes self-awareness, intercultural communication, and global knowledge as subdomains

3. **Global civic engagement**—The demonstration of action or predisposition toward recognizing local, state, national, and global community issues and responding through actions such as volunteerism, political activism, and community participation; subdomains include involvement in civic organizations, political voice, and glocal civic activism. Scottish sociologist Roland Robertson helped coin both globalization and glocalization, the latter of which reflects a synthesis of global and local aims (Kumaravadivelu, 2008). Glocalizing recasts curriculum from a traditional, local orientation to a global one (Zhao, 2009b).

Development of the GCS included two face-validity trials with experts, exploratory and confirmatory factor analyses with samples from 222 university students in twenty-two courses (eleven each with and without embedded international travel) at five campuses of Pennsylvania State University, and several applications of the nominal group technique. However, during the validation process, Morais and Ogden (2010) found social responsibility to be an unclear domain, collapsing its theorized subdomains global justice and disparities, altruism and empathy, and global interconnectedness and personal responsibility into the unidimensional social responsibility. Still, the researchers declared the measure ready to use for assessing study abroad outcomes, particularly with pre- and posttest designs. The GCS's stated purpose as a study abroad measure may problematize its use in K–12 schools.

Table 6.6: Domains, Reliability Coefficients, and Examples From the Global Citizenship Scale (GCS)

Domain	Items	Reliability	Example Item
Social Responsibility	6	.79	*I think that many people around the world are poor because they do not work hard enough.*
Self-Awareness	3	.69	I am able to get other people to care about global problems that concern me.
Intercultural Communication	3	.76	I often adapt my communication style to other people's cultural background.
Global Knowledge	3	.67	I feel comfortable expressing my views regarding a pressing global problem in front of a group of people.
Involvement in Civic Organizations	8	.92	Over the next six months, I plan to get involved with a global humanitarian organization or project.
Political Voice	4	.86	Over the next six months, I will contact or visit someone in government to seek public action on global issues and concerns.
Global Civic Activism	3	.74	I will boycott brands or products that are known to harm marginalized global people and places.

Note: All items are scaled strongly disagree (1) to strongly agree (5). Italics indicate reverse coded item.

Source: Morais & Ogden, 2010.

Global Perspective Inventory

If we are interested in measuring one's readiness to inhabit the global village, we could use the Global Perspective Inventory (GPI; Braskamp et al., 2014). Table 6.7 (page 126) reports reliability coefficients and six examples of the forty-six-item instrument that captures the GPI's three dimensions, each of which has two subscales.

1. **Cognitive**—One's knowledge and understanding of what is true and important to know; subdivided as knowing and knowledge

2. **Intrapersonal**—Becoming more aware of and integrating one's personal values and self-identity into one's personhood; subdivided as identity and affect

3. **Interpersonal**—One's willingness to interact with persons with different social norms and cultural backgrounds, acceptance of others, and being comfortable when relating to others; subdivided as social responsibility and social interaction

From 2007 to 2013, Braskamp et al. (2014) developed nine versions of the GPI, which they tested on more than one hundred thousand university students, staff, and faculty. The initial item pool included several hundred items before students and study abroad

Table 6.7: Domains, Reliability Coefficients, and Example Items for the Global Perspective Inventory (GPI)

Domain	Items	Reliability	Example Item
Knowing	7	.66	*Some people have a culture, and others do not.*
Knowledge	5	.77	I can discuss cross-cultural differences from an informed perspective.
Identity	6	.74	I am willing to defend my own views when they differ from those of others.
Affect	5	.73	I do not feel threatened emotionally when presented with multiple perspectives.
Social Responsibility	5	.73	I consciously behave in terms of making a difference.
Social Interaction	3	.70	*Most of my friends are from my own ethnic background.*

Note: All items are scaled strongly disagree (1) to strongly agree (5). Italics indicate reverse-coded item.

Source: Braskamp, Braskamp, & Engberg, 2014.

experts indicated items that were unclear or lacked credibility. High-factor loadings and convergence of multiple analyses suggest the GPI is a robust measure of its constructs of interest. Additionally, Philip H. Anderson and Leigh Lawton (2011) determined the GPI did measure the same characteristics as the Intercultural Development Inventory (IDI, discussed later in this section). However, GPI's most recent technical manual only cites sampling of 36,221 undergraduate students, 94 percent of whom identified as American, confounding the claim that it can be used with "persons of any age or specific cultural group" (Braskamp et al., 2014, p. 4). Similar to Van Dyne et al. (2008), Braskamp and colleagues (2014) oversampled on the basis of gender, with 69.7 percent of participants being female. Additionally, social interaction was the only subscale that did not seem susceptible to ceiling effects as a result of means that are close to the top of the scale (for example, the mean score of intrapersonal affect was 4.14 on a five-point scale). What might represent a larger challenge for K–12 schools is that all of the technical manual's seven advertised uses (for example, study abroad or service learning) would require infrastructural or programmatic overhauls to be actionable in most K–12 schools.

Intercultural Development Inventory

Mitchell R. Hammer (2011) has provided an instrument that is well equipped to measure one's personal growth in intercultural competence, which it defines as "the capability to accurately understand and adapt behavior to cultural difference and commonality" (p. 476). The Intercultural Development Inventory (IDI) is well positioned to measure growth in this construct because its fifty items and five open-ended context questions situate participants on a continuum. The continuum (see table 6.8) ranges from the most monocultural orientation, denial, to the most intercultural, adaptation. Hammer does not release items for publication. The IDI provides a gap analysis for participants as score reports contrast their perceived orientations (that is, where participants self-identify) with their developmental orientations (that is, where the IDI identifies participants) to determine over- or underestimation of their orientations. The IDI adds an additional dimension not reported in table 6.8: participants' levels of detachment from their own cultural groups, another indicator of intercultural development.

Table 6.8: Domains, Reliability Coefficients, and Score Ranges for the Intercultural Development Inventory (IDI)

Domain	Reliability	Score Range	Definition
Denial	.66	55–69	Recognizes more observable cultural differences (for example, food) but may not notice deeper cultural differences (for example, conflict resolution styles) and may avoid or withdraw from differences
Polarization	.72 (defense)	70–84	Views cultural differences in terms of "us" and "them"; can be subdivided as *defense* (an uncritical view toward one's own cultural values and practices and an overly critical view toward other cultural values and practices) or *reversal* (an overly critical orientation toward one's own cultural values and practices and an uncritical view toward other cultural values and practices)
	.78 (reversal)		
Minimization	.74	85–114	Highlights cultural commonality and universal values and principles that may also mask deeper recognition and appreciation of cultural differences
Acceptance	.69	115–129	Recognizes and appreciates patterns of cultural difference and commonality in one's own and other cultures
Adaptation	.71	130–145	Capable of shifting cultural perspective and changing behavior in culturally appropriate and authentic ways

Note: The IDI scales from 55–145. Additional reliability coefficients included cultural disengagement (.79), perceived orientation (.82), and developmental orientation (.83).

Source: Hammer, 2011.

Hammer conducted reliability and validity studies with more than ten thousand participants, but the IDI might be most salient for K–12 educators because he sampled 1,850 high school students. He drew participants from Austria, Brazil, Costa Rica, Ecuador, Germany, Hong Kong, Italy, Japan, and the United States, all of whom were students in what Americans call grades 10 through 12 to validate IDI for use with readers who are at or above grade level by age fifteen. Also, the IDI benefits from being back-translated into Chinese, German, Italian, Japanese, Portuguese, and Spanish, languages often spoken at home by U.S. students. A potential limitation stems from Hammer's oversampling male high school students at 63 percent. He oversampled females when studying 2,693 students from a major U.S. university at 65 percent.

Alternative Approaches to Measuring Global Competence

Portfolio-based assessment of global competence could employ either of two rubrics developed collaboratively by the American Council on Education/Fund for the Improvement of Postsecondary Education (ACE/FIPSE) or the Longview Foundation and the Asia Society. Designed for use in higher education institutions and reflecting earlier definitions of global competence, ACE/FIPSE's rubric enables educators to rate students' knowledge, skills, and attitudes as inadequate, minimal, moderate, or extensive. The Longview Foundation/Asia Society rubric does not assess students, but rather assesses educational systems, in twenty-one categories across five areas: (1) leadership, (2) resources, (3) preparing and certifying, (4) providing professional development for globally expert educators, and (5) curriculum and instruction for the Global Age. Systems are rated as beginning, developing, advanced, or exemplary. Neither rubric has published validity or reliability studies, but the Longview Foundation/Asia Society rubric provides exemplars from educational systems across twenty-three states and Washington, DC (Singmaster, n.d.). Shams and George (2006) offer a purely qualitative option, having validated increased global awareness, effective interactions across cultural settings, and expanded understandings of global interconnectedness using students' travel logs during service-learning programs abroad.

Where Do We Go From Here?

Global competence, like creativity, is an education outcome that has gained increasing recognition, but has not yet been integrated into practices of educational assessment. As illustrated in this chapter, the need is clear. Many efforts have been devoted to the development of the concept and its measures. Next, we need to make global competence part of our expectations of today's schools alongside math and reading.

There are a number of issues that need further investigation and effort before global competence can be measured reliably and validly. First, we need a more consolidated definition of the construct. Variety among definitions provides a rich source of ideas, but can make it difficult for systems to accept global competence as a core outcome. For example, a major issue within global competence is whether proficiency in an additional language should be included. This issue perhaps will not be resolved as it is context dependent. However, studying an additional language can be a powerful experience, and language courses may present a unique opportunity to orient students toward developing global competence. Such variance does not mean we will never reach an agreement about what exactly should be included (we haven't been able to do so even in mathematics, language arts, and science), but developing working definitions of specific systems would be necessary.

Second, most of the measures of global competence were developed for noneducation purposes. As an educational outcome, we want measures that can detect growth and reflect the impact of purposeful educational experiences. Thus, we need to adapt existing measures for educational uses.

References and Resources

Abbe, A., Gulick, L. M. V., & Herman, J. L. (2008). *Cross-cultural competence in army leaders: A conceptual and empirical foundation* (ARI Study Report No. 2008-01). Arlington, VA: U.S. Army Research Institute for the Behavioral and Social Sciences.

American Council on Education and the Fund for Improvement of Postsecondary Education (ACE/FIPSE). (n.d.). *ACE/FIPSE project on assessing international learning.* Accessed at www.acenet.edu/news-room/Pages/ACEFIPSE-Project-on-Assessing-International-Learning.aspx on March 23, 2015.

American Council on the Teaching of Foreign Languages. (2014). *Global competence position statement.* Accessed at www.actfl.org/news/position-statements/global-competence-position-statement on March 23, 2015.

Anderson, P. H., & Lawton, L. (2011). Intercultural development: Study abroad vs. on-campus study. *Frontiers: The Interdisciplinary Journal of Study Abroad, 21,* 86–108.

Ang, S., & Van Dyne, L. (Eds.). (2008). *Handbook of cultural intelligence: Theory, measurement, and applications.* Armonk, NY: Sharpe.

Bandura, A. (1994). Self-efficacy. In V. S. Ramachaudran (Ed.), *Encyclopedia of human behavior* (Vol. 4, pp. 71–81). New York: Academic Press.

Braskamp, L. A., Braskamp, D. C., & Engberg, M. E. (2014). *Global Perspective Inventory (GPI): Its purposes, construction, potential uses, and psychometric characteristics.* Accessed at https://gpi.central.edu/supportDocs/manual.pdf on July 25, 2015.

Brustein, W. (2009). It takes an entire institution: A blueprint for the global university. In R. Lewin (Ed.), *The handbook of practice and research in study abroad: Higher education and the quest for global citizenship* (pp. 249–265). New York: Routledge.

Churchman, C. W. (1967). Wicked problems. *Management Science, 14*(4), B141–B142.

Cisco. (2008). *Equipping every learner for the 21st century* [White paper]. San Jose, CA: Author.

Cohen, J. E., & Malin, M. B. (Eds.). (2010). *International perspectives on the goals of universal basic and secondary education.* New York: Routledge.

Deardorff, D. K. (2004a). Internationalization: In search of intercultural competence. *International Educator, 13*(2), 13–15.

Deardorff, D. K. (2004b). *The identification and assessment of intercultural competence as a student outcome of internationalization at institutions of higher education in the United States.* Unpublished doctoral dissertation, North Carolina State University, Raleigh. Accessed at http://repository.lib.ncsu.edu/ir/handle/1840.16/5733 on March 23, 2015.

Deardorff, D. K. (2014, May 15). *Some thoughts on assessing intercultural competence.* Accessed at http://illinois.edu/blog/view/915/113048 on March 23, 2015.

Deng, S., & Boatler, R. W. (1993). Worldmindedness among Canadian business students: Implications for curricula. *Journal of Education for Business, 69*(2), 94–98.

Falk, D. R., Moss, S., & Shapiro, M. (Eds.). (2010). *Educating globally competent citizens: A tool kit for teaching seven revolutions.* Washington, DC: Center for Strategic and International Studies. Accessed at http://csis.org/files/publication/100416_Falk_EducatingGlobally_Web.pdf on March 23, 2015.

Friedman, T. L. (1999). *The Lexus and the olive tree: Understanding globalization.* New York: Farrar, Straus & Giroux.

Friedman, T. L. (2005). *The world is flat: A brief history of the twenty-first century.* New York: Farrar, Straus & Giroux.

Hammer, M. R. (2011). Additional cross-cultural validity testing of the Intercultural Development Inventory. *International Journal of Intercultural Relations, 35*(4), 474–487.

Hett, J. E. (1993). *The development of an instrument to measure global-mindedness.* Unpublished doctoral dissertation, University of San Diego, California.

Hill, I. (2012). Evolution of education for international mindedness. *Journal of Research in International Education, 11*(3), 245–261.

Hunter, B., White, G. P., & Godbey, G. C. (2006). What does it mean to be globally competent? *Journal of Studies in International Education, 10*(3), 267–285.

Hunter, W. D. (2004a). Got global competency? *International Educator, 13*(2), 6–12.

Hunter, W. D. (2004b). *Knowledge, skills, attitudes, and experiences necessary to become globally competent.* Unpublished doctoral dissertation, Lehigh University, Bethlehem, Pennsylvania. Accessed at www.globalcompetence.org/research/WDH-dissertation-2004.pdf on March 23, 2015.

Huws, N., Reddy, P. A., & Talcott, J. B. (2009). The effects of faking on non-cognitive predictors of academic performance in university students. *Learning and Individual Differences, 19*(4), 476–480.

Katzarska-Miller, I., Reysen, S., Kamble, S. V., & Vithoji, N. (2012). Cross-national differences in global citizenship: Comparison of Bulgaria, India, and the United States. *Journal of Globalization Studies, 3*(2), 166–183.

Kumaravadivelu, B. (2008). *Cultural globalization and language education.* New Haven, CT: Yale University Press.

Lewin, R. (Ed.). (2009). *The handbook of practice and research in study abroad: Higher education and the quest for global citizenship.* New York: Routledge.

Madison, J. (1795). *Political observations.* Accessed at www.thefederalistpapers.org/founders /james-madison-quotes on July 25, 2015.

Mansilla, V. B., & Jackson, A. (2011). *Educating for global competence: Preparing our youth to engage the world.* New York: Asia Society.

Morais, D. B., & Ogden, A. C. (2010). Initial development and validation of the Global Citizenship Scale. *Journal of Studies in International Education, 15*(5), 445–466.

National Education Association. (2010). *Global competence is a 21st century imperative.* Washington, DC: Author. Accessed at www.nea.org/assets/docs/HE/PB28A_Global _Competence11.pdf on March 23, 2015.

Olson, C. L., & Kroeger, K. R. (2001). Global competency and intercultural sensitivity. *Journal of Studies in International Education, 5*(2), 116–137.

Parkinson, A. (2009). The rationale for developing global competence. *Online Journal for Global Engineering Education, 4*(2), 1–15.

Perry, L. B., & Southwell, L. (2011). Developing intercultural understanding and skills: Models and approaches. *Intercultural Education, 22*(6), 453–466.

Pratto, F., Sidanius, J., Stallworth, L. M., & Malle, B. F. (1994). Social dominance orientation: A personality variable predicting social and political attitudes. *Journal of Personality and Social Psychology, 67*(4), 741–763.

Ramachaudran, V. S. (Ed.). (1994). *Encyclopedia of human behavior.* New York: Academic Press.

Reimers, F. (2010). Educating for global competency. In J. E. Cohen & M. B. Malin (Eds.), *International perspectives on the goals of universal basic and secondary education* (pp. 183–202). New York: Routledge.

Shams, A., & George, C. (2006). Global competency: An interdisciplinary approach. *Academic Exchange Quarterly, 10*(4). Accessed at http://rapidintellect.com/AEQweb/cho3581z6.htm on March 23, 2015.

Singh, M., & Qi, J. (2013). *21st century international mindedness: An exploratory study of its conceptualisation and assessment.* Penrith, New South Wales, Australia: University of Western Sydney Centre for Educational Research.

Singmaster, H. (n.d.). *International education planning rubric: State strategies to prepare globally competent students.* New York: Asia Society. Accessed at https://asiasociety.org/files/states rubric.pdf on March 23, 2015.

Van Dyne, L., Ang, S., & Koh, C. (2008). Development and validation of the CQS: The Cultural Intelligence Scale. In S. Ang & L. V. Dyne (Eds.), *Handbook of cultural intelligence: Theory, measurement, and applications* (pp. 16–38). Armonk, NY: Sharpe.

Willard, J. (2006). *Global competency.* Sudbury, MA: Language Corps. Accessed at www.nafsa.org/_/file/_/global_competency_2.pdf on March 23, 2015.

Wolfe, S. (2014, February 12). *Global military spending to rise in 2014.* Accessed at www.npr.org/sections/parallels/2014/02/12/275885249/global-military-spending-set-to-rise-in-2014 on July 25, 2015.

Young, D. (2014, July 16). *Global competency: P21's call to action.* Accessed at www.p21.org/news-events/p21blog/1460-young-global-competency-p21s-call-to-action on March 23, 2015.

Zhai, L., & Scheer, S. D. (2004). Global perspectives and attitudes toward cultural diversity among summer agriculture students at the Ohio State University. *Journal of Agricultural Education, 45*(2), 39–51.

Zhao, Y. (2009a). *Catching up or leading the way: American education in the age of globalization.* Alexandria, VA: Association for Supervision and Curriculum Development.

Zhao, Y. (2009b). Needed: Global villagers. *Educational Leadership, 67*(1), 60–65.

Zhao, Y. (2010). Preparing globally competent teachers: A new imperative for teacher education. *Journal of Teacher Education, 61*(5), 422–431.

Brian Gearin, MEd, is a doctoral student at the University of Oregon and a graduate teaching fellow at the Center on Teaching and Learning. He was formerly an award-winning teacher at Dover High School in Delaware, where he led curricular improvements and professional development initiatives that helped move the low-income, majority-minority school out of turnaround status. Today, Brian designs curricular interventions that harness advancements in computer technology and cognitive psychology in order to make learning more effective and more enjoyable. He also writes about national and global trends in education policy.

Brian's interest in cognitive psychology and technology reflects his experience working in a school culture driven by high-stakes accountability. Baffled by the fact that most education policies were enacted for aspirational reasons rather than out of regard for how the brain actually works or the technological capabilities of schools, he decided to focus his research on translating science into practice. He is currently working on projects that examine the cognitive effects of physical activity, the digital divide's effect on academic achievement, and the conceptual history of social capital. The most exciting project, TrackTown USA, will unite mobile-gaming technology and activity trackers with a physical education curriculum that revolves around fitness metrics. The multidimensional intervention will help underserved children lose weight while promoting improved cognition and academic performance in science and math.

Brian graduated with high honors from Brandeis University, and obtained a master's degree in education from the University of Delaware.

To book Brian Gearin for professional development, contact pd@solution-tree.com.

CHAPTER 7

Friends and Enemies: Social Network and Social Capital

BRIAN GEARIN

Philip Knight, the cofounder of Nike, became a business magnate by harnessing the power of other people (Krentzman, 1997). His strategy for building Nike was relatively simple: noting that Japan had broken Germany's hold on the automotive and electronic industries through cheap, efficient labor, Knight would harness the power of Japanese factory workers to break the German-owned Adidas's hold on the running-shoe market. He already knew which Japanese factory he would use: the Onitsuka Company, a Japanese producer of cheap Adidas knockoffs called Tigers. However, he needed money to buy shoes and a market in which to sell them. He needed other people.

In 1964, Knight borrowed $500 from his father so that he could purchase shoes from Onitsuka (Callahan, 2003). He then approached Bill Bowerman, his former track coach at the University of Oregon, with a pair of Tigers to see what he thought of them. Bowerman did not think the shoes were perfect, but he was impressed enough that he was willing to match Knight's $500 investment with $500 of his own. The two were now in business. Knight, who was still living in his father's basement, went ahead and purchased three hundred pairs of sneakers from Onitsuka. Although he had to sell them out of the trunk of his car, he managed to sell every pair within three weeks (Wong, 2009). By 1974, Knight and Bowerman had renamed their company Nike, introduced the swoosh logo, redesigned their shoes to be more durable, and helped to create a fitness subculture that continues to be popular today. But Nike had not yet overtaken Adidas as the premier shoe seller in the United States.

To displace Adidas, Knight would again have to harness the power of others. Rather than relying on traditional advertising, Knight would connect his product with top athletes. In 1972, his partner, Bowerman, was coaching the U.S. Olympic track and field team. Knight and Bowerman made sure that the top U.S. runners, like Steve Prefontaine, were wearing Nikes when they crossed the finish line. Knight and Bowerman continued to seek celebrity endorsements throughout the 1970s and early 1980s, outfitting stars like John McEnroe, Michael Jordan, and Joan Benoit, as well as artists like Spike Lee (Brant, 2014; Madden, 2012). The Nike brand was no longer valued solely for its physical products. It was now a statement—a status symbol. By 1980, Nike had broken Adidas's domination of the U.S. running-shoe market (Krentzman, 1997; "Philip H. Knight," 2008). Crucial to Nike's success was Knight's capacity for harnessing the power of others.

Beyond Collaboration

Today, collaborative skills have been recognized as one of the core 21st century competencies. The Partnership for 21st Century Skills defines collaboration as working in teams, being willing to compromise to accomplish a goal, assuming responsibility for collaborative work, and valuing the individual contributions of each team member (Partnership for 21st Century Learning, n.d.). Along with creativity, critical thinking, and communication, collaboration is considered a super skill. To promote collaborative skills, Pearson and the Educational Testing Service (ETS) both seem to be in the process of designing large-scale assessments that require collaboration (Rosen & Tager, 2013; Von Davier & Halpin, 2013). Consistent with current education practices and beliefs about how collaboration should look in school settings, scores on these assessments might take into account observable interactions, such as interrupting team members, sharing resources and ideas, "social loafing," refraining from abusive language, and so forth (Von Davier & Halpin, 2013).

Unfortunately, collaboration does not go far enough. While collaboration is undoubtedly important, and while the inability to collaborate may, in some circumstances, be more damning than a lack of academic knowledge, collaboration alone is insufficient to harness the power of others. After all, being able to collaborate does not necessarily increase the likelihood that we will do so. We need a network of people with whom we can collaborate. We need the skills to understand the strengths and weaknesses of potential collaborators. We also need to know with whom we want to collaborate, and in what context collaboration makes sense. We therefore need to go beyond collaboration and consider how social interactions can be put to good use inside and outside of the classroom.

We know that social interactions are important to student success. Reviews of empirical literature (Cohen, McCabe, Michelli, & Pickeral, 2009; Thapa, Cohen, Guffey, & Higgins-D'Alessandro, 2013) found that positive school climates are associated with academic achievement, school success, effective violence prevention, student healthy development, and teacher retention. Similarly, a large-scale statistical study found that teachers' climate ratings were associated significantly and consistently with students' performance on standardized tests of academic achievement, and with indexes of their academic, behavioral, and socioemotional adjustment (Brand, Felner, Seitsinger, Burns, & Bolton,

2008). Social interactions outside of the school are also important. Sandra L. Dika and Kusum Singh (2002) note that nontraditional family structures and number of siblings are positively correlated with dropout rates (Israel, Beaulieu, & Hartless, 2001; Smith, Beaulieu, & Israel, 1992), while parental expectations, parent communication with the school, parental monitoring, and student involvement in activities are negatively correlated (Carbonaro, 1998; Smith et al., 1992; Teachman, Paasch, & Carver, 1997). Meanwhile, traditional family structure, parental expectation, intergenerational closure, and parent-teen interactions are positively associated with high school graduation and college enrollment (Furstenberg & Hughes, 1995; Yan, 1999). Correlations have also been found between low social capital and poverty (for example, Collier, 2002), obesity (for example, Kim, Subramanian, Gortmaker, & Kawachi, 2006), drug addiction (Winstanley, Steinwachs, Ensminger, Latkin, Stitzer, & Olsen, 2008), and poor dental health (for example, Pattussi, Hardy, & Sheiham, 2006). In light of these and other similar findings, the Centers for Disease Control and Prevention (CDC, 2009) and the U.S. Department of Education have recommended that schools adopt strategies to increase school connectedness and improve school social climate (Office of the Press Secretary, 2014).

What if students were explicitly taught strategies for improving school climate and enhancing their social capital themselves? An essential component of doing so would be to instill students with networking skills. The importance of networking has been cited by figures ranging from Albert Einstein, to eBay founder Pierre Omidyar, to once-upon-a-time community organizer Barack Obama (Carr, 2008; Dyer, Gregersen, & Christensen, 2009). Since networking is a skill that must be consciously utilized and carefully developed according to individual needs, students and teachers would benefit from a firm knowledge base that can be adapted to local contexts. This chapter provides an overview of that knowledge base.

Social Networks

Social network analysis is a technique for graphically representing how individuals (for example, people, animals, corporations) interact within a social network so that patterns can be detected and interpreted. In most texts, individuals are referred to as *nodes*, and they are connected by *ties*. Research questions dictate what constitutes a tie, but Stephen P. Borgatti, Ajay Mehra, Daniel J. Brass, and Giuseppe Labianca (2009) provide a useful typology that divides ties into four types: (1) social relations (for example, kinship, employer-employee, friendship), (2) interactions (for example, physical, email, conversation), (3) similarities (for example, shared location, shared attribute, shared membership), and (4) flow (for example, shared beliefs, shared information). Ties can be of various strengths, and they can be uni- or multidirectional. Social network analysis typically concerns itself with three features of a network: the location of nodes, the strength of the ties, and structural equivalence (that is, symmetry between whole networks, or parts of a network).

Figure 7.1 is an admittedly unsophisticated representation of the social network described in the anecdote about Philip Knight from the beginning of the chapter. The nodes represent the actors. The ties represent the existence of mutual obligations (that is, a social tie). This representation gives us a sense of why Knight's marketing strategy worked. Knight helped bridge disparate groups of people who otherwise would not have had anything to do with each other. Knight paid Kihachiro Onitsuka or some other executive at Onitsuka Company the $1,000 he received from his father and Bill Bowerman. The Onitsuka executive in turn paid the Onitsuka factory workers to make sneakers. In return for the payment, Knight received three hundred pairs of Tigers and sold them to consumers in the United States. Eventually, Knight would leverage Bowerman's connections to athletes on the U.S. Olympic track-and-field team to move sneakers and payment back and forth to an ever-increasing number of individuals (Krentzman, 1997; "Philip H. Knight," 2008).

The Onitsuka Factory Workers				University of Oregon Track Team
	Kihachiro Onitsuka		Bill Bowerman	
		Philip Knight		
	Matthew Knight		American Consumers of Tigers	

Figure 7.1: A representation of Philip Knight's social network as described in the opening anecdote where ties represent mutual obligations.

Different arrangements of social networks may be ideal for specific purposes but not for others. For example, Ronald S. Burt's (1992) theory of structural holes suggests that when nodes cluster tightly together, they tend to share a lot of redundant information: think of a CEO and a group of yes-men. Structural holes refer to gaps between clusters of nodes. The holes may be good for innovation because they allow for the generation of novel ideas. Burt (1992) therefore suggests that a vine-and-cluster structure may optimize entrepreneurial opportunity. Mark S. Granovetter's (1973) theory of weak ties holds that individuals who are loosely connected to a social network are more likely to break away and become a source of novel information for another network. A third insight is that individuals who act as bridges between networks are often in uniquely powerful positions because of their potential access to both groups (Lin, 2001). By the same token, however, they are also more likely to inherit problems from both groups.

Based on these insights and others, Borgatti et al. (2009) identify four types of patterns upon which social network analysts tend to focus. The first is transmission. An example of transmission would be the examination of how a dangerous idea, an innovative practice, or even a disease passes from one person to another. The second is adaptation. In a manner similar to convergent evolution in biology, nodes in similar positions tend to become more similar over time. For example, people in the same profession may develop similar beliefs and habits even if they never meet each other, and share few other commonalities. The similarities that arise are not necessarily a case of a shared race, class, or culture. Rather, they are similar responses to similar environmental pressures. The third is binding, which refers to the way that nodes sometimes connect in such a way that they produce emergent properties (for example, structural holes leading to novel information; loosely connected terrorist cells resisting infiltration). The fourth is exclusion. In competitive situations, nodes sometimes connect at the expense to other nodes. In such cases, node position can become a source of power. Imagine, for example, that Bill Bowerman had unexpectedly flown to Japan and went into business with Onitsuka Company himself. Not only would this have prevented Knight from doing so, it would have left Knight in a weaker position than when he started: he would now have an immediate competitor.

Students would benefit from an understanding of group dynamics that goes beyond "Don't be a bully," and social network analysis is one means by which they may achieve it, especially when it draws on findings from other areas of inquiry like game theory and sociology. As an instructional tool, social network analysis has considerable potential for use with adolescent learners, who tend to be very conscious of their social identities, and who are becoming increasingly capable of using social network analysis software. Teachers could even create assignments where students have to alter their social network in a constructive or interesting way. While this may seem like a strange suggestion, requiring students to perform volunteer work serves the same function. Using social network analysis would simply require students to step back and analyze how they fit into the bigger picture. The easiest tool for network visualization is probably NetDraw (Borgatti, 2002). For more sophisticated analysis, UCINET (Borgatti, Everett, & Freeman, 2002) may be more appropriate.

Social Capital

While there are a number of theories of social capital (see Fine, 2010), this chapter focuses primarily on that of Nan Lin (2001) because it draws heavily from the type of social network analysis just described. Lin (2001) defines social capital as an "investment in social relations with expected returns in the marketplace," which "may be economic, political, labor, or community" (p. 19). Just as in the previous examples, actors are represented by nodes, and social relations are represented by ties. However, Lin makes one crucial addition: the social network, comprised of nodes and ties, has resources embedded within it. When actors invest in a relationship, social capital is said to be generated because the actors have greater or easier access to each other's resources now that they are more closely connected. These resources are not necessarily physical. They also include wealth, power, reputation, and access to other social networks. The total amount of resources one can access at a given time is said to be one's social capital.

Lin's (2001) theory helps us understand phrases like "it's not just what you know but who you know" in a new light (p. 41). Social networks are like road maps for resource acquisition. Connecting with the right people can facilitate the exchange of useful information, the manipulation of other actors, and credentialing. After all, when one individual endorses another, it is implied (if not stated explicitly) that the endorsee is connected to the resources of the endorser, and is part of the same social network. Connections can also reinforce identity and recognition. Recognition, in turn, facilitates public acknowledgement of one's entitlement to certain resources.

Apart from the potential for practical application, teaching students about social capital could also help them understand the implications of the social standing before they learn it from experience, which can be an awfully cruel teacher. Borrowing from George C. Homans (1950), Lin describes relationships as either homophilous or heterophilous. Most relationships are homophilous: actors in the relationship occupy similar positions in the hierarchy, and control similar resources. As one moves laterally away from a node, the quality of the resources one encounters may differ, but the value remains about the same. In practical terms, this explains why members of a race, class, or profession tend to associate with fellow members.

A heterophilous relationship is one in which there is a differential in the amount of resources each person controls. These types of relationships are less common and demand more effort by both parties. The resource-poorer person has less to offer, and what he or she can offer might be exploited by the more powerful person. Meanwhile, the resource-rich person may have little to gain through the interaction. The primary motive for heterophilous relationships is that the richer individual wants to gain access to different types of resources, or access to additional nodes by increasing his or her total number of interactions. In heterophilous relationships, the lower person on the hierarchy is not expected to benefit as much as the higher. We see this principle in prizefighting. The more successful fighter not only earns more money, but he also sets the very terms of engagement. The lower-ranked fighter must agree to this arrangement if he wants to gain access to his opponent's resources (that is, the opportunity to take his title). At scale, this principle also seems to explain the apparent existence of social classes. Lin's hypothesis that actors with better starting points in the hierarchy continue to have better access to social capital seems to explain why classes tend to persist over time.

Teaching students about social capital could be a means by which they move beyond simply conceptualizing their social network, and instead consider how they can put their ties to use. Some will find it gauche or even unethical to suggest that children should be taught to see people as potential sources of resources to be exploited. The first charge may have merit. On the other hand, it could just as easily be argued that "social climbing" and "social mobility" are two ways of saying the same thing, and no one complains about the latter. The ethics charge, however, will not withstand scrutiny. Social capital is being recommended as a tool here. How it is used is up to students and teachers.

Social Intelligence

If students are to skillfully navigate their social networks in order to generate social capital, they will require social intelligence. Social intelligence, like social capital, suffers from competing definitions, and a tendency to resist objective measurement (see Kihlstrom & Cantor, 2000; Matthews, Zeidner, & Roberts, 2004). For illustrative purposes, we will consider the theory of social intelligence advanced by Daniel Goleman (2006) and Daniel Goleman and Richard E. Boyatzis (2008). For a fuller discussion of theoretical and measurement issues surrounding social intelligence, readers should refer to Matthews, Zeidner, and Roberts (2004).

Goleman and Boyatzis (2008) assert that to a certain extent, when people are engaged in a leader–follower dynamic, the brains of the leaders and followers are fused into a single system. Leaders are those individuals whose behavior leverages the power of the interconnected brain system. The authors identify three mechanisms through which brains form these interconnected systems: mirror neurons, spindle cells, and oscillators.

A mirror neuron is a neuron that fires both when the body to which it belongs performs an action and when it sees another animal perform the same action. While our understanding of mirror neurons is still developing, Goleman and Boyatzis (2008) claim that mirror neurons are responsible for mimicking what other beings are doing, and how they are feeling. Moreover, mirror neurons can be put to use by promoting certain behaviors and keeping others in check. For example, the authors recommend that leaders should maintain good moods, and not be afraid to laugh because their laughter and mood will rub off on their employees. Since studies have shown correlations between laughter from subordinates and the performance of top leaders, as well as correlations between good moods and the ability to take in information, there may be financial benefits in addition to the positive feelings employers share with their employees. Conversely, we have all had experiences where someone delivers one message, but his or her body language delivers the opposite one. Our moods affect others whether we want them to or not. These are important ideas to share with students because emotional affect has practical ramifications.

Spindle neurons, meanwhile, are large spindle-shaped cells with a single dendrite on one end and an apical axon on the other. Apart from humans, the cells have been found in the great apes, certain species of whales, elephants, and the macaque (Evrard, Forro, & Logothetis, 2012; Hakeem, Sherwood, Bonar, Butti, Hof, & Allman, 2009). The length of these cells seems to be crucial for their ability to quickly communicate with other cells. Goleman and Boyatzis (2008) claim that the speed with which spindle cells communicate allows people to "lead from the gut" (p. 77). Because they facilitate quick communication between cells, they may enhance our ability to recognize patterns and make snap judgments. They may even work fast enough that we can unconsciously reach a conclusion about a person or situation before engaging in the conscious processing of information. Goleman and Boyatzis (2008) suggest that leading from the gut need not be the sign of an incompetent leader. They acknowledge, however, that people would do well to consciously process as much information as time will allow before making important decisions.

Finally, neural oscillation describes rhythmic activity in the brain. Goleman and Boyatzis (2008) suggest that oscillating cells coordinate people physically. They suggest that these cells are at work when musicians play together, and when people seem to be unconsciously coordinating their movements. In conjunction with mirror neurons and spindle cells, they may also play a role in feelings of rapport and belonging that tend to be common among tightly knit groups. In such cases, the "shared feeling" is literally that: neurons firing in the same or similar patterns.

Goleman and Boyatzis (2008) make only a few suggestions for developing social intelligence, but they point the direction for the curious. For example, they discuss the concept of getting people "fired up," such as when a coach gives a rousing speech, or a charismatic politician enters the room. They note that what are really being fired up are neurons. Students could practice engaging in these types of behaviors, and as the authors note, it takes practice to pull them off. Trying to fake it can actually backfire because our moods can trump our message. The authors also recommend that leaders and potential leaders consider cultivating seven attributes that seem to be equated with social intelligence: (1) empathy, (2) attunement (for example, listening attentively, noting the others' moods), (3) teamwork, (4) inspiration, (5) organizational awareness (for example, appreciating group culture and values, understanding social networks), (6) influence, and (7) the ability to develop others. For a comprehensive review of empirical evidence related to the causes and effects of school leaders' emotions, readers should refer to Izhak Berkovich and Ori Eyal (2015).

In addition to the social intelligence described by Goleman and Boyatzis (2008), teachers would of course need to equip students with other important knowledge regarding human behavior if students are to develop any skill in traversing social networks. While it is beyond the scope of this chapter to summarize the myriad ways that this might be accomplished, it seems fitting to suggest here that students also learn about the irrational behaviors to which humans are prone, such as those described by Ariely (2008). Since some of the biases have been observed in other primates (for example, Chen, Lakshminarayanan, & Santos, 2006), humans may be hardwired for certain irrational behaviors. Students should be aware of this. For example, understanding that most humans prefer to avoid loss more than they desire to acquire gain may be of greater use to the average student than understanding the difference between the literary devices, epistrophe and polysyndeton.

As far as providing opportunities to practice developing social intelligence, ample literature exists to help teachers guide instruction. For example, David W. Johnson and Roger T. Johnson (2009) offer a history of social interdependence theory, which explains how group organization, group size, and positive and negative reinforcement tend to affect student interaction and achievement. It discusses the ideal conditions for cooperation, competition, and individualistic efforts in classroom contexts, as well as potential pitfalls. Slavin (2011) offers similar insights.

Measuring Collaboration and Social Interactions

Thus far, we have considered how and why schools might teach social networking and social intelligence. We now consider the difficult business of measuring these constructs. Measuring these constructs is difficult, not only because they are subject to heated theoretical debates (for example, see Haynes, [2009] for a discussion of challenges to measuring social capital; and Matthews, Zeidner, and Roberts, [2004] for challenges with measuring social-emotional intelligence), but also because measurement may require schools to shift away from the 19th century tradition of measuring the abilities of individual students, to measuring the abilities of groups of students, or even the school as a whole. (Of course, this is also what makes the prospect of taking social networking seriously so exciting.) Research-based measures exist for each of the individual, relational, and school levels. We will review some of the best-known instruments for each level.

Personal Level Measurement

Individual Assessment

Table 7.1 (page 142) lists common measures of social and emotional intelligence. While this chapter has focused on social intelligence, the existence of so many competing definitions for social intelligence and emotional intelligence prevents firm distinctions between the two constructs. Indeed, Goleman (2006) claims that his conception of social intelligence is essentially a more nuanced companion to his earlier conception of emotional intelligence. John F. Kihlstrom and Nancy Cantor (2000) also discuss at length the need to differentiate social intelligence from related constructs, like general intelligence and personality. Considering the great amount of debate that exists surrounding even

Table 7.1: Measures of Social Intelligence, Emotional Intelligence, and Collaboration Skills

Author(s) & Year	Assessment Name	Pros, Cons, & Content
Boyatzis & Sala (2004)	Emotional Competence Inventory (ECI)	**Pros:** Overlaps with the Big Five personality dimensions, and other psychological concepts in motivation and leadership literature (Conte, 2005)
		Cons: Discriminant and predictive validity evidence not provided; few peer-reviewed evaluations (Conte, 2005); research sample
		Content: 110 items and 20 competencies; 360-degree tool; assesses (1) self-awareness, (2) social awareness, (3) self-management, and (4) social skills; includes self-measures, peer measures, and supervisor measures
Bar-On (1997)	Emotional Quotient Inventory (EQ-i)	**Pros:** Adequate internal consistency reliability overall (.76); adequate test-retest reliability after four months (.75); adequate evidence of convergent validity (correlation amongst most subscales was .50); strong evidence of divergent validity from Wechsler Adult Intelligence Scale (.12); average correlation with Big Five personality measures about .50 (Conte, 2005); youth version available; scales correlate highly to adult version (Parker et al., 2004)
		Cons: Theory on which test is based is vague (Matthews, Zeidner, & Roberts, 2004); contrary to publisher's assertion, test may not predict academic success (GPA); more evidence of discriminant validity needed (Conte, 2005)
		Content: 133 item self-report; assesses (1) intrapersonal, (2) interpersonal, (3) adaptability, (4) general mood, and (5) stress management; 60 items on youth version
Mayer & Salovey (2000)	Mayer-Salovey-Caruso Emotional Intelligence Test (MSCEIT)	**Pros:** Adequate internal consistency overall (.75), and for subscales (.68 on average); quick to administer; intended to be ability-based (Conte, 2005)
		Cons: Uses expert and consensus scoring (examinee observes a face and must describe the emotion in a manner consistent with expert opinion); internal consistency for expert reliability (.71); internal consistency for consensus reliability (.68); authors cite studies of older version of the Multifactor Emotional Intelligence Scale (MEIS) for validity evidence, but tests differ considerably (Conte, 2005)
		Content: 141 items; assesses (1) perception of emotion, (2) integration and assimilation of emotion, (3) knowledge of emotions, (4) management of emotions (Conte, 2005)
Boyatzis, Goleman, & Hay Acquisition (2007)	Emotional and Social Competency Inventory (ESCI)	**Pros:** Similar to ECI but revised for increased statistical rigor; exploratory factor analysis confirms that questions load on expected factor; reliability similar to ECI
		Cons: No peer-reviewed research on instrument
		Content: Similar to ECI but cut scores replaced with descriptors

Note: It should be assumed that evidence of technical adequacy was gathered from an adult population unless otherwise stated.

ubiquitous assessments, like intelligence tests, this lack of clarity should not be seen as an insurmountable psychometric barrier for schools. That said, test-users should exercise the same professional judgment they would for any other cognitive test, beginning with an understanding of what the test is meant to measure. For example, John D. Mayer, Peter Salovey, and David Caruso's (2000) Mayer-Salovey-Caruso Emotional Intelligence Test (MSCEIT) is meant to be a test of ability (that is, "correct" answers were established by experts), whereas Bar-On's (1997) Emotional Quotient Inventory (EQ-i) is a self-report that is meant to be purely descriptive; and the Boyatzis, Goleman, and Hay Acquisition (2007) Emotional and Social Competency Inventory (ESCI) is a 360-degree assessment that incorporates data from the examinee, peers, and the evaluator. The different structures of these tests place different requirements on the test user. They also facilitate different types of interpretations that could easily become politically charged. Imagine a teacher trying to explain to parents that their children will receive a grade based on what other students in the class think of them on a social level: even if the test perfectly measured social intelligence, political realities could make for some very difficult conversations. Like any other test, educators should understand the technical adequacy of these tests, the theories that undergird them, and the consequences of the test scores (Messick, 1998). At present, the youth version of the EQ-i may be the safest option for educators. Because it is a self-assessment, students cannot be graded on performance; but by the same token, students may find it more useful for self-reflection and goal setting.

Group Assessment

An alternative to assessing students at the individual level is to assess them in teams or groups. As mentioned previously, large-scale standardized tests for this purpose are forthcoming, but it is unclear whether they will yield individual or group scores. In the meantime, teachers can use the collaborative two-stage test method of group assessment discussed by Brett Hollis Gilley and Bridgette Clarkston (2014). In such an instance, students would attempt to take a test or solve a problem independently. Immediately after, students would be placed with a partner or in a small group. They would then collaboratively attempt an alternative version of the test or problem, and teachers would evaluate the extent to which performance improved during the collaborative portion of the assignment. Teachers could vary the assessment by incorporating into the scores the behavioral ratings mentioned at the beginning of the chapter (for example, social loafing, refraining from abusive language), or the original test score. The few quasi-experimental studies that exist on this approach suggests that students actually learn more from this approach than they would have independently, perhaps because they are able to get immediate feedback on mistakes (Gilley & Clarkston, 2014). No systematic review of collaborative testing has been published as of yet, but as Gilley and Clarkston (2014) note, empirical research with post-secondary students has found that this approach can reduce anxiety (Lusk & Conklin, 2003; Zimbardo, Butler, & Wolfe, 2003), increase positive relationships amongst students (Sandahl, 2010), improve student perceptions of the class (Shindler, 2004), and increase student motivation (Shindler, 2004; Zimbardo et al., 2003). Considering how much attention cooperative learning has received, it is surprising that cooperative testing has received so little. More research is needed in this area, not just because group assessment may improve learning, but also because it could transform the way we conceive of K–12 education. Schools currently focus on individual accomplishments even though the adult workplace and civic spheres depend on primarily cooperation. Schools should actively prepare students to become leaders and collaborators.

Relational Level

If schools do decide to move away from treating individual students as the primary unit of analysis, they might measure emergent phenomena, like trust or psychological safety which cannot exist but for the presence of a group. Social capital is also an emergent phenomenon, but there are some barriers to measuring it. For example, the acclaimed sociologist James Coleman (1988) measured social capital by using proxies such as a student's number of siblings, the parental education level of his or her parents, the number of parents at home, and his or her mother's educational expectations, all of which may impact academic achievement. Unfortunately, there are two problems with Coleman's approach to measuring social capital. First, schools have no control over many of the proxies Coleman used for measuring social capital. Secondly, Coleman's formulation of social capital is tautological, which means that any instrument based on his definition will not live up to Messick's (1995) standards of validity (see also Fine, 2010; Haynes, 2009; Wilkinson, 1999). In the absence of any widely-used instruments for measuring social capital, schools might measure their internal climate as recommended by M. Lee Van Horn (2003) and Thapa et al. (2013) so that they develop smarter policies that will improve relationships within the school, and across their communities.

Measuring Emergent Phenomena

In terms of technical adequacy, two of the best surveys for measuring school climate are the School Climate Survey (SCS; Kelley et al., 1986) and the School-Level Environment Questionnaire (SLEQ). Both surveys have been evaluated in peer-reviewed journals. Van Horn (2003) found that the SCS had a consistent factor structure, and adequate to high internal reliability. Interrater reliability correlations from family scores were low (.06 to .12). However, Van Horn explains the low reliability by noting that families have fewer and more varied interactions with school than students and personnel. It therefore makes sense that this is reflected in survey responses. Survey items are on a five-point Likert scale. Separate versions of the survey exist for elementary and middle school students, high school students, family and community, and staff. Different versions evaluate different phenomena. For example, the high school student survey evaluates sharing of resources, order and discipline, parental involvement, student interpersonal relations, and student-teacher relations. The SLEQ, meanwhile, has been strengthened through several revisions following factor analyses (Johnson, Stevens, & Zvoch, 2007). The survey contains fifty-six items arranged in five scales. The five scales measure student support, affiliation, participatory decision making, innovation, and resource adequacy. Internal consistency for the whole test was .90. Subscales ranged from .77 to .86. Johnson et al. (2007) state that the SLEQ is a useful tool for evaluating and changing school climate.

Another survey that schools may find useful is the National School Climate Center's (NSCC's) Comprehensive School Climate Inventory (CSCI). The twenty-minute survey is intended to assess how students, teachers, parents, and community members perceive the school's climate. The NSCC offers complementary information on a five-stage school climate improvement process. The publishers claim that the survey was "scientifically vetted" in four independent evaluations, and that it has been recognized as a reliable resource by the U.S. Department of Education's Safe and Supportive Schools Technical Assistance Center (National School Climate Center, n.d.). However, the latter claim could not be confirmed. The survey has not been evaluated in a peer-reviewed journal.

Finally, Harvard Business School's Learning Organization Survey (LOS; Garvin, Edmondson, & Gino, 2008) is meant to evaluate how well organizations learn. The fifty-five-item survey focuses on three areas: environment, processes and practice, and leadership. Each area contains subcomponents such as psychological safety, experimentation, information collection, and so on. Singer, Moore, Meterko, and Williams's (2012) analysis of the LOS found that the survey had a strong factor structure overall, and that the survey reliably measures key features of organizational learning. However, their study focused on the survey's use in hospitals. Thus, their findings will not necessarily generalize to school settings or student use. The survey is free and available online. The constructs of interests are also likely to be valued by sports teams, clubs, and any goal-oriented group.

Education administrators already use school climate surveys to manage their schools. Why not equip students with the same tools so that they can begin to manage themselves? These surveys could also be used for goal setting within organizations in the same way schools and businesses are apt to use them.

Where Do We Go From Here?

Collaboration will be a vital skill in the 21st century, but by itself, it is insufficient. Cooperation is not a perfect good. It can facilitate exploitation, and amplify behaviors that are ultimately harmful to society as a whole, such as blind obedience and groupthink. In addition to practicing collaboration within the classroom, students need to extend what they learn about social interaction beyond the school building. Social network analysis, social capital, and social intelligence are conceptual and technical tools that educators can employ to help students achieve this goal. However, the exponential growth of scholarship in these areas of inquiry means that many of the theories and measures in circulation are only in the nascent stage. Educators should remember that we do not yet have anything approaching consensus regarding the nature of social intelligence and social capital. They should question the limits of these tools, and encourage their students to do the same. For example, Lin's (2001) theory assumes that social networks are pyramidal in structure, and those at the top have the most social capital. Is this a fair assumption? Are there any unique benefits to being on the bottom? How should one weigh the costs and benefits of forming a social connection? Researchers, meanwhile, will need to continue to follow the development of social network analysis, social capital, and social intelligence in order to determine how they can be unified so that they not only enhance classroom instruction, but reorient the goals of our education systems.

References and Resources

Akçomak, I. S. (2011). Social capital of social capital researchers. *Review of Economics and Institutions, 2*(2), 1–28.

Ariely, D. (2008). *Predictably irrational: The hidden forces that shape our decisions.* New York: HarperCollins.

Aukrust, V. G. (Ed.). (2011). *Learning and cognition in education.* Boston: Academic Press.

Bankston, C. L., III, & Zhou, M. (2002). Social capital and immigrant children's achievement. *Research in the Sociology of Education, 13*, 13–39.

Bar-On, R. (1997). *The Bar-On Emotional Quotient Inventory (EQ-i): Technical manual.* Toronto, Ontario, Canada: Multi-Health Systems.

Berkovich, I., & Eyal, O. (2015). Educational leaders and emotions: An international review of empirical evidence, 1992–2012. *Review of Educational Research, 85*(1), 129–167.

Borgatti, S. P. (2002). *NetDraw: Graph visualization software.* Harvard, MA: Analytic Technologies.

Borgatti, S. P., Everett, M. G., & Freeman, L. C. (2002). *UCINET for Windows: Software for social network analysis.* Harvard, MA: Analytic Technologies.

Borgatti, S. P., Mehra, A., Brass, D. J., & Labianca, G. (2009). Network analysis in the social sciences. *Science, 323*(5916), 892–895.

Boyatzis, R. E., Goleman, D., & Hay Acquisition. (2007). *Emotional and Social Competency Inventory.* Boston: Hay Group.

Boyatzis, R. E., & Sala, F. (2004). The Emotional Competence Inventory (ECI). In G. Geher (Ed.), *Measuring emotional intelligence: Common ground and controversy* (pp. 147–180). New York: Nova Science.

Brand, S., Felner, R. D., Seitsinger, A., Burns, A., & Bolton, N. (2008). A large scale study of the assessment of the social environment of middle and secondary schools: The validity and utility of teachers' ratings of school climate, cultural pluralism, and safety problems for understanding school effects and school improvement. *Journal of School Psychology*, *46*(5), 507–535.

Brant, J. (2014). The 1984 Los Angeles Olympics: A run to glory. *Runner's World*. Accessed at www.runnersworld.com/olympics/the-1984-los-angeles-olympics-a-run-to-glory on August 12, 2015.

Burt, R. S. (1992). *Structural holes: The social structure of competition*. Cambridge, MA: Harvard University Press.

Callahan, T. (2003). *In search of Tiger: A journey through golf with Tiger Woods*. New York: Three Rivers Press.

Carbonaro, W. J. (1998). A little help from my friend's parents: Intergenerational closure and educational outcomes. *Sociology of Education*, *71*(4), 295–313.

Carr, D. (2008, November 9). How Obama tapped into social networks' power. *The New York Times*. Accessed at www.nytimes.com/2008/11/10/business/media/10carr.html?_r=0 on March 23, 2015.

Centers for Disease Control and Prevention. (2009). *School connectedness: Strategies for increasing protective factors among youth*. Atlanta, GA: U.S. Department of Health and Human Services. Accessed at www.cdc.gov/healthyyouth/protective/pdf/connectedness.pdf on March 23, 2015.

Chen, M. K., Lakshminarayanan, V., & Santos, L. (2006). How basic are behavioral biases? Evidence from capuchin monkey trading behavior. *Journal of Political Economy*, *114*(3), 517–537.

Cohen, J., McCabe, L., Michelli, N. M., & Pickeral, T. (2009). School climate: Research, policy, practice, and teacher education. *Teachers College Record*, *111*(1), 180–213.

Coleman, J. S. (1988). Social capital in the creation of human capital. *American Journal of Sociology*, *94*, S95–S120.

Collier, P. (2002). Social capital and poverty: A microeconomic perspective. In C. Grootaert & T. Van Bastelaer (Eds.), *The role of social capital in development: An empirical assessment* (pp. 19–41). New York: Cambridge University Press.

Conte, J. M. (2005). A review and critique of emotional intelligence measures. *Journal of Organizational Behavior*, *26*(4), 433–440.

Daly, A. J. (Ed.). (2010). *Social network theory and educational change*. Cambridge, MA: Harvard Education Press.

Dika, S. L., & Singh, K. (2002). Applications of social capital in educational literature: A critical synthesis. *Review of Educational Research*, *72*(1), 31–60.

Duffy, F. M., & Dale, J. D. (Eds.). (1999). *Creating successful school systems: Voices from the university, the field, and the community*. Norwood, MA: Christopher-Gordon.

Dyer, J. H., Gregersen, H., & Christensen, C. M. (2009). The innovator's DNA. *Harvard Business Review*, *87*(12), 60–67.

Evrard, H. C., Forro, T., & Logothetis, N. K. (2012). Von Economo neurons in the anterior insula of the macaque monkey. *Neuron, 74*(3), 482–489.

Field, J. (2005). *Social capital and lifelong learning.* Bristol, England: Policy Press.

Fine, B. (2010). *Theories of social capital: Researchers behaving badly.* New York: Pluto Press.

Furstenberg, F. F., Jr., & Hughes, M. E. (1995). Social capital and successful development among at-risk youth. *Journal of Marriage and the Family, 57*(3), 580–592.

Garvin, D. A., Edmondson, A. C., & Gino, F. (2008). Is yours a learning organization? *Harvard Business Review, 86*(3), 109–116.

Geher, G. (Ed.). (2004). *Measuring emotional intelligence: Common ground and controversy.* New York: Nova Science.

Gilley, B. H., & Clarkston, B. (2014). Collaborative testing: Evidence of learning in a controlled in-class study of undergraduate students. *Journal of College Science Teaching, 43*(3), 83–91.

Goleman, D. (2006). *Social intelligence: The new science of human relationships.* New York: Bantam Books.

Goleman, D., & Boyatzis, R. E. (2008). Social intelligence and the biology of leadership. *Harvard Business Review, 86*(9). Accessed at https://hbr.org/2008/09/social-intelligence-and -the-biology-of-leadership on March 23, 2015.

Granovetter, M. S. (1973). The strength of weak ties. *American Journal of Sociology, 78*(6), 1360–1380.

Grootaert, C., & Van Bastelaer, T. (Eds.). (2002). *The role of social capital in development: An empirical assessment.* New York: Cambridge University Press.

Hakeem, A. Y., Sherwood, C. C., Bonar, C. J., Butti, C., Hof, P. R., & Allman, J. M. (2009). Von Economo neurons in the elephant brain. *Anatomical Record, 292*(2), 242–248.

Haynes, P. J. (2009). *Before going any further with social capital: Eight key criticisms to address* [INGENIO working paper series]. Valencia, Spain: Instituto de Gestión de la Innovación y del Conocimiento.

Homans, G. C. (1950). *The human group.* New York: Harcourt, Brace.

Israel, G. D., Beaulieu, L. J., & Hartless, G. (2001). The influence of family and community social capital on educational achievement. *Rural Sociology, 66*(1), 43–68.

John, P. (2005). The contribution of volunteering, trust, and networks to educational performance. *Policy Studies Journal, 33*(4), 635–656.

Johnson, B., Stevens, J. J., & Zvoch, K. (2007). Teachers' perceptions of school climate: A validity study of scores from the revised School Level Environment questionnaire. *Educational and Psychological Measurement, 67*(5), 833–844.

Johnson, D. W., & Johnson, R. T. (2009). An educational psychology success story: Social interdependence theory and cooperative learning. *Educational Researcher, 38*(5), 365–379.

Kelley, E. A., Glover, J. A., Keefe, J. W., Halderson, C., Sorenson, C., & Speth, C. (1986). *School Climate Survey (Modified): Comprehensive assessment of school environments.* Reston, VA: National Association of Secondary School Principals.

Kihlstrom, J. F., & Cantor, N. (2000). Social intelligence. In R. J. Sternberg (Ed.), *Handbook of intelligence* (pp. 359–379). New York: Cambridge University Press.

Kim, D., Subramanian, S. V., Gortmaker, S. L., & Kawachi, I. (2006). US state- and county-level social capital in relation to obesity and physical inactivity: A multilevel, multivariable analysis. *Social Science and Medicine, 63*(4), 1045–1059.

Krentzman, J. (1997). The force behind the Nike empire. *Stanford Alumni*. Accessed at https://alumni.stanford.edu/get/page/magazine/article/?article_id=43087 on August 11, 2015.

Latour, B. (2005). *Reassembling the social: An introduction to actor-network-theory*. New York: Oxford University Press.

Lin, N. (2001). *Social capital: A theory of social structure and action*. New York: Cambridge University Press.

Lusk, M., & Conklin, L. (2003). Collaborative testing to promote learning. *Journal of Nursing Education, 42*(3), 121.

Madden, L. (2012). Spike Lee is still the best Nike Jordan brand pitchman. *Forbes*. Accessed at www.forbes.com/sites/lancemadden/2012/12/05/spike-lee-is-still-the-best-nike-jordan-brand-pitchman/ on August 14, 2015.

Matthews, G., Zeidner, M., & Roberts, R. D. (2004). *Emotional intelligence: Science and myth*. Cambridge, MA: MIT Press.

Mayer, J. D., Caruso, D., & Salovey, P. (1998). *The Multifactor Emotional Intelligence Scale*. Unpublished report.

Mayer, J. D., & Salovey, P. (2007). *Mayer-Salovey-Caruso Emotional Intelligence Test*. Toronto, Canada: Multi-Health Systems.

Mayer, J. D., Salovey, P., & Caruso, D. (2000). *Mayer-Salovey-Caruso Emotional Intelligence Test*. Toronto, Canada: Multi-Health Systems.

Messick, S. (1995). Standards of validity and the validity of standards in performance assessment. *Educational Measurement: Issues and Practice, 14*(4), 5–8.

Messick, S. (1998). Test validity: A matter of consequence. *Social Indicators Research, 45*(1–3), 35–44.

National School Climate Center. (n.d.). *Frequently asked questions for researchers (doctoral students and social scientists) interested in Comprehensive School Climate Inventory (CSCI)*. Accessed at www.schoolclimate.org/climate/documents/faqs-csci-december-2014.pdf on August 11, 2015.

Neckerman, K. M. (Ed.). (2004). *Social inequality*. New York: Russell Sage.

Office of the Press Secretary. (2014, May 30). *Fact sheet and report: Opportunity for all—My brother's keeper blueprint for action* [Press release]. Accessed at www.whitehouse.gov/the-press-office/2014/05/30/fact-sheet-report-opportunity-all-my-brother-s-keeper-blueprint-action on March 23, 2015.

Parker, J. D. A., Creque, R. E., Sr., Barnhart, D. L., Harris, J. I., Majeski, S. A., Wood, L. M., et al. (2004). Academic achievement in high school: Does emotional intelligence matter? *Personality and Individual Differences, 37*(7), 1321–1330.

Partnership for 21st Learning (n.d.). *Framework for 21st century learning*. Accessed at www.p21 .org/our-work/p21-framework on March 23, 2015.

Pattussi, M. P., Hardy, R., & Sheiham, A. (2006). The potential impact of neighborhood empowerment on dental caries among adolescents. *Community Dentistry and Oral Epidemiology, 34*(5), 344–350.

Pebley, A. R., & Sastry, N. (2004). Neighborhoods, poverty, and children's well-being. In K. M. Neckerman (Ed.), *Social inequality* (pp. 119–145). New York: Russell Sage.

"Philip H. Knight." (2008). *Entrepreneur*. Accessed at www.entrepreneur.com/article/197534 on August 14, 2015.

Rosen, Y., & Tager, M. (2013). *Computer-based assessment of collaborative problem-solving skills: Human-to-agent versus human-to-human approach* [Research report]. New York: Pearson. Accessed at http://researchnetwork.pearson.com/wp-content/uploads/collaborative problemsolvingresearchreport.pdf on March 23, 2015.

Sandahl, S. S. (2010). Collaborative testing as a learning strategy in nursing education. *Nursing Education Perspectives, 31*(3), 142–147.

Shindler, J. V. (2004). "Greater than the sum of the parts?" Examining the soundness of collaborative exams in teacher education courses. *Innovative Higher Education, 28*(4), 273–283.

Singer, S. J., Moore, S. C., Meterko, M., & Williams, S. (2012). Development of a short-form learning organization survey: The LOS-27. *Medical Care Research and Review, 69*(4), 432–459.

Slavin, R. E. (2011). Cooperative learning. In V. G. Aukrust (Ed.), *Learning and cognition in education* (pp. 160–166). Boston: Academic Press.

Smith, M. H., Beaulieu, L. J., & Israel, G. D. (1992). Effects of human capital and social capital on dropping out of high school in the South. *Journal of Research in Rural Education, 8*(1), 75–87.

Staber, U. (2007). Contextualizing research on social capital in regional clusters. *International Journal of Urban and Regional Research, 31*(3), 505–521.

Sternberg, R. J. (Ed.). (2000). *Handbook of intelligence*. New York: Cambridge University Press.

Sun, Y. (1999). The contextual effects of community social capital on academic performance. *Social Science Research, 28*(4), 403–426.

Teachman, J. D., Paasch, K., & Carver, K. (1997). Social capital and the generation of human capital. *Social Forces, 75*(4), 1343–1359.

Thapa, A., Cohen, J., Guffey, S., & Higgins-D'Alessandro, A. (2013). A review of school climate research. *Review of Educational Research, 83*(3), 357–385.

Van Horn, M. L. (2003). Assessing the unit of measurement for school climate through psychometric and outcome analyses of the School Climate Survey. *Educational and Psychological Measurement, 63*(6), 1002–1019.

Van Regenmortel, M. H. V., & Hull, D. L. (Eds.). (2002). *Promises and limits of reductionism in the biomedical sciences*. Hoboken, NJ: Wiley.

Von Davier, A. A., & Halpin, P. F. (2013). *Collaborative problem solving and the assessment of cognitive skills: Psychometric considerations* (ETS Research Report No. RR-13-41). Princeton, NJ: Educational Testing Service. Accessed at www.ets.org/Media/Research/pdf/RR-13-41.pdf on March 23, 2015.

Walter, F., Cole, M. S., & Humphrey, R. H. (2011). Emotional intelligence: Sine qua non of leadership or folderol? *Academy of Management Perspectives, 25*(1), 45–59.

Wheatley, M. J. (1999). Bringing schools back to life: Schools as living systems. In F. M. Duffy & J. D. Dale (Eds.), *Creating successful school systems: Voices from the university, the field, and the community* (pp. 3–19). Norwood, MA: Christopher-Gordon. Accessed at www.margaret wheatley.com/articles/lifetoschools.html on March 23, 2015.

Wilkinson, R. G. (1999). Health, hierarchy, and social anxiety. *Annals of the New York Academy of Sciences, 896*(1), 48 63.

Winstanley, E. L., Steinwachs, D. M., Ensminger, M. E., Latkin, C. A., Stitzer, M. L., & Olsen, Y. (2008). The association of self-reported neighborhood disorganization and social capital with adolescent alcohol and drug use, dependence, and access to treatment. *Drug and Alcohol Dependence, 92*(1–3), 173–182.

Wong, G. M. (2009). *The comprehensive guide to careers in sports.* Sudbury, MA: Jones and Bartlett Learning.

Yan, W. F. (1999). Successful African American students: The role of parental involvement. *Journal of Negro Education, 68*(1), 5–22.

Zimbardo, P. G., Butler, L. D., & Wolfe, V. A. (2003). Cooperative college examinations: More gain, less pain when students share information and grades. *The Journal of Experimental Education, 71*(2), 101–125.

Yue Shen is a PhD candidate at the University of Oregon. Her research interests include educational assessment and evaluation, creative teaching, and creativity development. Her latest research work focuses on enhancing the learning experience of international students in higher education.

Yue Shen received a bachelor's degree in Xi'an International Studies University, Shaanxi, China, a master's degree in education from Humboldt State University, and is currently pursuing a PhD in Educational Methodology, Policy, and Leadership at the University of Oregon.

To book Yue Shen for professional development, contact pd@solution-tree.com.

CHAPTER 8

Nature via Nurture: Development of Nonacademic Skills

YUE SHEN

When considering the qualities of motivation, creativity, entrepreneurial spirit, and others as educational outcomes, a series of questions emerges. First, to what extent do our genes predetermine these qualities? Second, to what extent, and how, can experience change these qualities? Third, to what extent can school experience affect these qualities, or are most of them already shaped by children's experience before they arrive at school? We do not have enough research to satisfactorily answer all the questions. But there is emerging evidence to support some tentative answers.

Genetic Potential: The Role of Nature

There is now general acceptance that genes play a major role in who we are. Both popular beliefs and scientific evidence suggest biology plays a role in what we eventually become. Evolutionary psychologists have postulated that human behaviors, personalities, and values certainly are partly the result of the long process of human evolution that has encoded certain attributes in our genes to pass on from generation to generation (Barkow, Cosmides, & Tooby, 1992; Buss, 2004; Crawford & Krebs, 1998; Wright, 1994). We are not born a blank slate waiting to be scripted, as the Massachusetts Institute of Technology (MIT) cognitive scientist Steven Pinker (2002) argues in his book *The Blank Slate: The Modern Denial of Human Nature*.

Taking motivation, for example, Ohio State University psychologist Steven Reiss (2004) advances the work of William James and William McDougall and believes that human behaviors are driven by instinctual desires. He believes human beings are motivated by sixteen basic desires: power, independence, curiosity, acceptance, order, saving, honor, idealism, social contact, family, status, vengeance, romance, eating, physical exercise, and tranquility. "With the possible exceptions of the motives of idealism and acceptance," he suggests, "the 16 basic desires motivate animals as well as people" (Reiss, 2004, p. 186). Reiss (2004) further asserts that "the 16 basic desires are considered to be genetically distinct with different evolutionary histories" (p. 186). Furthermore, while all individuals possess the sixteen basic desires, there is tremendous variation in the intensity people experience with each desire. In other words, some people may be more driven by the desire for power, while others by romance. The individual differences reflect genetic variations. According to Reiss (2000),

> Some people are born with the potential for very strong tendencies toward aggression (indicating a desire for vengeance), whereas others are born with the potential for only weak aggressive tendencies. Others are born with the potential for enormous curiosity, whereas others are born with the potential for little curiosity. No two people have exactly the same potential for a particular desire. Across all sixteen basic desires, the strength of desire varies significantly, depending on both the individual and the desire in question. (pp. 21–22)

Entrepreneurial capacities also have genetic roots, argues Scott Shane (2010), Case Western professor of entrepreneur studies, in his book *Born Entrepreneurs, Born Leaders: How Your Genes Affect Your Work Life.* "Genes affect nearly everything," he says (p. 2). They "influence your work interests, work values, decision making, risk taking, management style, approach to leadership, creativity, entrepreneurship, and work performance" (Shane, 2010, p. 4).

Shane's assertions were primarily based on findings of studies of twins, an approach that has been used to separate genetic traits from environmental influences. By comparing the behaviors of twins in given situations, one can infer the source of the difference. There are two types of twins who have different genetic compositions. Identical twins have the same DNA, while fraternal twins only share half of their genetic composition. Thus, "if pairs of identical twins make more similar choices, such as starting a business, than pairs of fraternal twins, then genetics must affect the choices" (Shane, 2011). Shane (2011) also draws insights from molecular genetics research designed to study "the different versions of genes people have and see if entrepreneurs are statistically more likely to have one version over another."

Shane finds that DNA influences people's job preferences, job satisfaction, and job performance: 75 percent of differences in job preference in creative arts can be explained by genetic differences, and 40 percent of salary differences can be attributed to genetic differences, according to Shane (2011). Entrepreneurs are 40 percent born and 60 percent made (Mount, 2009). Shane and his colleagues studied over three thousand twins in the United Kingdom and found that "between 37 and 42 percent of the variance in the tendency of people to engage in entrepreneurship is accounted for by genetic factors" (Nicolaou, Shane, Cherkas, & Spector, 2008, p. 16).

Interestingly, entrepreneurial characteristics are closely related to personality traits, which are heavily influenced by our genes. Shane (2011) suggests:

> The same genes that affect whether we are extroverted, open to experience, disagreeable and sensation seeking also influence our decision to start our own business. Furthermore, the same genes that influence the tendency to be open to experience also affect the tendency to identify new business opportunities.

Experience Matters: The Role of Nurture

Our genes hold the potential qualities for what we may eventually become. But our environment and experiences play a critical role in determining who we are in a number of ways. First, the environment provides the necessary conditions for genetic potentials to be realized, just like water, soil, temperature, and light provide essential conditions for an acorn to grow into an oak tree. While the acorn has all the genetic ingredients, without the proper environment, it will never become an oak. One may be born with great entrepreneurial potential, but without the proper environment, that potential may never have a chance to be realized. Likewise, a person can be as talented in music as Mozart; unless she has the right environment, she is unlikely to become a great musician.

Second, the environment can affect which genetic potential is enacted. Human beings are endowed with the potential to develop different capabilities and characteristics. Environments and experiences affect which ones are realized and to what extent they are realized. For example, a child born into a family of artists may have his artistic potential developed more than his mathematics potential.

Third, environments and experiences also affect the degree to which certain traits are developed or suppressed. A person may be born with a strong inclination for entrepreneurship, but if he is discouraged to take risks, the person's entrepreneurial talent may not be developed. A child born with a more adventurous nature can be taught to become risk-averse. On the other hand, if creativity is encouraged in the culture, a person born to be less creative can certainly become more so.

Fourth, the environment affects how genetic traits may be realized or how the potentials are expressed. The same is true for how we satisfy our basic desires motivationally. For example, while it is human instinct to love their offspring, how parents express that love is determined by their culture and experiences. The same personality trait can have different manifestations in behavior in different cultures, as well. For instance, some behaviors that are considered to indicate aggressiveness in one culture may be viewed as normal or being frank in another.

Thus, it is safe to assume that our genes do not act alone to determine who we are. What we become is essentially the result of interesting interactions between genes and environment, as well as the result of previous interactions. Our development is a matter of nature expressed, enhanced, or suppressed via nurture (Ridley, 2003).

Mechanism of Mind: Examples of Nature via Nurture

Ultimately, as explained by developmental psychology and evolutionary psychology, life at any moment is full of unspecified and inexhaustible factors that would potentially influence the development of individual minds (Patel, Honavar, & Balakrishnan, 2001). What researchers know is that there are certain components that play a rather critical role in shaping the individual development of nonacademic skills over the life span.

Perception

As one of the most fundamental mechanisms in human development, individual perception constitutes the basis for the development of many other skills, including nonacademic skills like emotions, self-efficacy, and others (Bornstein & Arterberry, 2003). Nonacademic skills and their development over time rely first and foremost on the individual development of perception. Perception is the process between the input of sensory information and the output of behaviors (Bornstein, Arterberry, & Mash, 2011). Research studies in the development of perception over the life span of individuals have revealed mechanisms for the development of certain nonacademic skills as an interactive process of predisposed biological conditions and experiences.

Perception starts with senses, which heavily rely on the physical conditions of sensory-motor functions. For example, neurologists studied the behaviors of rats and found out the repeated correlation between rats' decision making was related to the activity in the sensory neurons in the brain (Nienborg, Cohen, & Cumming, 2012). They inferred from the study that mammals involve senses in their analytical thinking. In other words, the implication is that what individuals physically sense would influence their perception, which might lead to different behaviors under certain circumstances. The field of human physiology has made strong links of individual difference in the sensory functions to genetic predisposition and heredity (Konner, 2010).

However, more recent approaches to the study of perception have discovered alternatives to the theory of it being hardwired. Many researchers in genetic neurology have revealed relationships between genetic modeling and life experience. Psychopathology researchers Michael Rutter, Terrie E. Moffitt, and Avshalom Caspi (2006) discovered that there exists interplay between genetic heredity and environment in children and teenagers developing psychopathologies. They claimed that not only genetic heredity would moderate the environmental hazard children and teenagers might be exposed to in terms of mental disorders, but also that the environmental factors can enable the variation of genetic dysfunction into behaviors. Similarly, researchers Christian Kieling and his colleagues (2013) discovered that in their study of Brazilian children and teenagers, environmental effects had replaced the genetic disposition in influencing the teenagers' probability of demonstrating hyperactivity problems. In other words, the nurturing over time has erased the effects of nature in shaping some nonacademic behavioral aspects of individuals.

Perception has been found to be mostly effectively modified through self-consistent learning. Kukjin Kang and Shun-ichi Amari (2012) employed statistical models to simulate the process of human perception. They concluded that individual perception of the environment is as accurate as prior experiences, and that human minds prefer a process of self-consistent learning, in which the perception of a certain environment would converge to a static one over time. This finding is consistent with other research findings in the same field (Lee, Seo, & Jung, 2012).

Affects: The Becoming of Feelings

Affect is the mechanism through which situations trigger emotional expressions. Many nonacademic skills like emotional regulation, curiosity, and others are practiced through various affects. According to the affect theory first proposed by psychologist Silvan Tomkins (1962), affect has its innate qualities. Individuals are born with some basic affects that link certain stimuli in the environment such as sound, image, touch, and feelings, which are physically rushes of chemicals (Nathanson, 1992).

Allan Schore (1994) of the University of California–Los Angeles (UCLA) provides a comprehensive account of the developmental process of affective systems in infants in his book *Affect Regulation and the Origin of the Self: The Neurobiology of Emotional Development*. This development is a dynamic process of the infant interacting with the primary caregiver. In a year after birth, the orbitofrontal region in an infant's brain, which is responsible for forming and regulating affects, is dependent on environmental stimuli, particularly stimuli from interacting with the primary caregiver. Starting from ten to twelve months to the middle of the second year, the affective system continues to mature in the brain as other sensory-motor functions of the brain start to develop, and even picks up more affects like self-inhibition as the sensory-motor activities overly excite infant brains. Around the same time, when confronted by barriers that they can't overcome in moving around, infants are stimulated to go back to their caregivers. This phenomenon later develops into an attachment between the individual infant and the caregiver.

During the interaction between the infant and the caregiver, visual cues such as the expressions of the caregiver at different times are picked up by the brain as the basis of affects. Gradually, an imprint on the brain is formed to which each category of environmental stimuli is matched with one set of signals from the affective system, which subsequently leads to a rush of certain chemicals in the body and, behaviorally, an emotional expression. All basic affects—pride, joy, shame, and surprise—are by and large finalized by the end of the first two years of individuals' lives (Nathanson, 1992). The basics on which nonacademic skills are observed later in school-age children have thus completed their first and most significant stage of development.

It is well acknowledged among developmental psychologists that mother–infant interactions in the first two years after birth are particularly critical and influential, as the interactions encompass the majority of environmental factors that shape the individual brains when they are highly plastic (Coneus, Laucht, & Reuss, 2011; Konner, 2010). However, research also suggests that it is possible to introduce changes to individual affective systems at later stages of life. The changes can be introduced through amplifying the environmental stimuli that trigger positive affects for individuals so that these affects can be normalized in their minds.

In their study of emotion regulation, psychologists James Gross and Oliver John (2002) found that two major strategies of emotion regulation were frequently used: antecedent-focused strategy and response-focused strategy. Antecedent-focused strategy allows people to first analyze the situation they are in, elicit the aspects that would trigger affective behaviors, and then pay attention to some of the aspects instead of others in order to regulate the emotional expressions. Response-focused strategy prioritizes controlling emotions that surface through the affective system, usually through mentally inhibiting any display of emotions. People who mostly use some antecedent-focused strategy tend to experience more positive emotions and lesser negative emotions; in contrast, people who mostly inhibit emotional expressions tend to experience the same or more negative emotions. Built on other similar studies, Gross and John (2002) stated that attentive regulation over emotions would result in transient changes in individual affective systems. In other words, consciously exercising certain intervention over affects could eventually change these mechanisms within individuals.

Nonacademic Skills Are Teachable

So far, research suggests that many mechanisms in human minds that mediate the development of nonacademic skills emerge and form either before birth or soon after birth. Like perception and affects, these mechanisms for individuals always encompass inherited or predetermined components, like genetic predisposition and physiological conditions. Although the prime time of development is often the first couple of years in life, mechanisms that are fundamental to all skills, academic or not, remain unmalleable at later stages of life, which means schools are not helpless or responsible for nurturing nonacademic skills.

There have been many programs to help develop creativity, entrepreneurial capacities, grit, social skills, and a growth mindset. While research on the effectiveness of these programs is inconclusive, it has provided a growing body of ideas that can guide more effective actions for schools to take. Self-efficacy intervention and emotion regulation are two examples.

Self-Efficacy Intervention

Much research has been conducted in improving self-efficacy since psychologist Albert Bandura proposed this concept in 1977. Theories on self-efficacy development have concentrated on either improving individual belief in the feasibility of tasks they need to complete, or promoting individuals' awareness of their past achievements. Interventions on beliefs in feasibility include associating others' success to the feasibility of the tasks. In their research of mathematics and science self-efficacy, Darrell Luzzo, Patricia Hasper, Katrice Albert, Maureen Bibby, and Edward Martinelli (1999) randomly assigned some of the university freshmen participating in the study to watch a short video presentation given by two students who graduated from the same university. These two students narrated their transitions from being undeclared majors to finding an interest in mathematics or science-related majors and eventually working in mathematics or science-related fields after graduation. After watching the video, participants were measured on their career interest, mathematics and science self-efficacy, and course and major surveys, just like they did before they watched the video presentation. Comparing the results with those who did not watch the video suggests that the inspiration from the success of someone that the participants can relate to did influence their self-efficacy in a positive way. Similar research has found a positive relationship between strategies like motivation and inspiration and improved self-efficacy (Schunk & Zimmerman, 2008).

Moreover, there is evidence to show the effect of past performances on improving self-efficacy. A recent meta-analysis on 142 self-efficacy-related studies concluded that the past performance of an individual has a powerful effect on modifying his or her self-efficacy regardless of the contexts or the forms of performance (Sitzmann & Yeo, 2013). Simply put, the more positive past performance of tasks an individual has, the more improved his or her self-efficacy is going to be. Drawing from this research, school personnel aiming to improve their students' self-efficacy should consciously create opportunities for students to associate themselves with success through either observing others who complete tasks that they need to complete, or reminding them of their own past success in completing tasks or performances.

Emotion Regulation

Emotion regulation in its broad definition is to consciously regulate one's emotion from its occurrence to its expression to make sure that it does not jeopardize other cognitive tasks. In other words, it not only addresses the behavioral indicators of a negative emotion (for example, anger, aggressive or hostile behaviors toward peers, and agitation), but also preventively addresses the regulation of emotion understanding and awareness.

Psychologist Gayle Macklem (2011) dissected emotional regulation training into three parts: (1) emotion understanding, which is the ability to identify emotions of oneself and others through verbal and nonverbal indicators; (2) emotion expression, which is to express one's feelings in a situation-appropriate way; and (3) emotion regulation strategies, which is to use strategies to distract, down-regulate, or cognitively dissolve some aggregated emotions when emotion expression is not an option. Emotion understanding is the first step that integrates the cognitive process of understanding into the development of the noncognitive skill. Research has indicated that lacking knowledge of emotion expressions and emotion differentiation is related to poor emotion regulation skill (Barrett, Gross, Christensen, & Benvenuto, 2001). Meanwhile, emotion expression also plays a role in emotion regulation. Psychologists Abby Heckman Coats and Fredda Blanchard-Fields (2008) found that the ability of emotion regulation decreased from young adults to middle-aged adults and elder adults, partially due to the lack of emotion expression that middle-aged and elder adults have in comparison to young adults.

Emotion regulation strategies also include distracting from the trigger of emotion, utilizing cognitive reasoning to control reactionary behaviors, and drawing attention from the emotion to the procedural task (Gallo, Keil, McCulloch, Rockstroh, & Gollwitzer, 2009). Research on preschool children's emotion regulation indicated that young children who tend to use private speech (talking to oneself as if talking to someone else) in coping with stressful situations tend to regulate their negative emotions better (Day & Smith, 2013). In a sense, emotion regulation strategies are the least standardized part of emotion regulation development.

In response to the contextualized and individualized emotion regulation implementation in the school setting, Macklem's (2011) work *Evidence-Based School Mental Health Services: Affect Education, Emotion Regulation Training, and Cognitive Behavioral Therapy* has offered many comprehensive theoretical implications, as well as practical strategies from a school psychologist's perspective on improving students' emotion regulation. Similarly, Roslyn Arnold's (2005) *Empathic Intelligence* offers more pedagogical and instructional implications on nurturing the empathic skills in enhancing students' emotion regulation. Moreover, many publications have accumulated activities and event plans for teachers who are invested in improving students' emotion regulation skills as part of their intelligence development (Beachner & Pickett, 2001).

PBIS: An Example of School-Level Effort

The characteristics of schools as cross-level bio-ecological centers for individual development have been both a challenge and an opportunity for school personnel to impact nonacademic skills development among students. A recent intervention system, Positive Behavior Intervention and Support (PBIS), has gained popularity among K–12 schools that seek systematic implementation for improving schoolwide social and behavioral skills development (Barrett, Bradshaw, & Lewis-Palmer, 2008). PBIS starts with a leadership team of teachers, administrators, counselors, and other staff who actively interact with students in the school. With the help of PBIS facilitators, they collect the data, analyze the needs of students in prosocial behaviors and skills, and identify the resources within the school for intervention, then start a pilot program implementing a set of PBIS-proven policy and instructional changes. At the same time, program evaluation feedback is continuously collected and analyzed with the help of experts and the leadership team, which in turn refines the program's structure. From there, the evidence-based unique program of intervention and support for social skills and behavior development is implemented across the school. The schoolwide implementation of PBIS is the functioning unit of such intervention on a higher level, either on the district level or the state level (Dunlop, 2013).

The feature of PBIS is its multilevel approach to address behavioral problems of individual students, which creates a positive and prodevelopmental environment within the physical boundary of a school. A typical PBIS intervention starts on an all-student level. A few trained teachers, administrators, staff, and other constant figures in school create a list of positive behavior expectations and outline the main properties of the intervention. With more input collected from all staff at the school, a list of specific and concrete expectations is created for every visible space in school, such as the cafeteria, the playground, and the classrooms. An example of such concrete and specific expectations for behavior in the cafeteria would be to put the tray back in the collection bin after scraping away the leftover food on it. When students behave in the way that fulfills any of the specified expectations, adults in school need to observe these behaviors and praise the students right away, reinforcing the bonding effects of those positive expectations.

After implementing the all-student-level intervention, PBIS also provides protocols and strategies for the more challenging and behaviorally at-risk students in the positive environment. For these students, school administrators and staff create more targeted plans after analyzing the specific behavior data collected through a PBIS specific data collecting system. The plan utilizes the resources the school has to address the specific challenges these students experience in achieving the level of appropriate behavior in the school environment. These targeted or individualized plans for more behaviorally at-risk students are designed to concentrate the resources the school and district have on individuals who need them, instead of what traditional punitive strategies would inevitably cause: less environmental support for the wholesome development of students who are particularly challenged (Technical Assistance Center on Positive Behavioral Interventions and Supports, n.d.).

The strength of PBIS is that it is adaptive to the particular culture, structure, resources, and environment of the school or other educational organization it applies to. Ever since it was put into practice at the beginning of the 21st century, many schools where PBIS is implemented have reported significant improvement in student prosocial behaviors and positive interpersonal relationships, with fidelity being the biggest threat to its effectiveness (Mathews, McIntosh, Frank, & May, 2014).

Where Do We Go From Here?

Nonacademic skills as defined in the 21st century skills movement are more complex than ever before. Not only does the category include certain skills that are conventionally considered noncognitive, such as personality, emotions, and empathy, but it also covers many metacognitive skills such as curiosity and self-efficacy. Although these skills are not directly embedded in any subject-specific curricula or classroom instruction, the development of these nonacademic skills is critical to the long-term well-being of individuals, the ultimate purpose of education.

Interdisciplinary literature on human development has illustrated a comprehensive picture of individual progression. These fundamental processes of development such as perception and affect have demonstrated that any development of human potential, including nonacademic skills, is a continuing interplay of nature and nurture, heredity and environment.

For decades, researchers strove to detail these fundamental mechanisms whenever they took effect in reshaping certain behavioral outcomes like emotional expression, yet there has not been a how-to guidebook for educators to pick up and apply to their real-life scenarios. As the volume of research has increased, evidence-based interventions adaptive to schools have emerged. Promising approaches like PBIS could inspire more practices and systematic efforts in the school environment, so that students can develop the potential they were born with through attentive nurturing that educators are able to provide.

References and Resources

Anastasi, J. S. (2008). Cognition. In *International encyclopedia of the social sciences*. Accessed at www.encyclopedia.com/topic/Cognition.aspx on March 23, 2015.

Arnold, R. (2005). *Empathic intelligence: Teaching, learning, relating*. Sydney, Australia: University of New South Wales.

Ashcraft, M. H. (2002). Math anxiety: Personal, educational, and cognitive consequences. *Current Directions in Psychological Science, 11*(5), 181–185.

Bandura, A. (1977). Self-efficacy: Toward a unifying theory of behavioral change. *Psychological Review, 84*(2), 191–215.

Barkow, J. H., Cosmides, L., & Tooby, J. (Eds.). (1992). *The adapted mind: Evolutionary psychology and the generation of culture*. New York: Oxford University Press.

Barrett, L. F., Gross, J., Christensen, T. C., & Benvenuto, M. (2001). Knowing what you're feeling and knowing what to do about it: Mapping the relation between emotion differentiation and emotion regulation. *Cognition and Emotion, 15*(6), 713–724.

Barrett, L. F., & Salovey, P. (Eds.). (2002). *The wisdom in feeling: Psychological processes in emotional intelligence*. New York: Guilford Press.

Barrett, S. B., Bradshaw, C. P., & Lewis-Palmer, T. (2008). Maryland statewide PBIS initiative systems, evaluation, and next steps. *Journal of Positive Behavior Interventions, 10*(2), 105–114.

Beachner, L., & Pickett, A. (2001). *Multiple intelligences and positive life habits: 174 activities for applying them in your classroom*. Thousand Oaks, CA: Corwin Press.

Big Brothers Big Sisters of America. (n.d.). *We are here to start something*. Accessed at www.bbbs .org/site/c.9iILI3NGKhK6F/b.5962351/k.42EB/We_are_here_to_start_something.htm on March 23, 2015.

Borghans, L., Meijers, H., & Weel, B. T. (2008). The role of noncognitive skills in explaining cognitive test scores. *Economic Inquiry, 46*(1), 2–12.

Bornstein, M. H., & Arterberry, M. E. (2003). Recognition, discrimination, and categorization of smiling by 5-month-old infants. *Developmental Science, 6*(5), 585–599.

Bornstein, M. H., Arterberry, M. E., & Mash, C. (2011). Perceptual development. In M. H. Bornstein & M. E. Lamb (Eds.), *Developmental science: An advanced textbook* (6th ed., pp. 303–351). New York: Psychology Press.

Bornstein, M. H., & Lamb, M. E. (Eds.). (2011). *Developmental science: An advanced textbook* (6th ed.). New York: Psychology Press.

Bouchard, T. J. (1999). Genes, environment, and personality. In S. J. Ceci & W. M. Williams (Eds.), *The nature-nurture debate: The essential readings* (pp. 97–103). Malden, MA: Blackwell.

Bronfenbrenner, U. (1979). *The ecology of human development: Experiments by nature and design*. Cambridge, MA: Harvard University Press.

Buss, D. M. (2004). *Evolutionary psychology: The new science of the mind*. New York: Pearson.

Ceci, S. J., & Williams, W. M. (Eds.). (1999). *The nature-nurture debate: The essential readings*. Malden, MA: Blackwell.

Coats, A. H., & Blanchard-Fields, F. (2008). Emotion regulation in interpersonal problems: The role of cognitive-emotional complexity, emotion regulation goals, and expressivity. *Psychology and Aging, 23*(1), 39–51.

Coneus, K., Laucht, M., & Reuss, K. (2011). The role of parental investments for cognitive and noncognitive skill formation—Evidence for the first 11 years of life. *Economics and Human Biology, 10*(2), 189–209.

Conley, D. T. (2013, January 22). Rethinking the notion of "noncognitive." *Education Week*. Accessed at www.edweek.org/ew/articles/2013/01/23/18conley.h32.html?tkn=QVTF0ig0B4 WQVdhocP1D0iHKeFYHFYEpq2FV&cmp=clp-edweek on March 23, 2015.

Cosmides, L., Tooby, J., & Barkow, J. H. (1992). Introduction: Evolutionary psychology and conceptual integration. In J. H. Barkow, L. Cosmides, & J. Tooby (Eds.), *The adapted mind: Evolutionary psychology and the generation of culture* (pp. 3–15). New York: Oxford University Press.

Crawford, C., & Krebs, D. L. (Eds.). (1998). *Handbook of evolutionary psychology: Ideas, issues, and applications*. Mahwah, NJ: Lawrence Erlbaum Associates.

Cromwell, H. C., & Panksepp, J. (2011). Rethinking the cognitive revolution from a neural perspective: How overuse/misuse of the term "cognition" and the neglect of affective controls in behavioral neuroscience could be delaying progress in understanding the BrainMind. *Neuroscience and Biobehavioral Reviews, 35*(9), 2026–2035.

Cruickshank, C., & Haan, P. (2006). Using non-cognitive assessment in college recruiting: Applying Holland's self-selection assumption. *College and University, 81*(3), 31–39.

Day, K., & Smith, C. (2013). Understanding the role of private speech in children's emotion regulation. *Early Childhood Research Quarterly, 28*(2), 405–414.

Dunlop, T. (2013). Why it works: You can't just "PBIS" someone. *Education Digest, 79*(4), 38–40.

Ferrando, M., Prieto, M. D., Almeida, L. S., Ferrandiz, C., Bermejo, R., Lopez-Pina, J. A., et al. (2011). Trait emotional intelligence and academic performance: Controlling for the effects of IQ, personality, and self-concept. *Journal of Psychoeducational Assessment, 29*(2), 150–159.

Gallo, I. S., Keil, A., McCulloch, K. C., Rockstroh, B., & Gollwitzer, P. M. (2009). Strategic automation of emotion regulation. *Journal of Personality and Social Psychology, 96*(1), 11–31.

Gross, J. J., & John, O. P. (2002). Wise emotion regulation. In L. F. Barrett & P. Salovey (Eds.), *The wisdom in feeling: Psychological processes in emotional intelligence* (pp. 297–318). New York: Guilford Press.

Kang, K., & Amari, S.-I. (2012). Self-consistent learning of the environment. *Neural Computation, 24*(12), 3191–3212.

Kieling, C., Hutz, M. H., Genro, J. P., Polanczyk, G. V., Anselmi, L., Camey, S., et al. (2013). Gene-environment interaction in externalizing problems among adolescents: Evidence from the Pelotas 1993 birth cohort study. *Journal of Child Psychology and Psychiatry, 54*(3), 298–304.

Konner, M. (2010). *The evolution of childhood: Relationships, emotion, mind.* Cambridge, MA: Belknap Press of Harvard University Press.

Lamb, M. E., & Lewis, C. (2011). The role of parent-child relationships in child development. In M. H. Bornstein & M. E. Lamb (Eds.), *Developmental science: An advanced textbook* (6th ed., pp. 469–517). New York: Psychology Press.

Lee, D., Seo, H., & Jung, M. W. (2012). Neural basis of reinforcement learning and decision making. *Annual Review of Neuroscience, 35*, 287–308.

Luzzo, D. A., Hasper, P., Albert, K. A., Bibby, M. A., & Martinelli, E. A., Jr. (1999). Effects of self-efficacy-enhancing interventions on the math/science self-efficacy and career interests, goals, and actions of career undecided college students. *Journal of Counseling Psychology, 46*(2), 233–243.

Macklem, G. L. (2011). *Evidence-based school mental health services: Affect education, emotion regulation training, and cognitive behavioral therapy.* New York: Springer.

Mathews, S., McIntosh, K., Frank, J. L., & May, S. L. (2014). Critical features predicting sustained implementation of school-wide positive behavioral interventions and supports. *Journal of Positive Behavior Interventions, 16*(3), 168–178.

Mount, I. (2009, December 9). *Are entrepreneurs born or made? Scientists and academics battle out the nature-vs-nurture debate.* Accessed at http://money.cnn.com/2009/12/09 /smallbusiness/entrepreneurs_born_not_made.fsb on January 17, 2012.

Nathanson, D. L. (1992). *Shame and pride: Affect, sex, and the birth of the self.* New York: Norton.

National Research Council. (2012). *Education for life and work: Developing transferable knowledge and skills in the 21st century.* Washington, DC: National Academies Press.

Nicolaou, N., Shane, S., Cherkas, L., & Spector, T. D. (2008). The influence of sensation seeking in the heritability of entrepreneurship. *Strategic Entrepreneurship Journal, 2*(1), 7–21.

Nienborg, H., Cohen, M. R., & Cumming, B. G. (2012). Decision-related activity in sensory neurons: Correlations among neurons and with behavior. *Annual Review of Neuroscience, 35,* 463–483.

Patel, M., Honavar, V., & Balakrishnan, K. (2001). *Advances in the evolutionary synthesis of intelligent agents.* Cambridge, MA: MIT Press.

Pinker, S. (2002). *The blank slate: The modern denial of human nature.* New York: Penguin.

Prinz, J. J. (2002). *Furnishing the mind: Concepts and their perceptual basis.* Cambridge, MA: MIT Press.

Reiss, S. (2000). *Who am I? The 16 basic desires that motivate our actions and define our personalities.* New York: Berkley.

Reiss, S. (2004). Multifaceted nature of intrinsic motivation: The theory of 16 basic desires. *Review of General Psychology, 8*(3), 179–193.

Ridley, M. (2003). *Nature via nurture: Genes, experience, and what makes us human.* New York: HarperCollins.

Rosen, J. A., Glennie, E. J., Dalton, B. W., Lennon, J. M., & Bozick, R. N. (2010). *Noncognitive skills in the classroom: New perspectives on educational research* (RTI Press Publication No. BK-0004–1009). Research Triangle Park, NC: RTI International. Accessed at www.rti.org/pubs/bk-0004-1009-rosen.pdf on March 23, 2015.

Rutter, M., Moffitt, T. E., & Caspi, A. (2006). Gene-environment interplay and psychopathology: Multiple varieties but real effects. *Journal of Child Psychology and Psychiatry, 47*(3–4), 226–261.

Schore, A. N. (1994). *Affect regulation and the origin of the self: The neurobiology of emotional development.* Hillsdale, NJ: Erlbaum.

Schunk, D. H., & Zimmerman, B. J. (Eds.). (2008). *Motivation and self-regulated learning: Theory, research, and applications.* New York: Erlbaum.

Shane, S. (2010). *Born entrepreneurs, born leaders: How your genes affect your work life.* New York: Oxford University Press.

Shane, S. (2011, December 6). Are you a born entrepreneur? *Entrepreneur.* Accessed at www .entrepreneur.com/article/220804 on January 17, 2012.

Sitzmann, T., & Yeo, G. (2013). A meta-analytic investigation of the within-person self-efficacy domain: Is self-efficacy a product of past performance or a driver of future performance? *Personnel Psychology, 66*(3), 531–568.

Smith-Schrandt, H. L., Ojanen, T., Gesten, E., Feldman, M. A., & Calhoun, C. D. (2011). Beyond situational ambiguity in peer conflict: Unique and combined effects of cues from an antagonist and a best friend. *Child Development, 82*(6), 1921–1937.

Sommerfeld, A. (2011). Recasting non-cognitive factors in college readiness as what they truly are: Non-academic factors. *Journal of College Admission, 213*, 18–22.

Technical Assistance Center on Positive Behavioral Interventions and Supports. (n.d.). *Research: Making the case that school-wide positive support (SWPBS) is an evidence-based practice.* Accessed at www.pbis.org/research on January 16, 2015.

Tierney, J. P., & Grossman, J. B. (2000). *Making a difference: An impact study of Big Brothers Big Sisters.* Philadelphia: Public/Private Ventures. Accessed at www .issuelab.org/fetch/publicprivate_ventures_104.pdf on March 23, 2015.

Tomkins, S. S. (1962). *Affect, imagery, consciousness. Vol. 1. The positive affects.* Oxford, England: Springer.

Wittmann, W. W., & Hattrup, K. (2004). The relationship between performance in dynamic systems and intelligence. *Systems Research and Behavioral Science, 21*(4), 393–409.

Wright, R. (1994). *The moral animal: The new science of evolutionary psychology.* New York: Vintage Books.

Yong Zhao, PhD, is presidential chair and director of the Office of Global and Online Education in the College of Education at the University of Oregon and a professor in the Department of Educational Measurement, Policy, and Leadership. He is also a Professorial Fellow with the Mitchell Institute for Health and Education Policy, Victoria University in Australia. He was previously University Distinguished Professor in the College of Education at Michigan State University, where he was founding director of the Office of Teaching and Technology and the US-China Center for Research on Educational Excellence, and executive director of the Confucius Institute. He is an elected fellow of the International Academy of Education.

Dr. Zhao is an internationally known scholar, author, and speaker whose works focus on the implications of globalization and technology on education. He has designed schools that cultivate global competence, developed computer games for language learning, and founded research and development institutions to explore innovative education models. The author of more than one hundred articles and twenty books, he was named one of the ten most influential people in educational technology in 2012 by the journal *Tech & Learning*.

Dr. Zhao received a BA in English language education from Sichuan Institute of Foreign Languages in Chongqing, China, and an MA and PhD in education from the University of Illinois at Urbana-Champaign.

To book Yong Zhao for professional development, contact pd@solution-tree.com.

CHAPTER 9

Shifting the Paradigm: Assessing What Matters

YONG ZHAO

ounting or assessing is a necessary part of education. It's natural that all those who are involved in education, directly or indirectly, have a justifiable desire to do so: parents want to know how well their children are being educated; teachers and educational institutions want to know how well their students learn and progress; the public wants to know how well the education institutions supported by their tax dollars are doing in preparing future citizens; and their agents, the government, want to gauge the quality and efforts of education institutions and educators. Assessment is obviously a primary way to provide information and give answers.

Assessment drives education. What is assessed often becomes what is prioritized in the education process, especially when high stakes are attached. It is, therefore, critical to ensure that we assess what matters or, in other words, to count what counts. Despite the vast differences in educational viewpoints, be it the purpose or the process of education, all agree that education offers to produce desirable qualities in students. This book identifies a set of desirable qualities based on available research, which includes persistence, personality traits, motivation, social intelligence, and global competence.

While not all may agree with what has been included here—and indeed the short list is far from being exhaustive—there is sufficient evidence supporting the significant impact of each quality, especially on successful adulthood. They have, therefore, been identified and carefully selected as valuable educational outcomes. These qualities have been generally affirmed and advocated by educators and policymakers; however, they have not yet been included in current practices of making judgments about the quality or potential of an individual or a group of children or the quality or efforts of institutions or people responsible for students' education.

There is an urgent need for a new paradigm of assessment that should not only expand the types of educational outcomes by including many new, unconventional outcomes, but also offer to resolve a set of critical issues concerning the relationships between the various outcomes. These issues are deliberately presented as dichotomous as follows in order to highlight the differences between the new and traditional perspectives on educational outcomes.

Homogenizing vs. Diversifying

The traditional paradigm in education primarily assesses the success of homogenization: how well all the students have mastered the set of skills, or content, or developed the desired qualities as prescribed in curriculum or standards. For example, international assessments such as the Programme for International Student Assessment (PISA) and the Trends in International Mathematics and Science Study (TIMSS) use the average score and the variation of scores in a subject of a group of students from the same school or education system to gauge the quality of education of that school or system. Higher averages and smaller variation are considered positive. The effectiveness in homogenizing students is equated with the quality of education and the effectiveness of schools and teachers.

The traditional framework works well under a number of assumptions. First, there are only a limited number of outcomes worth pursuing for all students. Second, all students can achieve the expected outcomes with their efforts and through instruction. Third, all students are capable of achieving a similar amount of progress within a given time frame. And finally, all students are interested in pursuing the prescribed outcomes.

These assumptions are, nevertheless, not valid, at least not any longer. First of all, worthwhile educational outcomes have drastically expanded beyond what has traditionally been measured due to massive societal changes brought about by technology and globalization. Many traditionally undervalued human talents and attributes have become visibly valuable and cannot remain excluded from the realm of outcomes of education worth pursuing. Second, due to individual differences resulting from nature and nurture, students are differently talented, with weaknesses and strengths in different domains. Upon entering school, young children are already at different levels in the different domains. While it is, in theory, feasible to bring the "lower-proficiency" students ("low" according to the standards applied) up to "higher-proficient," it does not come without costs, such as the sacrificed opportunities to further develop what these students may be born talented in. Thus even though learning and teaching can help narrow the gap, the consequences are not necessarily desirable. Third, not all students have the same interests, nor should they. Students' interests are diverse, and that diversity is valuable in the new era.

Most importantly, an education that preserves or even amplifies human diversity is much more valuable than one that reduces it because modern society needs a diversity of human talents instead of a homogenous workforce with similar skills and knowledge. Technological advances and globalization have led to the rapid disappearance of traditional jobs that require routine, basic, and homogenous skills and knowledge, as many of them have been or are being rapidly replaced by automation. The world thus needs creative and entrepreneurial individuals who are talented in a variety of areas to create new jobs, invent new products, and provide new services to meet the diverse psychological and spiritual needs of human beings, tasks that cannot be carried out by machines (Zhao, 2012). One of the explanations for the fact that even though the United States has never ranked high in the international tests yet has maintained a prosperous economy is perhaps that the U.S. education system has not been effective in homogenizing, which, intentionally or not, has preserved more diversity than some other countries that have achieved consistently high rankings. It has been agreed that the preserved diversity of talents has been a major driver for innovation and invention that have pushed the U.S. economy forward despite the loss of jobs to automation and offshoring.

Thus, in the new evaluation paradigm, we need to assess how education contributes to enhancing individuals' talents rather than its effectiveness in homogenizing. In other words, the quality of education provided by a teacher, a school, or an education system should not be evaluated based on the mean scores or the variations of students' performance on a limited number of tests, but rather, it should be geared toward the growth of individuals (Center for Individual Opportunity, n.d.).

Short-Term Instruction vs. Long-Term Education

Traditional assessment normally measures the short-term effects of instruction. Typically, students are assessed during or at the end of a course to appraise how many of the objectives of the course they have achieved. The degree to which students master the predetermined content and skills defined by the course during a set period of time is used as evidence of the students' learning outcomes and their abilities. In cases where systemwide assessment exists, standardized tests are used to gauge students' mastery of knowledge and skills prescribed by systemically defined standards. Teachers and schools are held accountable for the progress students make in the course against the standards, with standardized test scores as evidence. Students, parents, and the public also look at the results of course-end assessment or standardized tests, be it a grade or test score, as an indication of quality of education or the ability of the student in the assessed domains.

Short-term instruction may, however, hinder long-term educational outcomes. For example, a study conducted by scientists at the Massachusetts Institute of Technology (MIT) found that direct instruction resulted in better short-term outcomes but hindered long-term educational outcomes (Bonawitz et al., 2011). In the study, the researchers looked at how four-year-old children learned about a new toy. In one condition, the experimenter told the children that she just found the toy and acted surprised when the toy squeaked, which is one of the four functions of the toy. In the other condition, the experimenter acted like a teacher. She told the children that she was going to show how the toy worked and asked them to watch her demonstrate. Then the experimenter left the children to play with the toy. The study found that the children from the first condition played with the toy longer and discovered more features of it than the second group. If we would measure the children's knowledge about the toy shared by the teacher, the second group might score well or possibly even better than the first group. But those children were less curious toward the toy than the first group, and therefore less likely to discover new information about the toy.

Another study conducted by researchers at the University of California–Berkeley, also with four-year-old children, found similar results (Buchsbaum, Gopnik, Griffiths, & Shafto, 2011). When the experimenter did not provide direct instruction like a teacher, the children did more exploration and found out a more intelligent way of getting the toy to play music. However, when the experimenter acted like a teacher, the children merely imitated her without discovering any novel solutions to better play music. Children in the latter setting became less curious and less creative, although if their learning as acquisition of what the teacher instructed had been measured, they would probably have done very well.

Creativity and curiosity are much more important qualities to cultivate than achieving good short-term learning outcomes. Although it is unlikely that a one-time direct instruction would cause a lifelong damage to creativity or curiosity, repeated direct teaching over time could (Zhao, 2014). The peculiar negative correlations between scores and confidence across education systems repeatedly found in the TIMSS and other international studies provide further evidence. In the TIMSS, for example, there is a consistent pattern that education systems with higher scores tend to show less interest, enjoyment, and confidence in the subject (Loveless, 2012; Zhao, 2012). Similar patterns exist also in the PISA (Sjøberg, 2012; Zhao, 2012).

Considering the importance of qualities such as creativity, curiosity, and confidence for lifelong success, short-term instructional outcomes can hardly reflect the potentials of children for future success. Given the potential of such focus in hurting the development of long-term educational outcomes, the new evaluation paradigm should take a long-term view. Rather than merely collecting data on students' raw knowledge/skill gain, evaluation should take into account the long-term educational outcomes by analyzing the extent to which each of those long-term outcomes is enhanced or damaged when it comes to making judgments about children's performance, progress, potential, the quality of teaching, and the effectiveness of the teacher, as well as the education systems.

Cognitive vs. Noncognitive

The primary focus of traditional education evaluation is on cognitive skills—that is, attending, memorizing, and applying logic. It is more often than not about students' ability to memorize, follow directions, and apply information to solve problems. Simply put, it is about a person's ability to do certain things in a certain way. It typically does not consider a person's desire to do certain things, which are often affected by a host of factors generally referred to as noncognitive skills. Therefore, very rarely are noncognitive domains such as motivation, persistence, confidence, and personality traits included in formal assessments.

The virtually exclusive focus on cognitive abilities in assessment results in neglecting the development of noncognitive skills in most schools. But many noncognitive skills have been demonstrated to be of crucial importance in an individual's lifelong success, and are well documented in research reviewed in this book as well as elsewhere (Brunello & Schlotter, 2010; Levin, 2012). The lack of consideration of noncognitive qualities in traditional assessment schemes is a main reason why test scores alone have not been reliable predicators of future success of individuals or nations (Baker, 2007; Goleman, 1995; Tienken, 2008).

Noncognitive skills may be difficult to teach explicitly. While it is almost unrealistic to fashion them into specific outcomes of a single course or two, the school environment can pose a significant impact on students' development of noncognitive skills, as can cultural norms, value orientation of schools and education systems, and teachers and families.

Thus, noncognitive skills should be included in the educational outcomes list, and they should be an integral part of educational assessment and evaluation. What comes with this inclusion is the inevitable change in our understanding of effective teaching and quality of education. For example, in a setting where only cognitive skills are assessed, a teacher whose students perform well on standardized tests would be considered an effective teacher. Likewise, when only test scores are used as a measure of the quality of education systems, East Asian education systems such as Shanghai, Korea, Hong Kong, Japan, Taiwan, and some other ones routinely ranking high in scores will automatically be considered as the best. However, when noncognitive skills are considered, the picture changes. For instance, if students in a class all develop a negative attitude toward the subject, the teacher may not be considered as effective, even if all achieve excellent test scores. The same is true for educational systems. For example, East Asian education systems should be considered as less effective as their students express less interest in the tested subjects of mathematics, science, and reading, and voice less appreciation of the values of these subjects.

While achievement in cognitive skills does not necessarily cause damage to the development of noncognitive skills, strong focuses on improving cognitive skills, particularly under the pressure of scoring high on standardized tests, can cause damage. For instance, while the practice of publicly ranking students based on test scores, as practiced in many schools in China, can certainly help motivate students to score better, it can also decrease students' confidence in their abilities. Except for a small group of students who are on top, the majority of students feel worse than the others. Likewise, rote learning and direct instruction may result in short-term gains on test scores, but they can cause a loss of interest and engagement in the subjects because the teaching method inevitably makes the subjects much less interesting than they actually are.

If we value noncognitive skills as an education outcome, as we should, we need to shift the paradigm of assessment and evaluation to a new paradigm where not only what the students have learned and improved in the cognitive domain is assessed, but also the degree to which students' noncognitive qualities are enhanced (or, conversely, stifled). In other words, a high-quality education should be not only about achieving excellent test scores, but also about improving noncognitive qualities such as interest, engagement, enjoyment, persistence, and appreciation of the subjects. Moreover, it should also have a positive effect on students' self-efficacy, future self, social-emotional skills, and growth mindset in general.

Measurable vs. Unmeasurable

The well-known saying that has been popularly but mistakenly attributed to Albert Einstein, "Not everything that can be counted counts, and not everything that counts can be counted," best explains a fundamental problem with the traditional paradigm of educational assessment and evaluation (Cameron, 1963, p. 13). These words, first uttered by sociologist William Bruce Cameron in 1963, aptly point out that what we measure in education may not matter, while what matters may not be measured or perhaps not even measurable. The fact that IQ scores or test scores in a few subjects have shown to be only weakly associated with the success of individuals and nations seems to support the first part of the observation. The second part of the observation expounds a challenge for education: if an educational outcome, as important as it is, cannot be tangibly measured or lacks good measure at the moment, how would we work with and incorporate it into the educational scheme for the benefit of students?

One of the reasons that testing, despite its apparent and widely recognized flaws, has been accepted and used widely in education for making a variety of high-stakes decisions such as admissions, evaluations of teachers and schools, and policies regarding curriculum, pedagogy, and financial investment is because it is considered to provide objective measures of what students should know and be able to do. But many of the human qualities and attributes that may matter even more for life success, such as the ones identified in this book, do not have such measures to have achieved the "objective" status. Some do not even have agreed-upon measures. The dearth of objective measures (or even measures) has made it difficult to include these qualities as important educational outcomes in practice. It has also contributed to a shortage of empirical research on the actual value of these attributes in education.

There are several reasons that not many objective measures exist for qualities in the noncognitive, nonacademic, or "soft" domains. First, the value of these qualities has just begun to be recognized with increasing evidence suggesting that the traditional measures are not as good an assessment of what matters in life. Second, research about these qualities has typically started in disciplines outside of education. Many of the measurement instruments were not designed for use with students in school settings. Additionally, there is a lack of consensus on the definition of these qualities because they have been studied in different disciplines. Without an agreed-upon definition, it is difficult to come up with agreed-upon measures. Furthermore, these qualities are more personal than solving a mathematics problem or memorizing facts, making observing these qualities less straightforward and more subjective. As a result, many instruments rely on self-reporting, obviously less objective than a reading test. Even more problematic is that many of these attributes are intertwined, and therefore it is difficult to sort out the discrete skills for proper assessment. In other words, it is difficult to enumerate these qualities, thus making them virtually unmeasurable.

Echoing the second observation that "not everything that counts can be counted," the new assessment and evaluation paradigm must find a way to "count" these noncognitive qualities as educational outcomes. This could mean concerted efforts to conduct further investigations of these qualities and develop valid instruments. It could also mean finding ways to include them other than assigning a numerical score.

Principles of a New Paradigm

Considering the issues facing educational assessment and evaluation today, what does a new paradigm look like? We propose a few principles that can be used to guide the development of education assessment and evaluation programs that can more accurately reflect the quality of students, teachers, schools, and education systems by considering a wider range of human qualities that matter to lifelong success. These principles are not meant as specific actions or strategies, but should be developed separately and specifically to fit the particular context and purpose.

Personalization

If we accept the premise that every individual is unique and all unique talents are worth developing and cultivating, enhancement of individual differences has to become a celebrated educational outcome, and such an education can only be realized first through personalization (Zhao, 2012). In a personalized education, there is no uniform curriculum or standards that would be used to apply to all students. Instead, each student would expect an individualized educational experience. Education is then the education of the individual, not of a group or to make an individual fit into the average of a group.

To meet the needs of a personalized education, we need to personalize assessments. We would need a broad range of tools, expanded to particularly assess the growth of individuals in whatever domain they pursue, rather than limited to uniform tests that measure the mastery of the same content and skills predetermined in a universal curriculum or set of standards in a constrained set of subjects, as is the case of the current educational system.

Personalized assessment also means looking at the growth of individuals and treating each individual truly as a population of one, not one among a group. That is, students' progress should be judged without reference to others, such as gap from the top or deviation from the average (Center for Individual Opportunity, n.d.; Rose, Rouhani, & Fischer, 2013).

Long-Term Orientation

To alleviate the potential damages to long-term educational outcomes caused by short-term instruction, it is important for assessment to avoid placing too much value on the short-term objectives. The practical implications are that, first, education systems should avoid making high-stakes decisions based on measures of short-term outcomes. For example, test scores should not be used to track students or stream them into different life paths. Second, teacher evaluation should not be based on students' performance on tests, but purposefully include long-term outcomes such as confidence, interest, motivation, curiosity, and creativity. Third, when it comes to evaluating a teacher, a much stronger emphasis should be placed on his or her role in "teaching" the noncognitive skills such as developing students' interest in the subject, instilling curiosity and a lifelong learning lifestyle, and building up students' confidence in themselves, to name just a few.

Awareness of Side Effects

Just as in medical research where both the effects and the side effects of any pharmaceutical products or medical procedures must be assessed because the cure can also cause damage, in educational assessment we have to be aware of the possible side effects in any educational practice and policy. For example, the overemphasis on test scores in the current educational systems' measures of accountability certainly has its numerous side effects, as discussed previously (Nichols & Berliner, 2007). New evaluation programs should be mindful of the reality of side effects and seek to include measures of a range of educational outcomes in order to gain a more comprehensive view.

Authenticity

The majority of assessment instruments used in education today are not authentic to real life. The tasks used to gauge students' abilities rarely occur in the world they live in now, let alone the one they will be living in as adults. For instance, writing short essays under pressure on topics the student might not be interested in does not happen often in the real life of adults, but it is a common task included in educational testing. An even bigger issue is the underlying assumption that all students are equally interested in all the tasks, which is, of course, not true. Furthermore, the tasks in most assessments are set with predetermined correct answers. As a result, there is little room for novel, unexpected, and possibly better solutions than what the test makers have in mind.

To account for the role of both cognitive and noncognitive skills, new assessments should be more authentic. A product-based assessment, for example, is one way to make this happen. As part of his proposal for a new paradigm of education, I suggest *product-oriented learning* as an effective pedagogical approach for cultivating creative and entrepreneurial individuals (Zhao, 2012). Product-oriented learning engages students in producing products or services that serve an authentic purpose—that is, that meet a genuine need of someone, including oneself. In product-oriented learning, the works of students provide evidence of learning, ability, and growth, just like a portfolio of artwork is evidence of the quality, personality, and talent of an artist. Outcomes providing information on both cognitive and noncognitive skills give a more comprehensive assessment of a student.

Collaboration

The final principle of the new assessment and evaluation paradigm is collaboration. In the traditional assessment approach, the person being assessed has virtually no say over what is assessed, how the assessment is delivered, and when the assessment is conducted. In fact, in some high-stakes assessments, the assessment is a well-guarded secret from the assessed. That is why testing security has always been a top priority in many countries. Testing is almost like an ambush on the assessed. Among the many negative consequences of this approach are anxiety, inauthenticity, and potential failure to capture individual's talent, and sure failure to identify an individual's uniqueness.

To comprehensively assess a broad range of educational outcomes, we need to shift our energy toward establishing a scheme that involves collaboration with the students. The students should play a role in deciding the what, how, and when of their assessments. This new approach does not mean teachers or authorities play a less significant role, but proposes a brand-new role for the assessor to collaboratively design and develop a personalized, more comprehensive and meaningful assessment with the assessor and for the benefit of the assessor.

Where Do We Go From Here?

Education is about preparing individuals to succeed in life, and we all know that to succeed in life individuals must have certain abilities, however *succeed* is defined. This book is an attempt to understand what abilities matter based on currently available research. However, what matters will change over time and likely vary in different societies. For example, in the age of globalization, global competency has risen to be a vital quality for life. Educational measures thus need to be constantly modified and tuned in with the changes and differences. Counting what counts should always encompass, for all involved, judging the quality of students, teachers, schools, and education systems.

References and Resources

Baker, K. (2007). Are international tests worth anything? *Phi Delta Kappan, 89*(2), 101–104.

Bonawitz, E., Shafto, P., Gweon, H., Goodman, N. D., Spelke, E., & Schulz, L. (2011). The double-edged sword of pedagogy: Instruction limits spontaneous exploration and discovery. *Cognition, 120*(3), 322–330.

Brunello, G., & Schlotter, M. (2010). *The effect of noncognitive skills and personality traits on labour market outcomes.* Munich, Germany: European Expert Network on Economics of Education.

Buchsbaum, D., Gopnik, A., Griffiths, T. L., & Shafto, P. (2011). Children's imitation of causal action sequences is influenced by statistical and pedagogical evidence. *Cognition, 120*(3), 331–340.

Cameron, W. B. (1963). *Informal sociology, a casual introduction to sociological thinking.* New York: Random House.

Center for Individual Opportunity. (n.d.). *The science.* Accessed at www.individualopportunity .org/overview on January 2, 2015.

Goleman, D. (1995). *Emotional intelligence.* New York: Bantam Books.

Levin, H. M. (2012). More than just test scores. *Prospects: Quarterly Review of Comparative Education, 42*(3), 269–284.

Loveless, T. (2012). *The 2012 Brown Center Report on American Education: How well are American students learning?* Washington, DC: Brookings Institution.

Nichols, S. L., & Berliner, D. C. (2007). *Collateral damage: How high-stakes testing corrupts America's schools.* Cambridge, MA: Harvard Education Press.

Rose, L. T., Rouhani, P., & Fischer, K. W. (2013). The science of the individual. *Mind, Brain, and Education, 7*(3), 152–158.

Sjøberg, S. (2012). PISA: Politics, fundamental problems and intriguing results. *Recherches en Education, 14*, 1–21. Accessed at www.recherches-en-education.net/spip.php?article140 on March 23, 2015.

Tienken, C. H. (2008). Rankings of international achievement test performance and economic strength: Correlation or conjecture? *International Journal of Education Policy and Leadership*, *3*(4), 1–15.

Zhao, Y. (2012). *World class learners: Educating creative and entrepreneurial students.* Thousand Oaks, CA: Corwin Press.

Zhao, Y. (2014). *Who's afraid of the big bad dragon? Why China has the best (and worst) education system in the world.* San Francisco: Jossey-Bass.

Index

A

Abbe, A., 123

Abridged Big Five–Dimensional Circumplex (AB5C) model, 52, 54

Ackerman, P. L., 48–49

Acquisition, H., 143

ACT, 13, 17–18

ACT Inc., 17

Adidas, 133, 134

Adult Dispositional Hope Scale (ADHS), 82, 83–84

Affect Regulation and the Origin of the Self: The Neurobiology of Emotional Development (Schore), 157

affects, 157–158

Albert, K., 159

Alvarez, L., 15

Amari, S., 157

American Council on Education/Fund for the Improvement of Postsecondary Education (ACE/FIPSE), 128

American Council on the Teaching of Foreign Languages (ACTFL), 117

Anderson, C., 35

Anderson, P. H., 126

Anderson, R. C., 92–111

Ang, S., 122

Ariely, D., 141

Aristotle, 72

Arnold, R., 160

Art of Innovation: Lessons in Creativity From IDEO, America's Leading Design Firm, The (Kelley), 58

Asia Society, 128

Assessing What Really Matters in Schools: Creating Hope for the Future (Newell and Van Ryzin), 77

assessments

authentic, 177

cognitive versus noncognitive skills, 173–174

collaboration, 177

group, 143–144

homogenizing versus diversifying, 170–171

individual, 141–143

need for personalized, 41–42, 169–170, 175–177

short-term instruction versus long-term outcomes, 171–172, 176

side effects, 176

Auerswald, P., 96–97

Australia, 6

authenticity, 177

B

Baker, K., 21, 25

Bandura, A., 120, 159

Bar-On, R., 142, 143

Bates College, 18

Beckham, D., 35

Beghetto, R., 94

Behavioral and Emotional Rating Scale (BERS), 42

Behavior Assessment System for Children (BASC), 42

Berkovich, I., 140

Berlyne, D., 78

Bibby, M., 159

Deeper Learning
James A. Bellanca
Education authorities from around the globe draw on research as well as their own experience to explore deeper learning, a process that promotes higher-order thinking, reasoning, and problem solving to better educate students and prepare them for college and careers.
BKF622

Inspiring Creativity and Innovation in K–12
Douglas Reeves
Encourage a culture of innovation and creativity. Explore the four essentials for developing a creative, mistake-tolerant culture; investigate teaching and leadership beliefs and practices that undermine creativity; and discover strategies for successfully navigating challenges that your team may face along the way.
BKF664

Bringing Innovation to School
Suzie Boss
Activate your students' creativity and problem-solving potential with breakthrough learning projects. Across all grades and content areas, student-driven, collaborative projects will teach students how to generate innovative ideas and then put them into action.
BKF546

Contemporary Perspectives on Literacy series
Edited by Heidi Hayes Jacobs
Today's students must be prepared to compete in a global society in which cultures, economies, and people are constantly connected. The authors explain three "new literacies"—digital, media, and global—and provide practical tips for incorporating these literacies into the traditional curriculum.
BKF441, BKF235, BKF236, BKF415

Solution Tree | Press
a division of
Solution Tree

Visit solution-tree.com or call 800.733.6786 to order.